The Monmouth Rebellion

W. MacDONALD WIGFIELD, MA

The Monmouth Rebellion

A SOCIAL HISTORY

Including the complete text of 'Wade's Narrative', 1685
and a Guide to the Battlefield of Sedgemoor

MOONRAKER PRESS

BARNES & NOBLE BOOKS:
TOTOWA, NEW JERSEY

TO THE MEMORY
OF THOSE STALWART MEN
OF DEVON, DORSET, SOMERSET AND WILTSHIRE
WHO FAITHFULLY AND COURAGEOUSLY
FOLLOWED THEIR LEADER TO SEDGEMOOR

© 1980 W. MacDonald Wigfield
First published in 1980 by
MOONRAKER PRESS
26 St Margaret's Street, Bradford-on-Avon
SBN 239.00195.8 (paper SBN 239.00241.5)
First published in the USA 1980 by
BARNES & NOBLE BOOKS
81 Adams Drive, Totowa, New Jersey
ISBN 0.389.20149.9
Printed by T. H. Brickell & Son Ltd
The Blackmore Press, Shaftesbury and
bound in England at The Pitman Press

Preface

The West Country has at times acted together against the dominant power in eastern or central England. Perhaps Arthur's campaign against the West Saxons came first. Harold's sons led a rising based on Exeter against William the Norman. In 1496 Cornishmen with some Somerset support marched as far as Kent, and in 1549 the West rose against the government which acted in the name of Edward VI. We can know very little of the personnel involved in these rebellions, but it is very different with the men who rose to follow the Duke of Monmouth. We have the names of 3500 or more of these rebels, about three-quarters of Monmouth's army. Their surnames are surnames we still know in the West Country; the villages from which they came are villages we know; the places where they fought are places we know or can find. So the rebellion of 1685 has a special and lasting interest, especially to Westcountrymen, as well as the interest of a popular rising and the search for its cause or causes.

This study began as a roll-call of the rebels who can be traced. It moved on to become a collection of survivors' narratives, and thence to a more general history, preserving as far as seemed suitable the language of the survivors, and the accounts of some rather exciting escapes. There must have been several hundred rebels 'presented' (or accused) at the Assize at Wells, who were not there to be tried, either because they had fallen and been buried at Sedgemoor, or because they had got away and found refuge where they could remain until March 1686, when King James issued his General Pardon (albeit with a list of 178 exceptions). Of most of those who fell at Sedgemoor it is appropriate to quote from the praise of famous men in chapter 44 of the book Ecclesiasticus: 'And some there be which have no memorial, who are perished as though they had not been'. We cannot say that their name liveth to all generations, but we can pay tribute to their devotion and courage.

Through some 12 years of part-time research I received consistent encouragement and help from my friend of many years, the late Ivor Collis, F.S.A., then Somerset County Archivist, and from his assistant and successor, Mr David Shorrocks, M.A.; from Dr Robert Dunning, F.S.A., Editor of the Victoria History of Somerset; and from Mr Robin Bush, B.A., now Somerset's Deputy Archivist. Mr Stephen Morland, M.A. has discussed with me the identity of the nine Quakers in Monmouth's army, and directed me to the Quaker documents in Somerset Record Office.

I owe thanks for ready and courteous help to the staffs at the British Library, the Public Record Office, and the County Record Offices of Somerst, Dorset, and Wiltshire; at Bristol University; and to Mr David Bromwich, M.A. at the Local History Library at Taunton Castle. Professor Ivan Roots of Exeter University has been consistently encouraging and helpful with the loan of books I should otherwise not have seen.

My friend, Mr Peter Matthews, has sought and typed for me the documents that have been printed in *Somerset and Dorset Notes and Queries*. I am indebted to another friend, Mr Maurice Philpott, for most of the illustrations. For introducing me to family and local traditions I must thank the Rev. C. E. E. Meredith, B.A., Vicar of Weston Zoyland, Lt-Col. Newton Wade, Mrs Joan Bower and Miss Margery Smith; and Mr and Mrs Hughes, lately of Barbados. The Rev. W. A. Hawkins kindly showed me the Ashill Parish Register for 1685. Mr Stevens Cox of Guernsey very kindly sent me a photostat of the defence of Joseph Holmes.

Dr J. H. Bettey kindly introduced me to Anthony Adams of the Moonraker Press, who has been a helpful critic and patient publisher. The book might never have been completed but for the help, encouragement and patience of my wife.

Mr David Chandler, M.A., Deputy-Head of War Studies at the Royal Military Academy, Sandhurst, has very kindly given permission to reproduce the Sedgemoor battle-plans he drew for the Souvenir Programme of the re-enactment of the battle by the Society of the Sealed Knot.

CONTENTS

	Introduction	page 9
1	The Duke	15
2	The Men who came with him	24
3	The Welcome in the West	32
4	Into Action	38
5	'King Monmouth'	43
6	The Advance	48
7	Retreat	57
8	Sedgemoor	63
9	The Next Few Days	71
10	The Bloody Assizes	82
11	Prison, Transportation and Escape	96
12	The Social Consequences of Sedgemoor	111
13	Some Survivors	121
	A Guide to the Battlefield of Sedgemoor	127
	Notes	132
	Bibliography	144
	Appendix: *Wade's Narrative*	149
	Index	173

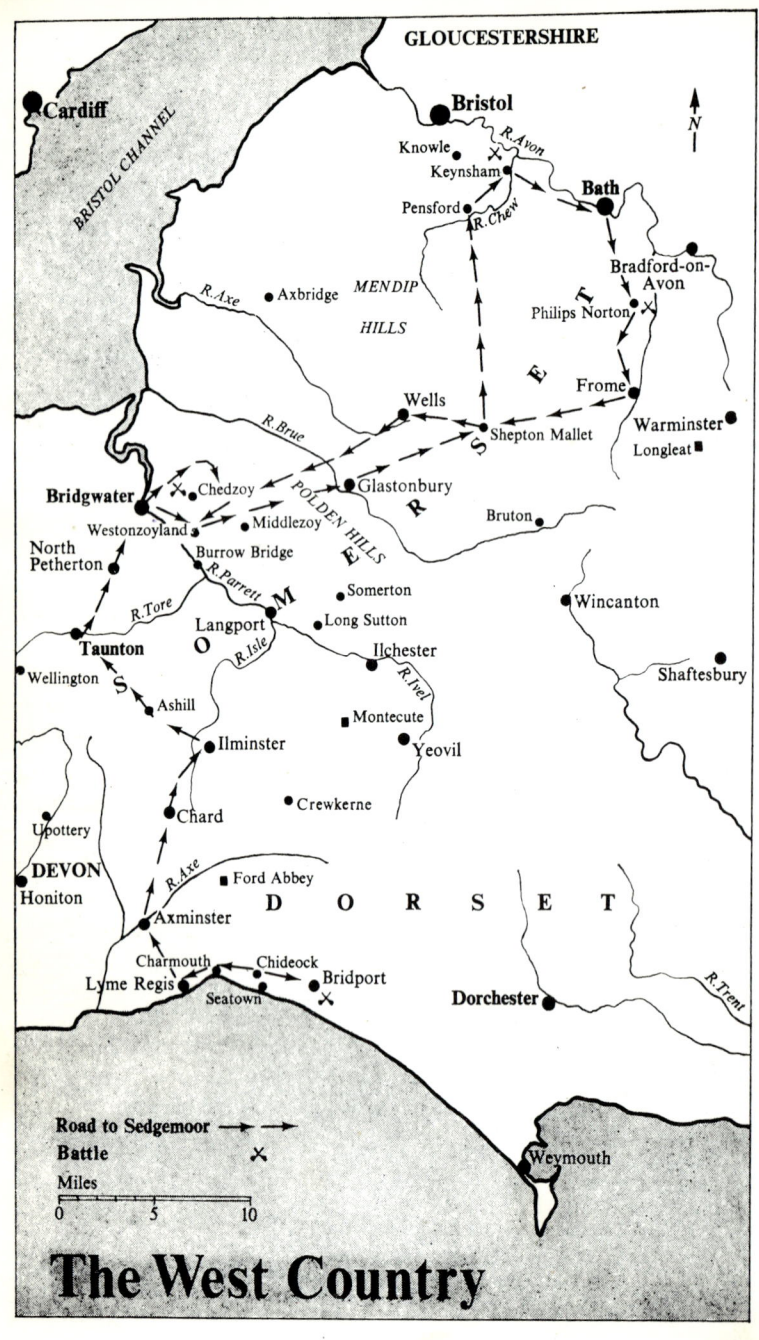

Introduction

The Western Rebellion led by the Duke of Monmouth was much more than an attempt to substitute a popular royal bastard for the legitimate heir, a Prince Charming for his 'wicked uncle'. It was, rather, the next-to-the-last chapter in the century-long struggle for parliamentary government against autocracy, for Puritan Protestantism against High Anglican episcopacy, for some measure of religious freedom against the rigidity of an Establishment.

The century of Stuart rule witnessed a succession of confrontations between the monarch and parliament, culminating in but not terminated by the Civil Wars of the 1640s. Disputes began with King James I's lack of understanding of, and lack of respect for, the Privileges of Parliament, especially their Freedom of Speech. The disputes were aggravated by disagreements over finance. Increasing costs of administration and the fall in the value of money, partly caused by the large imports of gold and silver from Spanish America, drove the king to demand grants from Parliament and to seek revenue from unparliamentary taxation. In the Middle Ages the king had been expected to 'live of his own'. Henry VIII barely managed to pay his expenses by plundering the monasteries and debasing the coinage; Queen Elizabeth, hers, by exercising extreme parsimony and by assuming that her chief minister expected neither salary nor expenses. James I never understood this need for economy. To him England was 'the land of plenty', and his extravagance and his gifts of crown land to favourites made recourse to Parliament unavoidable. The House of Commons took the line: No taxation without redress of grievances.

The doctrine of the Divine Right of Kings was devised by weak kings—by Richard II in the first place—to bolster their position against opposition. There could have been no worse training for Charles I, who, after quarrelling with three parliaments in four years, determined to rule without calling another. Most ill-advisedly he added religion to the causes of contention with the suppressed opposition. In face of increasing

Presbyterian (and Calvinist) opinion, King Charles encouraged the Anglo-Catholic policy of Archbishop Laud, even attempting to impose bishops and an English service-book on the Presbyterian Church of Scotland. The Scots signed the Covenant and rose in arms to resist these innovations. Charles could not finance the 'Bishops' Wars' without appealing to Parliament, but Parliament was more interested in redress of grievances and injustices than imposing High Anglicanism on the Scots. King Charles soon dissolved the Short Parliament (1640), but very shortly had to call another, which became the Long Parliament.

At first the king had few supporters apart from his courtiers and the bishops, but the Puritan majority in the House of Commons, after abolishing the prerogative Courts of Star Chamber and High Commission, which had been used to try and to punish those who could not be punished by the normal process of law, went on to attack the position of bishops in the English Church. This drove many 'moderates' over to this king's side. It is doubtful if there would have been a Civil War without this religious dispute.

Both sides had officers who had seen service on the Protestant side in the Thirty Years War, or in the resistance of the Dutch to the Spaniards. At first the Parliamentary officers were predominantly Presbyterian, but the breakdown of royal and episcopal authority meant that political and religious discussion was able to shape new and free opinions. As humbler men won promotion and the Army was 'new modelled', the strength of the Independents (mainly Congregationalists and Baptists) increased, until the Army that won the Second Civil War in 1648 was unquestionably both Independent and republican, determined 'to make an end of that man of blood, Charles Stuart'.

It cannot be claimed that the government of the Commonwealth or of the Protectorate was popular, but life went on without major discontents and England had never known such religious freedom, though officially the use of the Book of Common Prayer was forbidden. Bishops had been abolished; High Anglican incumbents were dispossessed of their livings, though allowed a very small fraction of their endowment for the support of their families. Ministers were appointed by 'Triers' who satisfied themselves of the ministers' sound Protestant theology. The great majority of the new incumbents were university-educated, and most of them graduates. There was much Bible-reading, and many folk found in congregational services a reality they had not experienced in 'Common Prayer worship'.

The Restoration of the monarchy in 1660 was accompanied by a restoration of the dispossessed rectors and vicars, and shortly afterwards by the ejection of all Puritan ministers who could not subscribe their full assent and consent to all that was included in the Prayer Book of 1662. Altogether 1760 beneficed clergy were ejected from their livings between 1660 and 1662. Many of these, perhaps the majority, continued to minister to the faithful of their congregations, in schools or barns or farmhouse kitchens. Before his return King Charles II had in his Declaration of Breda promised liberty to tender consciences, but the Cavalier Parliament of 1661 refused to honour the king's pledge, using as excuse a tiny revolt in London of the Fifth Monarchy Men,[1] one of the wilder of the Puritan sects. In 1664 the first Conventicle Act forbade any meeting for worship outside the parish church except family prayers, at which no more than five could be present beside the family. On 7 August that year Samuel Pepys wrote in his diary 'Lord's day ... I to Whitehall ... met with Mr Spong ... While we were talking came by several poor creatures carried by, by constables, for being at a conventicle. They go like lambs, without any resistance. I would to God they would either conform, or be more wise, and not be catched!' Others were 'more wise' and held their conventicles in woods, or even in caves, often varying the time to lessen the risk of detection. The Congregationalists of Axminster and Chard hardly missed a Sunday between 1664 and 1688, but very few other congregations were so fortunate, and many prisons were often full of Nonconformists. The Quakers seem to have suffered most. Often a whole meeting was marched off to prison. At Reading and at Bristol, their parents being in prison, the Quaker children met to hold their meeting for worship. Being under 16, they could not be arrested under the Act, but they were 'driven forth'.

The lapse of the Conventicle Act in 1668, as Parliament was not then sitting, allowed the Dissenters to re-establish their services, and to show their numerical strength. So, when Parliament met again in 1670, a second Conventicle Act was passed, more easily enforceable than the first, and fiercer in its fines. Many magistrates were zealous in harrying Nonconformists, and some took pleasure in making bonfires of pulpits and pews. Two years later King Chrales tried to honour his old promise by issuing his Declaration of Indulgence, under which Nonconformist preachers and meeting-houses could be licenced, but as soon as he wanted a grant of money from Parliament, he was told plainly that there would be no grant until the Declaration was withdrawn. For three weeks the king held out; then, with his own hands he broke the seal on the Declaration. Thereafter the persecution of the Dissenters was intermittent.

In 1678 the country was alarmed by the announcement of the discovery of a Popish Plot, described by Titus Oates. Though he was a completely unscrupulous liar, he had hit on some facts that were confirmed by investigation, and the House of Commons agreed *nem con* 'that there has been and still is a damnable and hellish plot, contrived and carried on by popish recusants for the assassinating and murdering the king, and for subverting the government and rooting out and destroying the Protestant religion'. Oates had named as one of the conspirators Edward Coleman, secretary to the Duchess of York. His papers were seized and examined, and among them was his correspondence with Père la Chaise, the French king's confessor. To him Coleman had written

'We have a mighty work upon our hands, no less than the conversion of three kingdoms, and by that the subduing of a pestilent heresy, which has domineered over a great part of this northern world a long time; there was never such hopes of success since the death of Queen Mary as now in our days, when God has given us a prince who is become (may I say a miracle) zealous of being the author and instrument of so glorious a work.

Coleman went on to mention 'the favour of my master the Duke'[2], who was in fact the heir to the throne.

However remote the chance of converting England to Roman Catholicism in the seventeenth century now seems to us, the fear of a serious attempt to achieve it, with the aid of the Irish and a French army, was very real in the 1670s and 1680s. English folk of that time had been brought up on the stories of Protestant martyrs burnt by Queen Mary, of Catholic plots against Queen Elizabeth, of the Gunpowder Plot, and of the Irish massacre of Protestants in 1641. The inscription on the Monument informed its reader that London had been burnt in 1666 through the malice of the Papists. Protestants had had to fight for their survival in France, in Germany, and in Holland; and were at the time being harried in France in spite of the toleration promised in the Edict of Nantes (which King Louis XIV was to revoke entirely in 1685). While innocent Catholics were being put to death on the perjured evidence of Oates and others, the House of Commons was attempting to exclude the king's Catholic brother, the Duke of York, from the succession.

The first Exclusion Bill (1679) proposed that at the death of Charles II the throne should pass to the next heir, as if James, Duke of York, were dead. That would have brought Princess Mary of Orange, James's elder Protestant daughter, to the throne. When the Bill had passed the Commons, the king dissolved Parliament before the Lords had considered the proposition. In the new Parliament, meeting in 1680, a new Exclusion Bill got as far as the House of Lords, but was defeated there before the king dissolved that Parliament. When yet another Parliament met in 1681 at Oxford, the Commons agreed to consider a third Exclusion Bill, and Lord

Shaftesbury asked the king to guarantee the Protestant succession by declaring that the Duke of Monmouth should be his successor. 'Let there be no delusion', said the king; 'I will not yield, nor will I be bullied'; and within a week he dissolved the Oxford Parliament.

Annual subsidies from King Louis XIV freed King Charles from the need to summon another Parliament. There was a reaction of public opinion against the Whigs, and in 1681 the persecution of the Nonconformists was revived. The disappointed Whig leaders began to discuss the possibility of an armed rising to force the king to recall Parliament and accept the exclusion of his brother from the throne. Shaftesbury had been eager for simultaneous risings in London, Cheshire and the West, but divided counsels prevented prompt action. Some looked for the restoration of the Commonwealth, but the peers in the group were opposed to this, as implying the removal of the king. In 1683 informers told their stories of the Rye House Plot, deliberately linking the talk of rebellion with a republican plot to murder the king and his brother as they returned from the Newmarket Races. The plot miscarried because the king returned a week earlier than usual. The government seized the chance to get rid of the Whig leaders. Shaftesbury had died in 1681; Lord William Russell and Colonel Algernon Sidney were executed on inadequate evidence of treason; the Earl of Essex died in the Tower, either by suicide or by murder. John Hampden the younger was to have been tried, and the Duke of Monmouth was subpoena-ed to give evidence against him, but fled to Holland before the trial began.

The king and the Tories had triumphed; and when King Charles died early in 1685, his Catholic brother succeeded to the throne as King James II without opposition.

The Duke of Monmouth (from a painting by Lely engraved by Blooteling)

1

The Duke

James Scott, Duke of Monmouth and Buccleuch, was the eldest of King Charles II's many illegitimate sons, his mother being Lucy Walters. He was born in Rotterdam on 9 April 1649. He appears in Pepys' Diary on 7 September 1662 as 'Mr Crofts, the King's bastard, a most pretty sparke of about 15 years old'. On 27 October Pepys' friend Mr Creed told him 'what is whispered at Court, that young Crofts is lawful son to the King, the King being married to his mother. How true this is', comments Pepys, 'God knows; but I believe the Duke of York will not be fooled in this of three crowns'.

Although King Charles always emphatically denied that he was married to Lucy Walters, many, such as the Rev. John Hickes, believed that this denial[1] was a 'necessary lie', and the Whig leader, the Earl of Shaftesbury, an ex-Lord Chancellor, encouraged Monmouth to drop the bar sinister from the royal arms on his coach. In 1700 when the Princess Anne's last surviving son, William, Duke of Gloucester, died, an Act of Settlement of the Succession became necessary. Before Parliament had settled on the Electress Sophia of Hanover, a grand-daughter of King James I, as the nearest Protestant heir, Daniel Defoe suggested in a pamphlet that it might be worth investigating the claim of Monmouth's son, James, Earl of Dalkeith, a grandson of King Charles II.

In more recent times Colonel Lord Herbert Scott told friends that his father, the 6th Duke of Buccleuch, found in a black box in the muniment-room at Dalkeith Palace the marriage certificate of Charles Stuart and Lucy Walters, and thinking its production in Queen Victoria's reign would be embarrassing, burned it. The story[2] may well be true, but if so the certificate was probably a forgery, prepetrated when Shaftesbury was trying to substitute the Protestant Duke of Monmouth for the Catholic Duke of York as heir to the throne. Monmouth occasionally spoke of incontrovertible proof of his legitimacy, but he never attempted to produce it during his father's lifetime.

King Charles's brother and heir, James, Duke of York, always maintained, perhaps through wishful thinking, that young James was not the son of his brother, but of Colonel Robert Sidney, the younger brother of Algernon Sidney. Portraits, however, of King Charles as a boy (painted by John Hoskins and William Dobson) and of Monmouth as a boy (drawn by Samuel Cooper) show a distinct resemblance. There is also a remarkable similarity of feature between some members of the Buccleuch family (who are descended from Monmouth) and King Charles II as painted by Mary Beale. Charles never doubted that he was Monmouth's father; and Queen Henrietta Maria received and looked after the boy as her eldest grandson.

The boy became a favourite with most people who met him. He was athletic, and had inherited his mother's beauty and his father's affability and charm of manner. He danced well, and took part in several masques at court. Some couplets from Dryden's *Absalom and Achitophel*, written in 1681, describe the king's affection for his son and the young man's charm. After mentioning several sons, Dryden continues

> Of all this numerous progeny was none
> So beautiful, so brave, as Absalom . . .
> Early in foreign fields he won renown
> With kings and states allied to Israel's crown . .
> Whate'er he did was done with so much ease,
> In him alone 'twas natural to please;
> His motions all accompanied with grace,
> And Paradise was opened in his face.
> With secret joy indulgent David viewed
> His youthful image in his son renewed;
> To all his wishes nothing he denied
> And made the charming Annabel his bride . . .
> Thus praised and loved, the noble youth remained,
> While David undisturbed in Sion reigned.

It was when the boy was fourteen that King Charles arranged his marriage to Anne Scott, Countess of Buccleuch, the richest Scottish heiress. He made the boy Duke of Monmouth and a Knight of the Garter shortly before the wedding, and created the young couple Duke and Duchess of Monmouth and Buccleuch. The bridegroom took his wife's surname.

Two years after his marriage the young duke served at sea under his uncle, the Duke of York, and was praised for his conduct in the Battle of Solebay. After his return from sea he was made a Captain of Horse, and when he had learned his duties, Captain in the Life Guards.

About this time Mr Pepys was told by Lord Brouncker (on 16 December 1666) that 'the Duke of Monmouth spends his time the most viciously and idle of any man, nor will be fit for anything'; but by 11 September 1667 Mr Moore was assuring Pepys 'he do verily believe that the King do resolve to declare the Duke of Monmouth legitimate, and that we shall soon see it'. When Sir Hugh Cholmley repeated this opinion on 4 November, Pepys added to his record 'which God forbid'. Monmouth certainly struck a bad patch, sowing wild oats with a group of rich and riotous companions. Promotion to be Colonel of the Life Guards and, on the death of General Monk, Duke of Albermarle, to succeed him as Captain General of His Majesty's Land Forces gave Monmouth more to occupy his time.

In 1672 the young duke was sent to command an English brigade lent to the French, to serve under the great Turenne against the Dutch. Both Monmouth and his friend, Captain John Churchill, distinguished themselves by the courage and promising military ability they showed, especially at the siege and capture of Maestricht. In the next war (1678) Monmouth was fighting on the other side, for the Dutch and against the French. He held Ostend with a small force, and showed personal courage at the Battle of St Denis and the defence of Mons.

As Captain General[3], Monmouth achieved an agreement with Sir Stephen Fox, the Paymaster General, to expedite the payment of the troops, which was always in arrears; and later, after his service abroad, he introduced the French army-drill, which he considered more efficient and more up-to-date.

Persecution of the Scottish Covenanters led in 1679 to a rising of the Cameronians in the south-west of Scotland. At Drumclog they outnumbered and defeated Graham of Claverhouse. King Charles sent Monmouth north to take command against the rebels. He caught them at a disadvantage on a Sunday and defeated them at Bothwell Brig, and then exerted himself to stop the slaughter of 'my father's subjects'. His clemency won him the respect and goodwill of the Scots, but disapproval by[4] the government.

Between the dissolution of the Cavalier Parliament in 1679 and the meeting of the new Parliament in 1680, Shaftesbury sent Monmouth on a semi-royal 'progress' through the western counties. He received a rapturous welcome, and was entertained by friends: at Longleat by Tom Thynne; at Whitelackington by George Speke (who had fought as a Royalist in the Civil War); at Ford Abbey by Edmund Prideaux, the son of Cromwell's Attorney General; at Colyton by Sir Walter Yonge; at Barrington by William Strode (son of a Parliamentarian colonel); at Hinton St George and at Brympton d'Evercy by Sir John Sydenham, the guardian of young Lord Poulett. At Whitelackington there was a great feast 'under a spreading chestnut tree' whose enormous trunk, now fallen, may still be seen. At Hinton St George Monmouth, probably without intending it, touched for the King's Evil (scrofula), and the patient, Elizabeth Parcet, claimed to be cured. This, Monmouth's adherents averred, proved his royal blood.

There is an unforgettable account of Monmouth's passage through Ilchester in the autobiography of John Whiting, a young Quaker farmer who was in prison there for refusing to pay tithes, because Quakers held that tithes belonged to the era of the Old Testament, and are nowhere commanded in the new Testament. Similarly, as is also relevant to the story, they refused to pay 'hat honour' to any man, all men being equal in God's sight. After a year in the gaol itself, Whiting was moved to easier confinement at the Friary 'a great house at the other end of the town, where were many Friends prisoners', and where they were able to hold their Meetings for Worship. They were allowed to take their exercise walking into the town, their gaolers knowing that they would return.

In August 1680 the Duke of Monmouth, wrote Whiting,

came through Ivelchester[5] with some thousands on horseback attending him; the country flocking to him and after him, the eyes of the nation being towards him as the hopes and head of the protestant interest at that time, in opposition to the Duke of York and the Popish party; so that the affections of the people ran exceedingly after him. We stood in the Friary-gate as he rode through the town; and as he passed by, taking notice of so many Quakers together with their hats on, he stopped and put off his hat to us . . . We could not but have a respect for his affability, and therefore were the more concerned for him when his fall came[6].

In 1681 England had been not far from a renewal of civil war. The Whig leaders had come to Oxford with crowds of armed supporters, and when the King dissolved Parliament a week after it met, Shaftesbury felt that Monmouth missed his opportunity to lead a successful rebellion. Monmouth had no wish to rebel against his father, though he had hoped to force him to recall Parliament and allow the passing of the Exclusion Bill.

In the next year Monmouth attempted another semi-royal progress in and around Cheshire, and won easy popularity by showing that he could win races on foot as well as on horseback; but when he reached Stafford he was met by the King's messenger with orders to arrest him and return him to London. Monmouth submitted, and Shaftesbury felt that he had let slip another chance of rebellion. The duke was released on bail and went to Sussex, ostensibly to hunt with his friend Lord Grey at Uppark, but hoping for another successful progress. A royalist reaction had set in, and there was no progress. A warrant was issued for the arrest of Shaftesbury, and when he was eventually released on bail he fled to Holland and before long died there.

For a year and a half after the Rye House Plot Monmouth lived hopefully and happily in Holland, hopeful and expectant of a recall from exile and restoration to his father's favour, for which Lord Halifax was working steadily. Monmouth had long been a favourite with Princess Mary, and was treated with friendship by William of Orange. He danced at state balls and skated with Princess Mary on frozen canals. He was at this time living happily with Henrietta, who was Lady Wentworth in her own right. She had been a Maid in Waiting to Mary of Modena, Duchess of York, James's second wife, and had acted and danced with Monmouth in court masques. She fell deeply in love with him, and he with her, and he had found refuge in her home at Toddington in Bedfordshire, when he was ordered abroad by King Charles in 1681. In those premissive days in high society, Henrietta's mother made no difficulties for the lovers, and when Monmouth went to Holland in 1683, both Henrietta and her mother followed him into exile. Monmouth's marriage to Duchess Anne having been arranged for him when he was a minor, he did not regard his marriage vows as binding and believed that Henrietta was his true wife in the sight of heaven.

Monmouth's personality eludes us. Contemporaries wrote of his beauty and charm, but apart from portraits little survives to recreate his actual personality, except the pocket-book which was taken from him when he was captured, and sent to King James. It went to France in 1688 when King James fled, and was among those papers he lodged in the library of the Scots College in Paris, whence it was removed during the French Revolution. After various misadventures it found its way to a second-hand bookstall beside the Seine, whence it was bought[7] by an Irish theological student. Perhaps he was the John Barrette of the Irish College, Paris, who wrote his name on the blank page 90 on 31 December, 1827. The small book was taken to Ireland and came into the possession of Mr Robert Rae of County Kerry, and was sold by him in May 1851, probably to Sir Philip Grey Egerton, with some of whose collections it came to the British Museum. It is now Egerton MS 1527 in the British Library.

Monmouth's pocket-book measures $3\frac{3}{8}$ by $5\frac{7}{8}$ in., is bound in black leather, and once had silver clasps. It contains about 80 leaves, of which a few are blank. Almost all it contains is in Monmouth's handwriting, and some entries are in French. The contents are an amazing mixture. Some of the earliest are a collection of recipes, such as 'for to make Bouts and choos hold out water; to kip Iron from Rusting; to make the face fair; to keep the goms (gums) well'. There is a horoscope dated 1680 and some pages of rules for fortune-telling. There are several pages of 'casualties' (marvels or mishaps) in each reign from William I to Queen Mary. The next page is headed Queen Elizabeth, but no 'casualties' follow.

In a more serious mood, and reflecting his real military ability, are a couple of pages about 'the Batteryes that can be made at Flushing to keep ships from coming in . . . (for) Sheeps may come in with a wind without tacking'. At the end of the book are notes about the equivalent of Dutch 'ducatoons' in English money, and several addresses in the Low Countries, not in the Duke's writing.

Other pages give us surprising insights into Monmouth's character. He copied several pages of commentary on various Psalms; he filled about 30 pages with prayers, most, no doubt, copied, a few original. The earlier pages of prayers are for morning and evening use, some 'to be said after confession of sins', and one 'after assurance of forgiveness', and assurance he was clearly seeking in prayers at the end of the book. An evening prayer may be quoted:

Watch over me in my sleep, O Lord, that whether I sleep or weak I may be thy servant. Be thou first and last in all my thoughts, and the guide and continuall assistance of all my actions.

The Duke was clearly revolted at the idea that some are predestined to Hell. 'O God the Father, who canst not be thought so cruel as to make me only to distroy me, Have mercy on me . . .' In his later prayers Monmouth was earnestly seeking peace with God. He deplores 'the sins of unfaithfulness'. He prays 'Save me O God as a Brand snatched out of the fire. Receive me, O my Jesu, as a sheep that hath wandred, but is now returned to the great Shepherd and Bishop of my soul'. Most moving among the later prayers is this:

I aske not of thee any longer the things of this world; neither Power nor Honours, nor Riches, nor Pleasures. No, my God, dispose of them to whom thou pleasest, so that you givest me mercy. O that I could hear thee once say, as thou didst to him in the Gospel, My son be of good cheer; thy sins are forgiven thee.

Turning from Monmouth's prayers to the poetry he tried to write is only to continue the search for his personality. He copied a long poem entitled The Twin Flame, about his love for 'Clovis' (or perhaps Cloris) and 'Philis'. The poet is not implying 'How happy could I be with either,
     Were t'other dear charmer[8] away',
for he despairs of continued happiness with the demanding and selfish Clovis, whom he has loved, but he hesitates to seek Philis as his mistress.

  That love wee to our Prince or Parents pay
  I'le beare to you, and love a humble way.

> I'le pay you Veneration for your love
> And your Admirer, not your lover prove.
> Oh, bee contented with the sacred name
> Of friend, and inviolable flame
> For you I will preserve, and the first place
> Of all the few I with that title grace;
> And yet this friendship doth so fast improve
> I dread least it in time should grow to love.

It did; for whether Clovis represented to him Anne, his wife, or his earlier mistress, Eleanor Needham, Philis was almost certainly Henrietta Wentworth, his last and dearest love, with whom he lived the happiest days of his life.

Sir Charles Sedley and John Milton[9] had both used the name Phyllis with the suggestion of a country girl, and Monmouth followed his longer poem with two shorter songs of his own about his happiness in the country, even adding a row of notes to suggest an air to which they might be sung.

> With joie we do leave thee
> falce world and do forgive
> all thy beace treachery,
> for now w'ill happy live
> As w'ill to our Bowers
> and there spend our howers
> happy there we will bee.
> Wee noe striffs there can see,
> no quareling for crowns,
> nor fear the great ons frowns
> nor slavery of state
> nor changes in our Fate.
> from Plots this place is free.
> heer w'ill ever bee
> w'ill sit and bles our stars
> that from the noise of wars
> did this Glorious place give
> that Thus we happy live.

In the margin Monmouth wrote an alternative to the penultimate line: 'or did us Tedington give'.

The first verse of the next song runs:

> O how blest and how inocent
> and happy is a country life
> free from tumult and discontent
> heer is no flatterys nor strife
> for t'was the first and happist life
> When first man did injoie himselfe.

Lastly we come to notes of itineraries, which give us some of the very few dates Monmouth entered in his note-book. 'The way from London to East Tilbery' bears a tiny note in the margin '1 of Decem 84', and so confirms that Monmouth did make a secret visit to England towards the end of 1684. The sequel is 'The rode that is to be taken from Bruxels to Diren, the Prince of Oranges house'. It includes as one stage 'from Nimegen to Arnem 3 leagues', and later 'The way that I took when I cam from England December the 10th 84'; and squeezed in the margin he wrote a note on the weather: 'frost, much snow, then rain'. Right at the end of the book is the route Monmouth loved best:

from London to Hamsted,
from Hamsted to Hendon,
from Hendon to Edgeworth [Edgware],
from Edgeworth to Astre [Elstree]
from Astre to St Steephens [just below St Albans]
from St Steephens to Dounstable
and from Dounstable to Tedington [as he always spelt Toddington].

So long as his father lived Monmouth kept away from the numerous Whig exiles, who among themselves charged him with the ingratitude which was characteristic of the Stuarts. At the end of 1684 he was almost daily expecting a letter from Lord Halifax summoning him home, but early in 1685 he heard instead of King Charles's early and unexpected death, and of his uncle James's unopposed accession. William and Mary expressed their friendship but explained that they could no longer welcome him as their guest. Monmouth is said to have promised them to make no further bid for the crown. William suggested that the Duke should apply for a general's commission in the Emperor's army, then fighting the Turks.

Monmouth and Henrietta withdrew to Brussels, then in the Spanish Netherlands, and after his initial bitter disappointment Monmouth seems to have contemplated a retired life of domestic bliss with Henrietta. Whig exiles and conspirators, however, worked on his ambition and persuaded him that the English people were eager to support him and his claim to the throne. Exiles easily believe that the government at home is unpopular and the people anxious to overthrow it, if the right leader should appear. Monmouth was told of 10,000 supporters in London; and of the Earl of Argyll, also in exile, but planning to raise a revolt in Scotland. He expected his friends in Cheshire to rise if and when they heard of his landing; and he expected many army officers who had served under his command to desert from the royal army to join him. It is said that he held back until the plotters enlisted the support of Henrietta. Then Monmouth agreed to a meeting with Argyll, and went to Amsterdam to begin preparations for the invasion of England.

Many potential supporters were republicans who wanted to restore the Commonwealth. Argyll agreed with them that Monmouth should not claim the crown, but proclaim that freely elected Parliaments in England and Scotland should be chosen to settle the future government of the two countries. Argyll could not afford to keep his followers waiting in exile until Monmouth was ready, so, urging speed in preparations, he set sail for Scotland on 2 May. Monmouth promised to follow within three weeks, but did not sail until 30 May.

Messengers went to and fro between Monmouth and the Whig conspirators in London, Major Wildman and Colonel Danvers. These were both republicans and very suspicious of the royal duke. When he applied urgently to them for money, Wildman told Monmouth's messenger that there was no need to send money for arms, as the London 10,000 were already armed. Monmouth and Henrietta raised what money they could on their jewels, all except his 'smaller George' and his watch. Three small ships were obtained, four small cannon, 1500 muskets and pikes; and 1500 breastplates (which were never used).

Taunton was to be the rallying point, and this secret was well kept; Lyme Regis was chosen for the landing. King James got the Dutch authorities to promise to prevent the sailing of Monmouth's ships, but by trickery and some connivance they got away to sea on 30 May with Monmouth and 82 followers aboard.

2

The men who came with him

Of the 82 men who came from Holland with Monmouth one was an English nobleman, one a Scottish laird, a few were old Cromwellian officers, two or three came from English regiments in the Dutch Service, two more from the Army of Brandenburg, two were gunners. Of civilians, four were Whig lawyers, three of them from London, the other a Westcountryman; two were clergymen. There were two doctors, and a medical student, two other students; a goldsmith and his son; and at least six of the Duke's personal servants. There were others to whom Monmouth gave commissions while they were at sea. Altogether we have the names of nearly 60 who landed with him in Dorset.

The English nobleman was Ford Grey, Lord Grey of Warke, his odd Christian name being his mother's maiden name. Her mother, Grey's grandmother, was the sister of General Ireton, Cromwell's son-in-law. Ford Grey inherited rich lands in Northumberland, where Warke Castle stands, some in Essex and some in Sussex, where Uppark was his favourite seat. Before he was twenty he was married to Lady Mary Berkeley, who at seventeen had lost her heart to the charming Duke of Monmouth. The two peers became friends, and the Duke used to come to Uppark to hunt with Grey. The Popish Plot drove Grey into Whig politics, and making friends with the Earl of Shaftesbury and Lord William Russell, he played a large part in securing the election of two Whigs for Essex in 1679. He was reckoned one of the Whig 'Council of six', which also included Monmouth.

Early in the 1680s rumour had it that Monmouth had a liaison with Lady Grey. Lord Grey remained friends with the Duke, caring much more for his wife's younger sister, Lady Henrietta (Harriet to the family) than for his wife. He scandalised society by seducing Lady Harriet, and after her escape from her father's house Grey was prosecuted for abduction, Mr Sergeant Jeffreys conducting the prosecution. Grey may have aided and abetted Harriet's flight, but there is little doubt that she went of her own free will, and she came to Grey's trial to give her own evidence. The Earl of Berkeley demanded her return to his home and care; but Harriet had secured herself against this claim by a marriage with Grey's henchman, William Turner. Though quite legal, it was certainly a marriage of convenience, and Harriet remaind Grey's mistress for some years. As the law term was at its end, bail was granted to Grey, who settled £1000 a year on his wife, Mary. The family accepted the settlement, and a *Noli Prosequi* in the next term set Grey at liberty; though not for long. The government had a couple of bones to pick with him, one concerning a midsummer-day riot, and the other about a larger collection of weapons than the government thought necessary. Then Colonel Rumsey turned informer about the Rye House Plot, and denounced Grey as a conspirator. A sergeant-at-arms, Dereham, was sent to arrest him and conduct him to the Tower. As it was late they dined, at Grey's expense, and slept at the Rummer Tavern near Charing Cross. Early the next morning they took a coach to the Tower. After a late night and some share of 14 bottles of claret, Sergeant Dereham, who was apparently neither drunk nor drugged, fell fast asleep in the coach, and it was Lord Grey who got out to knock at the Bulwark Gate of the Tower and dispatched the sentinel to fetch the Lieutenant to receive a prisoner. As Dereham was still fast asleep, Grey suddenly realised and seized his chance to escape. It was Sergeant Dereham who became the prisoner. Grey got himself rowed across the Thames, collected a servant and two horses, and rode to Uppark. There he was joined by Lady Harriet and William Turner, and making contact with 'a seafaring man with one leg'—one Robert Lock—got his little party transported to Flushing, on to Middelburg, and thence by way of Rotterdam to Cleves, then a possession of the Elector of Brandenburg. Grey's cousin and lawyer, Henry Ireton (the younger) managed to send him money, part of which came from Grey's brother and part from Lady Grey, who must have been fonder of her husband than he realised.

The lack of any message from Monmouth made Grey think him most ungrateful, but the Duke did arrange to see him in The Hague on the eve of his semi-secret visit to England in November 1684, and sent for him again at the end of January 1685, just before he got the news of the King's death. Their friendship was renewed, and when the Duke planned his invasion of England, Grey, as the only nobleman in the expedition, was nominated Second-in-command and commander of the Horse. Grey, though a skilled horseman and a keen huntsman, was not cut out to be a cavalry general.

His instinct for self-preservation was much too strong; but he was not the poltroon for which he has too often been taken, as two incidents during the Rebellion and his subsequent career[1] under King William III will show.

The Scottish laird was Andrew Fletcher of Saltoun in East Lothian, described by Bishop Burnet in his *History of My Own Times* as 'a Scotch gentleman of great parts and many virtues, but a most violent republican, and extremely passionate'. Fletcher's father died when the boy was ten, and Burnet, then minister of Saltoun parish, supervised the boy's education until he was fifteen. Fletcher went on the Grand Tour, and came back to take his place in public life. He represented East Lothian in the Convention of Estates, voting steadily with the Duke of Hamilton against the Duke of Lauderdale, who was the King's representative in Scotland. As a result, he had soldiers quartered on him by the government, but he continued his opposition in the Scottish Parliament of 1681, when the Duke of York represented the King. When the Earl of Argyll was put in prison on a preposterous charge of treason, Fletcher and others went abroad. Visiting London, Fletcher was taken into the confidence of Monmouth, Russell and Shaftesbury, and later joined Monmouth in Holland. In spite of his fiery nature, Fletcher advised Argyll and Monmouth against rebellion but, being an experienced Militia officer, he agreed to accompany Monmouth to command the cavalry[2] under Grey.

Nathaniel Wade, a lawyer of Bristol and London, dictated, while he was a wounded prisoner, the best contemporary account we have of the rebellion.* Born in 1646, the third son of an Ironside Major who rose to be a Major-General, Nathaniel grew up a Nonconformist and a republican. He inherited distinct military ability, and is reported to have taught military drill to nonconformist volunteers in 1681, when civil war was again a possibility. Two years later in London he was involved in discussions of a possible armed rising with the Whig leaders. For this he was denounced by Colonel Rumsey, who also falsely accused him of complicity in the Rye House Plot to murder the King. With Richard Nelthorpe, who was also accused, Wade fled via Scarborough to Holland and on to Switzerland, where he made friends with Colonel Ludlow, a famous Parliamentarian soldier who had signed the death-warrant of King Charles. One of the Whig conspirators asked Wade to enquire whether Ludlow would be the Infantry Brigadier if and when the Whigs were able to renew the Civil War. Ludlow replied that his fighting days were done. The exiles asked Wade to rejoin them in Holland. 'All this while', Wade recorded, 'the Duke of Monmouth and his party knew nothing of this affair'. Then came the news of the death of King Charles, and soon after

---

*See Appendix, p. 149.

that the Duke was persuaded to invade England. 'All the money for both Expeditions', (Argyll's and Monmouth's) says Wade, 'came out of the purses of the people beyond the seas'. Monmouth and Grey recognised the reliability and efficiency of Wade, and entrusted him[3] with the laying out of £3000 on ships, cannon, arms and 200 barrels of gunpowder.

Of special interest is Wade's list of the officers Monmouth commissioned on the voyage to Lyme Regis. Before he dictated his account, he had been at pains to find out who had been killed, and who had got safely abroad, and he contrived to forget the names of those who might still be arrested. Captain Venner, John Foulkes and Abraham Holmes were to be Lieut-Colonels of the Red, White and Green Regiments. Wade himself, James Fox and Robert Parsons were to be Majors in the Red, Yellow and Green Regiments. The Red Regiment was to be Monmouth's own regiment. Richard Goodenough, Joseph Tily, Lieutenant Thompson and Captain James Hayes were made captains in the Red; Francis Goodenough in the White, and Patchall in the Green. Taylor, Dolly (or Dalby), Mitchell, Lillington, and William Hewling became Lieutenants in the Red; with John Cragg, Thomas Dare junior, Mr Sanford, Babbington and Vincent as Ensigns in the Red, and Blake as Ensign in the Green. Wade professed that he could not remember the others who were commissioned. William Hewling's elder brother, Benjamin was one, and Ensign Josiah Ascue—the son of a tallow chandler in Long Acre—was another.

Those Wade mentions with a previous military rank were either old Cromwellian officers, or officers in one of the English regiments in the Dutch service, as were Foulkes and Fox. King James had asked William of Orange to cashier several officers whom he, King James, regarded as of doubtful loyalty.

Little is known of Samuel Venner, who may well have been a relative of the Thomas Venner who was hanged in 1661 for leading the brief revolt of the Fifth Monarchy Men. Samuel was glib enough of speech to impress Monmouth, who often used him as Acting Brigadier of the Foot but, as will appear in the narrative of the Rebellion, Venner had lost his nerve, and his advice seems invariably to have favoured retreat. He was not present at Sedgemoor.

A very different man was Abraham Holmes, who had served as a Major in Scotland under[4] General Monk. He was a zealous Baptist and an avowed republican. Though popular with his men, he was suspected by Monk of being an agitator, and Monk sent him to London to be under Cromwell's eye. He was back in Scotland after Cromwell's death, but Monk cancelled his commission. Involved in a plot to assassinate King

Charles before his coronation, Holmes spent some years as a prisoner in Windsor Castle. He was free by 1681 and provided a refuge for the Earl of Argyll in his lodgings in London. Two years later Holmes was imprisoned in the Gatehouse for alleged complicity in the Rye House Plot, but though charged with High Treason, he was not brought to trial. Either he escaped or was released, and crossed to Holland, and was brought to see Monmouth. Afterwards he said he 'hesitated because he thought it [the rebellion] not feasible with those men and the correspondents the Duke had'; but he agreed to accompany the Duke and accepted the command of the Green Regiment. The subsequent account of two battles will bear witness to his courage and toughness.

Richard and Francis Goodenough were London Lawyers and had held the office of Under Sheriff alternately, serving the Whig interest by nominating juries guaranteed to return 'Ignoramus' verdicts whenever Whigs were prosecuted by the government. Losing control in 1683, and denounced as Rye House conspirators, they fled to Holland. Being absent when the Grand Jury found a True Bill against them for High Treason, they were outlawed.

Of Thompson we are told that he was 'an officer and a linnen draper of London', and that he 'commanded the Scythemen'. So said John Kidd when interrogated[5] after Sedgemoor.

Benjamin and William Hewling were respectively 22 and 19 in 1685. They were the grandsons of a prominent London merchant, a leader among the Baptists, William Kiffen. They were in Holland as students, possibly preparing for the Baptist ministry. They seem to have been young men of singular charm and courage. When they were captured after Sedgemoor, Captain Richardson 'found in young Hewling's pukett' a paper[6] with a list of 34 mostly officers, who came from Holland with the Duke.

Monmouth brought with him at least six personal servants: his steward, William Williams; Matthews, his equerry; Robert Hampton, who had been his butler for 14 years and was to be 'in charge of the carriages'; Moses Wagstaffe, a servant of five years' standing, who 'attended on the carriages'; Thomas Boad, his groom; and Richard Hubbard, his servant. Four of them were eventually captured and questioned, and Williams[7] mentioned a score who came from Holland with the Duke. To those listed by Wade, we can add a dozen named by Williams: Lord Grey, Captain Buys, Bruce, Dare, Chamberlain, Nelthorpe, Ferguson, Manley, Fletcher, young Barnardiston, Temple and Walters (or Woolters), a pilot.

Anton Buys, often referred to as 'the Brandenburger', had been recruited to command Monmouth's artillery of four light guns. A skilled and experienced Dutch gunner, whose name we do not know, and an English gunner, Mr Rose, were also enlisted to serve the guns. Captain Robert Bruce, a Scot of Fife, also came from the army of Brandenburg, in which he had served for 14 years. Major John Manley, whom Wade 'forgot' as he had not been captured, was another experienced officer who won Monmouth's confidence.

Thomas Heywood Dare had been until 1680 a goldsmith and a prominent member of Taunton Corporation, but in 1679 he took it upon himself in the name of the inhabitants and freeholders of Somerset to present to the King a petition for the sitting of parliament. This he thrust before the King as he was leaving the House of Lords in procession. King Charles exclaimed 'How dare you?' and was not amused when the petitioner replied 'Sire, my name is Dare'. Dare had an indiscreet tongue and was unlucky in having his unguarded remarks reported to someone in authority, so he found himself arraigned at the Assizes in 1680 for sedition, having said that 'The subject has but two ways of redress, by petition or rebellion'. The Grand Jury first disowned the Somerset Petition, and then sent Dare for trial, at which he was fined £500, with imprisonment until it was paid, and was turned off Taunton Corporation. Unless he could be sure of the discretion of his hearers, Dare really did ask for trouble by replying to a friend who mentioned the Privy Council, that 'he knew no Council the King had but the Duchess of Portsmouth, the French Ambassador, Lord Duras[8], and the Duke of Lauderdale'. This also was duly reported, and when, after ten months in prison, Dare apologized and begged for mercy it was not forthcoming. Somehow Dare contrived to escape, and not unnaturally betook himself to Holland late in 1680 or early 1681. There his lodgings became a meeting-place for the Whig conspirators, among whom he was described as 'the principal manager'. In due course Monmouth nominated him[9] as his Paymaster (though there was never money to pay the rebel troops).

Hewling's list describes both Hugh Chamberlain and Samuel Barnardiston as 'Reformade', which seems to mean an officer of a disbanded regiment, who had enlisted in a new regiment without rank[10], but hoping for a new commission. It was Chamberlain's son who persuaded Josias Askew to join Monmouth, so probably he, and certainly Dare's son and perhaps Barnardiston's son came with the Duke.

Richard Nelthorpe was a barrister of Gray's Inn, and perhaps the nephew of Captain John Nelthorpe of the New Model Army. On the fringe of the Rye House Plot, Richard was in June 1683 denounced by Colonel Rumsey, and fled with Nathaniel Wade via Scarborough to Rotterdam. His chambers in the Temple were searched, but nothing incriminating was found. In July a Grand Jury found a True Bill against him for High Treason, and he was outlawed.[11]. Hewling calls him a captain.

The Duke brought two clergymen with him: the Rev. Robert Ferguson to be Chaplain to the Army, and the Rev. Nathaniel Hook as his domestic chaplain. Ferguson was already notorious, a wanted man. After studying at Aberdeen University, during the Interregnum he had been the Presbyterian vicar of Godmersham, Kent, and was ejected in 1662. He continued to preach whenever he could, and wrote pamphlets both theological and political. He became increasingly involved in Whig plots, especially the Rye House Plot, after which he was described in a government poster as 'A tall lean man, dark brown hair, a great Roman nose, thin jawed, heat in his face, speaks in a Scotch tone, a sharp piercing eye, stoops a little in the shoulders; he hath a shuffling gait that differs from all men; wears his periwig down almost over his eyes; about 45 or 46 years old'. Outlawed, Ferguson escaped to Holland and moved restlessly among the exiles. Monmouth, Grey tells us, 'had not the best opinion of Mr Ferguson's secrecy . . . and resolved to conceal from him' names, times and places. Ferguson eagerly drafted a proclamation to be read at the Duke's landing, and he it was who committed Monmouth to accusing King James of murdering his brother, King Charles. It is said that Ferguson hoped to be made Archbishop of Canterbury as a reward for his services. Monmouth's final assessment of Ferguson[12] was that he was 'a bloody rogue'.

Nathaniel Hook was not much more than 21 when the Duke appointed him his domestic chaplain. Hook had entered Trinity College, Dublin, and after a year there moved to Glasgow University, and thence in 1680 to Sidney Sussex College, Cambridge. As a nonconformist he came down without a degree, and he seems to have been considered a Congregational minister. His later career[13] shows him to have been a man of great ability.

Having been in action several times Monmouth realised an army's need of surgeons, and engaged Dr Benjamin Temple, a Nottingham man then in Holland, as his chief physician and 'chirurgeon'. He also brought with him 'Gillard, Chirurgeon' and William Oliver, then 26, probably the only Cornishman in his army. Oliver was a second-year medical student at Leyden University, but was regarded in Monmouth's army as one of their surgeons.

Another man who chanced to be in Holland at this time was John Kidd, who had come over to buy horses for the Earl of Devonshire, the 4th Earl who became the 1st Duke. Kidd had been gamekeeper at Longleat, was an experienced N.C.O. in the Militia, and had considerable local influence.

Monmouth offered him a captaincy when William Turner and Captain Parsons persuaded him to come over with the Duke. We cannot be certain that Turner came with Lord Grey, but it is probable, as a William Turner was pardoned 'for all treasons committed by him' on 10 December 1686.

The last half-dozen we can name of Monmouth's company are John Tellier, who had been kept on board as a prisoner lest he should give information, but accepted a commission on the way to England; Samuel Storey, a Scot who became Monmouth's Commissary General; James Burton, another of the Rye House outlaws; and three named on Hewling's list, Colonel Stevenson, a second Lieut. Tomson, and Ensign Showers.

3

The Welcome in the West

On 14 May 1685 two men were drinking in a tavern at Wellington; one, William Way of Combe St Nicholas, the other, Mr Cross, the County Coroner. Cross was gloomy, but Way spoke hopefully of the future, for 'our Gile', Mr Cross thought he said, was in Scotland with an army, and the Duke of Monmouth would be here before the end of the month. Wine must have loosened Mr Way's tongue, for otherwise the secret had been kept. Mr Cross passed on the information to the Rev. Thomas Axe,[1], who sent it on to London, but the government took little notice of this careless talk.

A fortnight later someone in London was addressing a letter to 'Mr James Carryer at Ilminster in Somersett'. It took two days to reach the Post House there; but before it could be delivered, the Postbag was searched by Captain William Speke (the only Tory in that family) and the vicar, the Rev. Henry Clarke. They thought it odd that a letter should be addressed to the blacksmith (for that was James Carrier's calling); and they opened the letter and read

Friend,
These are to advise thee that honest Protestants forthwith prepare and make themselves very ready, for here is now orders to apprehend all honest men, that are any wise noted, and to secure them, for they have notice here at Court that a certaine person will forthwith appear in the West, which puts them here at Court into a most dredfull fear and confusion; tis hoped therefore that all honest men that are true Protestants will stick togeather, and not let their friends be brought out of the Country by any Messengers or the like, you know how to deale with your two Neighbouring and such like Fellowes; Argile have had great Successe in Scotland and have already distroyed great part of the Kings forces there, and we heare from good hands that he hath such an Army that doe encrease so mightily daily that nothing can oppose them, And if they be once up in the West, they would suddenly be up in all parts of England, all the Protestants being certainly prepared by this, and resolved rather to dye then to live Slaves or Papists: make good use hereof, and Impart it to such as you can trust, that you may all be

prepared and ready against the appearance of a certain person which will be forthwith if not already

from your freind
F.R.

Captain Speke, having sent a messenger to the Mayor of Taunton advising him to search the Mail Bag there, set off to show the king the intercepted letter. Almost all the Taunton mail had been delivered, but among the remaining eight letters was one addressed to 'Mr Christofer Cooke, Aulnager in Taunton' dated, fraudulently, as from St James's, and truthfully as 28 May 1685. The letter uses some of the same phraseology and the same false news from Scotland. After signing the letter 'S C', the writer added 'I hope you understand the meaning of these lines'.

The initials F.R. have been thought to be those of Robert Ferguson reversed. The extravagant lies about Argyll's success are quite in the vein of Ferguson, but as he was in Holland at that date, he must, if he was the author, have sent the letters to London by one of Monmouth's messengers.

The following Sunday, 31 May, two Ilminster men, Joseph Standerwick and Samuel Key, left home (so Sir William Portman was informed) and did not return until the following Tuesday. Two stories reached Sir William of about 80 mysterious horsemen[1] passing Obridge Mill on the night of 1 June. Standerwick and Key were subsequently in Monmouth's army, so the accounts probably record a combined recruiting drive and an 'exercise'.

The Rev. Thomas Axe estimated that 'all confiding Dissenters had full intelligence of Monmouth's comeing into the West . . . and . . . were soe true to one another that nobody perceived it'. We do not know when the Congregationalists at Axminster first heard of Monmouth's coming, but their Book of Remembrance[2] recorded

Now the Lord stirred up James, Duke of Monmouth (reputed son of the former king C.2.) who had bin in an Exile state for some time . . . Tydings of his landing was spread abroad far and near very speedily . . . Now were the hearts of the people of God glad-ded, and their hopes and expectations raised that this man might be a deliverer for the nation, and the interest of Christ in it, who had bin even harrous'd out with trouble and persecution.

The voyage from Holland had been slow, and it was 11 June before Monmouth's little fleet was off the Dorset coast. That day they sent a small boat ashore near Chideock to land Thomas Heywood Dare and Hugh Chamberlain to spread the news of Monmouth's arrival and to collect what support they could. They set off towards Hawkchurch, and thence to Ford Abbey; where else we do not know. When Dare and Chamberlain rejoined the Duke at Lyme, they brought 40 horses, most of them with riders. How many of the horses came from Edmund Prideaux's stables at Ford Abbey we cannot tell, but the best of them—ridden by Dare—almost certainly did. Prideaux was thought to have aided and abetted the Duke with a gift of money; £500 was mentioned, but after the rebellion, Dare being dead, the government could not obtain satisfactory evidence of this although they offered free pardons to several rebels if they would 'swear against Mr Prideaux'.

When Monmouth's three ships hove to off Lyme Regis, the inhabitants were puzzled because they showed no colours, fired no gun, and made no attempt to land passengers or cargo on the Cobb. Instead armed men came ashore in small boats to the beach west of the Cobb, still called Monmouth's Beach. There, when his small company had assembled, the Duke called for silence, knelt down, and said a prayer of thanksgiving for a safe voyage and asked a blessing on his venture. Then, with their banner aloft, inscribed 'Fear nothing but God', the little army of 83 men marched into Lyme with swords drawn. Some of the crowd that gathered shouted 'A Monmouth! A Monmouth! The Protestant Religion!'

Samuel Dassel, Deputy Searcher of Customs at Lyme, had been with the Mayor, Gregory Alford, while he was dithering about what he should do. Dassel had gone to fetch powder for the town gun from a ship inside the Cobb when he saw the first boat come ashore. Shortly afterwards, as he delivered the powder to two magistrates, he saw the Mayor departing on horseback. He then went to meet the advancing procession, wondering whether the biggest of the three ships was a King's frigate and had captured the Duke of Monmouth, who was reported in the Newsletter to be sailing down the Channel with three ships. Dassel was soon informed that the man marching in front of the standard was the Duke himself, and noticed that he was advancing with difficulty through the crowd of folk trying to kiss his hand. Dassel joined the procession and got into conversation with 'a man that looked of a pleasant humour', enquiring the meaning of the armed landing.

'We come to fight the Papists', the man replied. 'Then', said Dassel, 'your business is done, for here is none to fight you'. 'Why? Is not the Duke of York a Roman Catholic?' 'I know no such man, for he that was Duke of York is now our Sovereign Lord the King'. Dassel then enquired their destination, but one thinking him too inquisitive, threatened to arrest him. Dassel therefore took himself off, and met a friend, Anthony Thorold, with whom he went to the fields east of Lyme. The standard had been erected and they watched the enlisting. The Duke was shaking hands with and speaking affably to the recruits. A bystander pointed out Lord Grey standing by with a musket on his shoulder and a pair of pistols in his

Monmouth's Beach, Lyme Regis, where the Duke landed from a rowing-boat.

sash. Dassel and Thorold went home for money, but not daring to reappear in riding-boots, they walked on to the mayor's house, meeting on their way two groups of men hurrying to Lyme, though it was near midnight. The men told them that they came to join the Duke. At the mayor's house they found only his daughter-in-law, whom they asked for a couple of horses. They had to be content with one and 'rode double to the next stage, which was to Crewkerne'. From there they sent warning letters to the Duke of Albermarle at Exeter, to Sir Edward Phelips and Colonel Luttrell at Taunton. When they reached London, they sought Sir Winston Churchill, the M.P. for Lyme. He and his son, Brigadier Lord Churchill, took them to the king, who heard their story, allowed them to kiss his hand, ordered them to be rewarded with £20 each, and arranged for them to repeat their story[3] at the Bar of the House of Commons.

In the centre of Lyme Monmouth's proclamation[4] had been read. Written by the loquacious Ferguson, it was far too long and scurrilously unfair to the king. The three points that would interest those who heard it were, first 'that no protestant of what persuasion soever, shall be molested or troubled for the exercise of his Religeon'; secondly, that Parliament should be chosen annually; and thirdly, that though the Duke had incontrovertible proofs of his legitimacy, he would not at once claim the throne, but would leave a freely elected Parliament to settle the future government of England.

That night Major Wade was ordered to get the guns and other weapons ashore, while others took the names of the recruits and sent them to the outposts, where the officers taught them their drill and the handling of their weapons. Ninety-five men of Lyme joined Monmouth's army, and were allowed the privilege of remaining an independent company right up to Sedgemoor, by which time they had dwindled to 80. In addition recruits marched in from east Devon and west Dorset. They must have known that the Duke was coming, for they told Wade and those who took their names that they had gone to bed before the news came, but got up immediately to come to join the Duke. These formed the nucleus of the Red and the Green Regiments.

Small groups of zealous supporters rode down from London. Hundreds had been promised, but less than a dozen can be named. Tom Chadwick, who had been a 'gentleman private'—a potential officer—in the Life Guards, rode down with young Holmes and John Jones, once a Cromwellian trooper and then a cabinet-maker in London. Monmouth made them Captains, Chadwick and Holmes in the Green Regiment, Jones in The Horse. Another batch of three or four were former students of the Nonconformist Academy at Stoke Newington, and one of them was Daniel Foe, better known to us as Defoe. Single horsemen who came included Christopher Battiscombe, a Dorset gentleman, a law student at the Temple; and William Jenkyn, son of a Nonconformist minister who had died in Newgate prison, his only crime the holding of religious services outside the parish church. This young man was stopped at Ilchester on suspicion of rebellious intent and lodged there in prison until Monmouth sent a party to release him and others. Some others from London joined the Duke at Taunton.

The men of Lyme who joined Monmouth represented[5] most of the usual contemporary occupations. William Hardy was an apothecary, and comes into the story later. There were two bakers, a barber, and three blacksmiths; five carpenters and three carriers; two clothiers, a coachman and a cooper; six fullers, two glaziers, three 'helliers' (? hauliers); three husbandmen, two joiners and two masons. Sea-faring men were represented by five mariners, a 'mercator' and seven seamen. There was a mercer, a miller, an ostler, a pipemaker, a tobacco-cutter, and two tobacconists; two porters, a poyntmaker and a printmaker, a 'sopeboyler', nine shoemakers and 13 tailors. A thatcher, a yeoman, a worsted comber, a 'woolbreaker', and seven undescribed make up the 95. Beside the recruits, another 19 men of Lyme strutted about wearing swords as if they too had joined Monmouth's army; but when that army marched to Axminster, these 19 stayed behind and were later at pains to protest their innocence of rebellion when the constables were collecting the names of those absent from their homes at the time of the rebellion.

Monmouth's legitimacy or illegitimacy mattered little to his army. A few of his officers were republicans who looked for a restoration of the Commonwealth, with the Duke as Lord Protector. Some sons of old Cromwellian soldiers may also have been republicans, but far more were Nonconformists, at heart or openly. Almost all the recorded 'dying speeches' and the last letters[6] that have been preserved mention the defence of the Protestant religion as the motive that took them into the rebel army. Indeed, John Whiting the Quaker[7] wrote 'Had liberty of conscience been granted sooner . . . there might have been no rebellion in the west'; and Whiting was in a position to know, for he had several brothers-in-law in Monmouth's army, and shared his prison with Monmouth rebels.

4

Into Action

Narratives of the rebellion are dependent on the account dictated by Nathaniel Wade, Major and Second-in-command of the Red Regiment, when he was a wounded prisoner in Windsor Castle. He seems to have been a born soldier, efficient and trusted alike by Monmouth and by the men he led. Monmouth treated him as his Brigade Major, though that title was never used. He was often Acting Commanding Officer of the Red Regiment, which has led some writers to call him Lieut-Colonel, but he gives no hint in his narrative[1] of having a higher rank than Major.

Monmouth had landed on Thursday, 11 June. On the Friday morning recruits continued to come in until there were over a thousand. Someone reported a party of would-be recruits at Bridport, unable to set off because the constables had posted a militia guard. Major Manley collected a mounted party of 15 young gentlemen who had come from Holland, rode to Bridport and charged the guard of militia Horse, killing two and driving off the rest of the guard. Finding the militia reinforced, Manley drew off his party and returned to Lyme.

Other news came in, suggesting that the Duke of Albermarle was marching the Devon militia to make a night attack on the rebels at Lyme. Monmouth therefore marched most of his army up out of Lyme, 800 Foot, 150 Horse, and three of his guns, and posted them as an ambush concealed by hedges. The men slept on the ground, still in their ranks, the horsemen holding their bridles in their hands. Left behind to guard Lyme were 200 Foot and the fourth gun. On the Saturday morning Mr Tyler came in with news form Exeter that Albemarle would not be ready to move to attack for several days. Dare and Chamberlain returned with their 40 horses, and numbers approached 1500. The Red and Green Regiments, numbering about 500 each, were divided into companies. Colonel Foulkes' White Regiment numbered about 350, and Major Fox began enrolling the Yellow Regiment, of which Matthews was to be Colonel.

Late on Saturday the Duke gave Wade orders to detail 300 of the Red

Regiment and 100 of the White, with 40 of the Horse, for a raid on Bridport. Lord Grey was to be in command, and Colonel Venner was to command the Foot and advise Lord Grey. Captain Francis Goodenough was to command the company of the White Regiment, Lieutenant Mitchell was to lead the Vanguard of 40 Musketeers, supported by 100 men under Captain Thompson. The Horse were to march in the rear.

A most unfortunate accident deprived Monmouth of two valued officers. Lt-Col. Fletcher as Officer Commanding the Horse selected for himself the best of the horses from Ford Abbey, and was riding to take command when Thomas Dare seized the animal's bridle and, considering the horse his own, ordered Fletcher to dismount. Fletcher was more used to giving than to obeying orders, and spoke his mind sharply. Dare made as if to strike the colonel with his switch. Fletcher snatched out his pistol and shot Dare dead, bitterly regretting his hasty action as soon as Dare fell. The Taunton goldsmith, whom Monmouth had made Paymaster, was popular with the Westcountrymen, and his son demanded vengeance. Reluctantly the Duke ordered Fletcher back to the ship, nominated Richard Goodenough as Paymaster, and left Grey in command of the Horse. He could ill spare Fletcher and Dare.

The raiding-force marched off after nightfall, reaching Bridport soon after daybreak, hidden at first by a thick mist. The outguard and the mainguard of the militia fell back on their camp beyond the eastern bridge, leaving the town and a number of horses in the hands of the rebels. Ensign Askew was left in command of a small rearguard near the western bridge. Lieutenants Lillingstone and Brinscombe were in charge of small outposts north and south of the crossroads. (It was safe for Wade to name these officers in October, as they were out of the government's reach. Venner and Manley had escaped abroad; Askew had been hanged; Francis Goodenough and the subalterns were killed at Sedgemoor.)

Venner, preparing to attack the eastern bridge, which was held by Major Erle of the Dorset Militia, sent Wade 'to desire Lord Grey to advance with the Horse'. Wade returned to find some shooting from neighbouring windows. Lieut. Coker of the Dorset militia wounded Venner in the belly, and Venner shot him dead. Another militia officer, Wadham Strangways, was also killed, and William Harvey of Wike[2] subsequently died of his wounds. At the bridge each side fired a volley. Two of Monmouth's Foot fell dead, and the Horse bolted. The rebel vanguard started to scatter to take cover, but Wade, bringing up the support, rallied them, and felt sure that he could have carried the bridge at a second assault, had not Venner ordered a retreat and then galloped off after Lord Grey. Wade called in his outposts and fell back on the west bridge, where he prepared an ambush, but as the militia stayed beyond musket-range he marched the Foot back towards Lyme with a dozen prisoners and about 30 captured horses.

The fugitives reported to the Duke that Wade was killed and the Foot cut to pieces, so Monmouth set out with the rest of the Horse to rescue what he could of his expeditionary force. About two miles from Lyme he met them marching along in good order and in good heart. 'He thanked me', says Wade, 'for bringing off his men, and demanded of me if it were true, as it was reported, that my Lord Grey ran away. I answered him Yes, at which he seemed much surprised, yet nevertheless continued him in his command'.

Wade and his men were tired, but got little rest. Monmouth's 'intelligence' warned him that Albemarle with the Devon militia was marching to meet the Somerset militia at Axminster in order to confine the rebels in a narrow coastal strip. An early march was imperative and Wade, confirmed as Acting Commanding Officer of the Red Regiment, was asked to assemble all the officers to receive their orders. Having done so by 2 a.m., he snatched an hour's sleep on the ground. The drums beat the 'Fall in' at 3 a.m. Wade commanded the vanguard of 300 men, and after marching several miles realised that the march had become a race, with the men of Devon away to his left and those of Somerset on his right. Quickening their pace, the rebels reached Axminster first. The Duke posted a guard of musketeers with one of his guns to cover each approach. Wade, with 'the German gent' as assistant, was posted towards Shute. The Devon Horse advanced to within a furlong of his post but, seeing the hedges lined by musketeers, withdrew. Wade began to advance after them but the Duke called him back, explaining that marching on to Taunton was more important than seeking a fight with untrained troops.

On the other side of Axminster part of the Somerset militia advanced and retreated. There is in Somerset Record Office a letter written by Colonel Sir Edward Phelips to Colonel Berkley, dated from Montacute on 16 June 1685, the day after the race to Axminster. Phelips refers to 'the shamefull story'. Albemarle had written that 'he would be at Axminster yesterday by 12 a clock. Will Luttrell with his regiment and a Company of mine and the horse went towards it', but when the enemy appeared 'some of both sorts run ... most shamefully; yet they returned to Chard ... weary and hungry'. The pious scribe of the Axminster Book of Remembrance saw the hand of God in this. 'The Lord eminently appeard, filling this new Army [Monmouth's] with wonderfull courage, and sending an Hornet of fear* amongst those that came to oppose them'. The more

---

*Cf. Deuteronomy VII. 20.

prosaic Wade learned 'that the retreat of the Somersetsheire forces was little better than a flight, many of the souldiers' coats and arms being recovered and brought in to us'. One of those Somerset militiamen was John Coad[3] of Stoford near Yeovil, a godly carpenter who was most unhappy among foul-mouthed soldiers. When Colonel Phelips ordered the 'About turn', Coad pretended not to hear and marched on, quickly putting some bushes between himself and his former comrades. Crossing a stream, he reached Axminster the next morning 'and tendered myself and armes to the Duke, was kindly accepted, where I found Mr Ferguson at prayer'. Coad seems to have been posted as a pikeman to the Red Regiment. He quotes the Army orders 'giving strict charge against swearing, thieving, and plundering, etc. with penalties on the breach thereof'.

Altogether 500 men of East Devon joined Monmouth's Army, but how many of them joined at Lyme, Axminster, Chard or Taunton we do not know. Over 80 men of Axminster were in the rebel army, and among them at least eight members of the Congregational Church, including their minister, the Rev. Stephen Towgood, and their Ruling Elder, Thomas Lane. The Book of Remembrance records the landing of the Duke,

> who immediately gave forth his declaration to restore liberty to the people of God for the worship of God . . . Tydings of his landing was spread abroad far and near very speedily, and divers persons from several quarters hasted to resort to him . . . A great number of sober and pious men marched forth with the Army . . . Divers also of the Brethren belonging to this Church marched along with them.

After sleeping at Axminster the Duke's army marched on to Chard, where recruiting went on rapidly. Chard Town provided 99 recruits; Chardland 58; Combe St Nicholas 22; and Winsham 8. Only three occupations are mentioned in the Presentment of the Chard rebels: John Legg was a roper, William Burrage a cutler, and John Streete a mason. To Chard also came John Speke, son and heir of old George Speke of Whitelackington, and with him 'a company of ragged horse'. John Speke is subsequently mentioned as Colonel Speke. From Chard Monmouth marched to Ilminster and camped just beyond the small town, at Winterhay. Ilminster recruits numbered 54. As the Duke crossed the Square, he shook hands with Charles Speke, John's younger brother. Three months later it pleased Lord Chief Justice Jeffreys to construe this as Aiding and abetting rebellion, and to sentence Charles Speke to be hanged in Ilminster Square.

Folk came in from nearby villages as the rebels marched on towards Taunton. Local tradition makes the army turn left at Hatch Green, the modern road through Hatch Beauchamp not then being made. The rebels approached Taunton by way of Stoke St Mary and Shoreditch, where

'Fight Ground' Ashill, the site of a cavalry skirmish on 19 or 20 June 1685; the road is modern.

Walter Upham the blacksmith and Daniel Manning, his apprentice, shod Monmouth's 'cattle and horses', the cattle presumably being oxen drawing either the guns or the baggage-wagons. Some of the officers thought they should enlist another blacksmith-farrier, and so, with his master's consent, they conscripted[4] Daniel, then 19 or 20. His home was in Stoke St Mary.

As usual, Monmouth prepared his defences. Hearing that Albemarle had occupied Wellington, the Duke had trenches cut for an outpost astride the Wellington road and posted the Red Regiment there, under Wade's command, for that night and the following day. When they were relieved, they were allotted quarters and, says Wade, 'we lay in beds the first time after coming over'.

On the other side of Taunton the Duke sent out a cavalry patrol of 17 or 20 men under Cornet Legg to scout southwards to ascertain how closely Brigadier Churchill's cavalry was following the rebel advance. Churchill also sent out from Chard a cavalry patrol of 20 of The Royals under Lieutenant Phillip Monoux and a Quartermaster to reconnoitre the rebels' position. The patrols approached each other through dead ground alongside the modern road over Barrington Hill (in Ashill parish) to Broadway Hill, and suddenly came upon each other too close for anything but fighting or flight. They fought: Lieut. Monoux and Cornet Legg were both killed. Another rebel, Samual Rampson, one of the Axminster dissenters, was mortally wounded. All told perhaps four rebels were killed and two or three of the Royals wounded. The action was fought on 19 June; and nearly three months later the Vicar of Ashill buried 'Thomas Hewes, a souldier'. Perhaps Hewes was one of the wounded Royals and died of wounds. The Quartermaster of the Royals drew off his force and returned to Chard, where Lieut. Monoux was buried, though his body was later taken back to his home and re-buried in the church at Wootton in Bedfordshire.

The site of the skirmish is still known locally as Fight Ground. Its map reference is ST.300165.

5

'King Monmouth'

That Monmouth aimed at the crown was assumed by all his opponents and half his friends. The London republican conspirators, Major Wildman and Colonel Danvers, were not interested in substituting James Scott for James Stuart on the throne, and sent no money to Holland to equip the rebel army. The Earl of Argyll had extracted a promise from Monmouth that he would not proclaim himself king, but would leave such a decision to parliaments freely elected in England and Scotland; and when the Duke landed, that was in his proclamation. But, as the rebels marched northwards, counter-pressure was put on the Duke.

Lord Grey and Robert Ferguson raised the proposition when they reached Chard, arguing that the landed gentry, who were conspicuous by their absence, held aloof through fear that the rebels aimed to restore the Commonwealth (as indeed some of the officers certainly hoped). They also made play with Henry VII's Statute of Treason, in which Parliament, remembering the many executions for treason during the Wars of the Roses, laid it down that no man was to be held guilty of treason for supporting a *de facto* king against the king *de jure*. No man of substance, it was argued, would risk his children's patrimony, unless Monmouth made himself *de facto* king. (If any of the rebels thought that James Stuart or his Lord Chief Justice would be restrained by this law, passed by Parliament nearly 200 yers before, they were indulging in unrealistic optimism.) It is said that some of the non-conformist ministers supported the argument, but at Chard the republican officers talked it down.

On 18 June the people of Taunton gave the Duke a rapturous welcome. The streets were thronged with people, all endeavouring to manifest their joy at his coming; and their houses, doors and streets were garnished with green boughs, herbs and flowers. So wrote the anonymous author of the account of the rebellion printed in King William's reign in a book[1] called *The Bloody Assizes*. The author who had come from Holland with Monmouth, and was an eye-witness of the rebellion until the Council of War at Frome, may have been Lt. Col. Venner.

The following day Monmouth's original proclamation was read, and the Duke was presented with 27 flags for his troops made by the girls of the school whose joint headmistresses were Miss Mary Blake and Miss Susanna Musgrave. Miss Blake led the procession with a Bible in one hand and a naked sword in the other. Monmouth accepted the Bible, declaring that he had come to defend the truths it contained. The 27 maids who followed were each rewarded with a kiss. Mary Mead's flag was embroidered with a crown and the letters J.R. standing for Jacobus Rex, which revived the suggestion of a new proclamation. Characteristically, Wade 'did not know' the names of the maids of Taunton, but when the Duke of Albemarle arrived from Wellington he had no difficulty in ascertaining the names of half of them and noted them on the back of a letter[2] he sent to the Earl of Sunderland, one of the Secretaries of State. His additional notes have an obvious bearing on the ransoms subsequently demanded for the pardons of these youngsters, though Albemarle may only have thought of fines.

> 27 Colours given by Maids introduced by Col. Bovet's daughter.
> Katherine Bovet, her Father a Colonel
> Mary Blake rich
> Sarah Blake
> Susannah Peck
> Eliza Gammon Hacker, kinswoman to the Captain
> Anne, Susan and Grace Herring, their father a captain
> Mary Mead the Golden Flagg, J.R., a crown, etc. Fringed lace round.
> Eliza Simpson Shop keep rich
> Sarah Reynolds rich
> 2 of Mr Thomas Baker's daughters, he one of Monmouth's Privy Councill Very rich

Later that day the Duke called a Council of War, the first he held says Wade, who was present. Should they march back and fight Albemarle, or march on? When the council had decided to march on, Monmouth took Wade and some others aside 'and persuaded us that we should consent to his being proclaimed king', alleging as reason the gentry's fear of a Commonwealth, and promising to include in the proclamation fresh promises of popular liberties. 'We submitted to it', says Wade laconically. So on 20 June in the presence of magistrates fetched at sword-point[3] by Captain Samuel Storey and Captain Zachery Wyatt, Captain Tily read the proclamation[4]:

Whereas, upon the decease of our Sovereign Lord Charles the Second, late King of England, &c. the right of succession to the Crown of England, Scotland, France and Ireland, with the dominions and territories thereunto belonging, did legally descend and devolve upon the most illustrious and high-born Prince James Duke of Monmouth, son and heir apparent to the said King Charles the Second; but James Duke of York (taking the advantage of the absence of the said James Duke of Monmouth beyond the seas) did first cause the said late King to be poysoned, and immediately thereupon did usurp and invade the Crown, and doth continue so to doe: We therefore, the noblemen, gentlemen, and Commons at present assembled, in the names of ourselves and all the loyal and Protestant noblemen, gentlemen, and Commons of England, in pursuance of our duty and allegiance, and for the delivering of the Kingdome from popery, tyranny, and oppression, do recognise, publish, and proclaim the said high and mighty Prince James Duke of Monmouth, our lawful and rightful sovereign and king, by the name of James the Second, by the Grace of God, King of England, Scotland, France, and Ireland, Defender of the Faith, &c.

God save the King.

To avoid the confusion of having both rival kings called James the Second, the rebels styled their leader King Monmouth.

Monmouth had already issued a proclamation forbidding the seizure of horses without a written order from him. He now issued others headed 'By the King a Proclamation'. One denounced the Parliament then sitting at Westminster as an unlawful assembly; another forbade the payment of current taxes; another denounced the Duke of Albemarle and his adherents as rebels and traitors, because he, once Monmouth's bosom friend, had spurned his call to join forces with him. A worthier document was an Order 'in his Majesty's name . . . to all officers and soldiers of our army, and to all others our loving subjects' to suffer the post to pass[5] without interruption.

Of Monmouth in Taunton we get an unexpected glimpse in the autobiography of John Whiting, the Quaker who had seen him at Ilchester in 1680. Still officially a prisoner at Ilchester, John was sufficiently trusted by his guards to go 'by connivance' to his home at Nailsea to make arrangements for his marriage to Sarah Hurd of Long Sutton. On his leisurely return John heard of Monmouth's landing, stopped a couple of nights with Sarah's father at Somerton, and attended the Quaker Quarterly Meeting at Gregory Stoke. There he found Sarah's sister Joan in considerable distress, as her husband Francis Scott, a small farmer of Hambridge near Curry Rivel, had gone to sell horses to Monmouth. She begged John to ride with her to Taunton to persuade Francis to come home. In Taunton they traced Francis, but found him obstinate. They put up their horses at the Three Cups Inn (where the County Hotel now stands) opposite Captain Hucker's house, where Monmouth and Lord Grey were staying. Joan Scott and her sister, Alice Roman,

went over to speak with the Duke, to desire him not to take it amiss if her husband went home, for it was contrary to our (i.e. Quaker) persuasion to appear in arms... She had a pretty deal of discourse with him, for she was a woman that could use her tongue as well as most. The Duke seemed to take it well enough, and told her he did not desire that any should appear with him against their consciences. So they left him and came away... Soon after, the Duke and Lord Grey came forth and took horse... and rode down the street... So we took horse and rode down after. The street was full of people... Looking about me to see the Duke, I asked somebody which was he; he shewed me him, just at my right hand... I thought he looked very thoughtful and dejected in his countenance, and thinner than when I saw him four (actually five) years before, as he passed through Ivelchester... so that I hardly knew him again, and was sorry for him as I looked at him.

Richard Bovet*, appointed Lieut-Colonel of the Blue Regiment, claimed all the Taunton men for his regiment, even those who had joined the Duke at Lyme, and so reached a strength of 800. Supporters who had ridden down from London included Captain Edward Matthews, who became Lieut-Colonel of the Yellow Regiment, and with him Robert Perrett, once a Lieutenant in the Parliamentarian Army, and subsequently Colonel Blood's accomplice in his attempt to steal the Crown Jewels; Monmouth made him a Major in the Yellow Regiment. Others who came were a Mr Brand, to be a Captain of Horse, Joseph Flighe of Broad Street to be a Cornet of Horse, and a Mr Hooper. Two, who came to Taunton through curiosity but were persuaded to join Monmouth's army, were Henry Pitman, a young doctor, and his brother William of Sandford Orcas.

Of the 356 men of Taunton presented by the Constables[6] as 'Assisting, aiding and abetting' the rebellion, we have the occupations of 271. As would be a natural in a clothing town the majority, two-thirds in fact, had been engaged in the cloth industry. There were 56 weavers, plus a silk-weaver, a serge-weaver and 11 sergemakers; 53 were worsted combers, 23 combers and 3 comb-makers. There were also 20 fullers, five tuckers, 10 tailors, a dyer and a feltmaker; a mercer, a haberdasher, and an upholsterer. The leather trade was represented by six shoemakers, a cobbler, two cordwinders, a currier, a tanner, a saddler and a glover. Metal workers included a brazier, a tinman and a tinker, a blacksmith, three smiths, two locksmiths, two goldsmiths and a cutler. Of woodworkers there were nine carpenters, a joiner and a cooper. The building trade provided three masons, three bricklayers, a glazier, a thatcher; and with them may be numbered a millard, two labourers, two porters, two

---

*A letter from the Commissioners for Sequestrations to the County Committee for Somerset, dated September 30, 1659, says 'In your communication there is a mistake, Col. Bovett's name being written Buffett.' Wade's amanuensis misread this spelling as Bassett in days when a 'long s' looked like an f. (*Calendar of the Committee for Compounding*, 1643-60, Vol. 1. p. 754.)

innholders, three brewers, a maltster and an exciseman, a pipemaker and a tobacco-cutter. Also among the rebels were a butcher and a baker, three barbers, an apothecary and two 'sopers'; three gentlemen and a yeoman, eight husbandmen, two clerks, and a 'mercator' (a merchant or shopkeeper).

The men from the neighbouring villages must also have been included in the Blue Regiment to make up the total of 800. The 74 men from Wellington and the 62 from Milverton probably marched to Taunton to enlist. Two of the Milverton men are given their rank in the Constables' Presentments: Roger Colborne, Captain, and William Farmer, Serjant.

It was Saturday 20 June when the Duke was proclaimed King. He issued orders for the march to Bridgwater on the Sunday morning. Robert Ferguson had reckoned that he would preach in the church of St Mary Magdalene that Sunday, and had borrowed the vicar's gown and stole without his leave, all to no purpose. There is a curious account of Ferguson leaving Taunton on horseback, a drawn sword in his hand, proclaiming to all and sundry that he was 'the famous Ferguson[7], for whose head so many hundred pounds have been offered'.

Fortunately for the troops on the march, the weather was fine.

6
The Advance

Bridgwater also gave the Duke and his army a welcome, and the Mayor and Aldermen attended the proclamation of King Monmouth. More to the point for the soldiers, Wade noted 'We had very good quarters at Bridgwater, and for the most part free'. There they were joined by contingents from neighbouring places, and even a couple of yeomen from Dulverton, five from Minehead, and a dozen from Dunster. These last were led by Richard Jeul, chirurgeon. Larger groups came in from the moorland; 28 from North Curry, 26 from Gregory Stoke—a village strong in nonconformity—13 from Thurloxton, and 14 from [1] North Petherton.

It is interesting to note that it was at Bridgwater that Daniel Manning, the blacksmith's apprentice, gave the rebel army the slip. After lying low at his uncle's house in North Petherton for a week or ten days, he joined the royal army, enlisting in Captain St. John's company[2] of the Second Foot, generally known as Kirke's Lambs. The First Regiment of Foot were the Royal Scots, who had been re-enlisted from General Monk's army, and claim a much longer pedigree than that. The Second Foot had been raised in 1661 to provide a garrison for Tangier, part of the dowry brought by Princess Catherine of Braganza on her marriage to King Charles II. As the regiment was the Queen's Regiment, its men wore the badge of the House of Braganza, the Paschal Lamb. Percy Kirke had been their colonel since 1682, and regiments were then and for long afterwards called by their colonel's name.

The royal troops in the West had been under the command of Brigadier Lord Churchill, but the day before Monmouth was proclaimed king, King James appointed Lieut-General Lord Feversham to the supreme command. Louis Duras Earl of Feversham, was a nephew of the great French general (subsequently Marshal) Turenne, and like him (in Turenne's early days) a Protestant. He had come to England in the entourage of James, Duke of York, was naturalized in 1663, commanded a troop of the Horse Guards, was given an English peerage and made Master of the Horse. As a Lord of the Bedchamber, and as one considered absolutely trustworthy, Feversham had been allowed to remain at the bedside of the dying King Charles while he was received into the Roman Catholic Church. Feversham seems to have been much more competent[3] than Macaulay and some other historians have thought. Lord Churchill was irked at his supercession, but he supported Feversham loyally.

From Bridgwater Monmouth's army marched on, on 'an exceeding rainy day' to Glastonbury, alarmed as they marched by a party of Lord Oxford's Horse, the Blues, part of the force with which Churchill was following and harassing the rebels. In Glastonbury, the rebel infantry were quartered in the churches of St John and St Benedict and in the Abbey grounds, where they lit 'very great fyers to dry and refresh our men'. Fortunately the commissaries were able to provide an adequate meal. The next day the rebels reached Shepton Mallet and were quartered in houses. It was at Shepton Mallet that the Rev. John Hickes[4] joined Monmouth. There the Duke consulted Wade about his plan to attack Bristol. So far Monmouth's strategy was sound. Bristol was then the second city in the kingdom, and it was strong in Nonconformity. The capture of Bristol would have added enormously to Monmouth's prestige, as well as giving him much material aid in recruits, munitions, money and food. In 1684 the government, suspecting plans for a rising, had ordered a search for arms in Bristol and had confiscated the weapons found in a considerable number of houses. In a list of members of Broadmead Baptist Church 32 are mentioned as having had arms confiscated, and eight are described as 'strong supporters[5] of the Duke of Monmouth'. Few of these in the event, were able to join the Duke.

Monmouth was thinking of a direct attack on the south (Somerset) side of the city but Wade, a Bristolian born, warned him that that side was the most readily defensible, and that he would be wise to cross the Avon by Keynsham Bridge and attack the city from the Gloucestershire side. The Duke accepted Wade's advice. On Wednesday 24 June, therefore, the rebels marched to Pensford, harassed on their march by Churchill's Horse and Dragoons (who in those days were considered Mounted Infantry). 'Nevertheless', says Wade

we lodged quietly that night in Pensford, within five miles of Bristol, where we met with nothing remarkable but that we perceived a great fire in or near Bristol, that night by the redness of the sky. We supposed that they had set the suburbs on fire lest we should have possessed ourselves[6] of it; but it seems it was a ship accidently set on fire'.

Monmouth's route lay through Keynsham and over the bridge there, but in June King James had sent instructions[7] to the Duke of Beaufort,

'Whitehall, June 21, 1685. My lord Duke of Beaufort, The preservation of the Citty of Bristol from the Rebells being a matter of great importance, I have directed the Duke of Somerset to joyne with you with his Militia in the defense of that place, and being informed there is a Bridge at a place called Keinesham halfe way between Bathe and Bristoll I would have you by all means to endeavour to breake the same immediately upon the receipt hereof which will in a great measure delay, if not hinder their passage that way. James R.

Informed of this, Monmouth sent a troop of Horse under Captain Tily, like Wade a Bristolian, to occupy Keynsham and repair the bridge. Tily found a troop of Horse of the Gloucestershire Militia in Keynsham, but they retired, leaving a trooper and two horses to be captured by the rebels. Tily found one arch of the bridge broken, but managed to repair the gap with planks and about 10 a.m. on Thursday 25 June, Monmouth's army filed across into Sydenham Mead, and awaited further orders.

Lord Faversham had been appointed Commander-in-chief against the rebels on 19 June. He left London with a cavalry escort on the following day. With a reduced escort he reached Bristol at midday on the 23rd, met the Dukes of Beaufort and Somerset and conferred with them about the defence of the city. A message from the Earl of Pembroke told him that the rebels talked of marching to London, so Feversham planned to block their way at Bath and at Westbury. He was at Bath on the 24th and sent his favourite scout, Colonel Oglethorpe, to ascertain Monmouth's position. Churchill with his cavalry was coming up from Glastonbury; the infantry under the Duke of Grafton (Monmouth's half-brother) were approaching Bath; and the artillery under Henry Sheres (Feversham calls him Mr Shiers) was on its way from Marlborough to Devizes. As soon as Oglethorpe reported the rebels at Pensford, Feversham gathered the Horse that were available and returned that night[8] to Bristol.

The rebels were driven from Sydenham Mead by a heavy downpour of rain, and were ordered to take quarters in Keynsham as if they meant to spend the night there. Two parties of royalist Horse broke independently into Keynsham, one under Colonel Oglethorpe and the other under Captain Parker. John Coad[9] tells us

The enemy came upon us at unawares, and assaulting 3 passages to the Towne, but could not prevaile, but retreated with the loss of about 20 men, where I came to push of pike with them, yet through the protection of God had no harm.

Wade says 'our Horse unadvisedly engaged, and after the loss of about fourteen of our own party, amongst whom was Brand, Captain of Horse, they [the enemy] retired, leaving us 3 prisoners'. The royal cavalry lost six men, according to their own account, perhaps including the three taken prisoner, who were interrogated by Monmouth and told him that the royal army, numbering about 4000 men, was at hand. Major Fox of the Yellow Regiment was wounded and was succeeded as Second in Command by Major Perrett.

Monmouth called a council of war. He had intended a night assault on the city led by the Bristolians who knew their way there. He had learned that the Duke of Beaufort had threatened to burn the city if Monmouth assaulted it or the citizens tried to open the gates. He did not then know that the fire his men saw was a ship burning accidentally, and thought it was evidence that Beaufort meant to carry out his threat. Monmouth's normal kindness of heart revolted against bringing such distress upon the people of Bristol, and late evidence suggests that Lord Grey stressed this objection. The Bristolian officers, knowing ways into the city and knowing the strength of Whig and Nonconfirmist opinion there, argued in favour of the assault. Monmouth was depressed, first by finding Beaufort and Feversham there before him, then by the drenching rain, then by the lack of success of his men against the heavily out-numbered royal cavalry, and lastly by the prisoners' report of 4000 royal troops 'at hand'. The account written[10] by the grandson of the Rev. Andrew Gifford, Baptist Minister of Broadmead Chapel, Bristol, says that Monmouth's council voted against attacking Bristol. We have no means of checking the accuracy of this, but we do know that the Duke asked advice whether to by-pass Bristol, make for Gloucester and march beyond Severn to Cheshire, where Lord Delamere was expected to raise a supporting rebellion; or to turn into Wiltshire, where he had been promised the support of 500 Horse by Captain Adlam, and march towards London. The fear of the royal cavalry on either march was daunting, and Gloucester was considered four days' march away. The regimental officers knew that their men's shoes were badly worn (some of them had already marched a hundred miles.) The officers voted for Wiltshire, and Monmouth issued orders to march to Warminister.

This was the real turning point of the rebellion. We do not know whether Monmouth could have captured Bristol, but the attempt would have given him the greatest chance of success in the whole venture. Sir John Reresby, a strong supporter of King James, wrote in his Memoirs, 'Had Monmouth obtained a victory, it was much to be feared that the disaffected would have risen in such numbers in the several parts of England[11] as to have made the crown precarious'. The elation of the successful march was lost.

THE BATTLE OF PHILIP'S NORTON

One of the Royalists recorded in an anonymous account[12] of Lord

Feversham's marches that the rebels 'in the dead of the night marcht away on the south side of the river towards Bath'. That was on the night between Thursday 25, and Friday 26 of June. The rebels had given the royal army the slip, and were heading in the direction of London. Their direct route would be through Bath, where they 'summuned it, only in bravado', says Wade, 'for we had no expectation[13] of its surrendry'. One of the Bath sentries shot the messenger dead.

Alternative routes to London would be through Norton St Philip, then usually called Philip's Norton, or through Warminster; and the rebels trudged on to Philip's Norton, having to use manpower as well as horses to get their guns up some of the hills. They were thankful to spend Friday night at Norton—the Duke, Lord Grey and the non-regimental officers in The George, the cavalry in the small town, the infantry and their officers in two fields just west of the manor-house. To guard against a surprise attack the infantry erected a barricade across North Street, which was guarded by 50 musketeers of the Red Regiment under Captain Vincent.

That night Monmouth 'was very disconsolate', says Wade, 'and began to complain that all people had deserted him, for there was no appearance of the Wiltshire Horse Mr Adlam talked of, although we were near enough to have joined them if they had any stomach to it. Indeed the Duke was so dejected that we could hardly get orders from him'. The Duke had expected that some at least of the royal troops who had served under him in Flanders or in Scotland or in London would transfer their allegiance to him, but no one came.

Meanwhile as soon as Feversham realised that Monmouth was marching away from Bristol towards Bath, he set his troops in motion in that direction on the north side of the Avon, and reached the city some time after the rebels' unsuccessful summons. There the royal troops achieved a concentration. The Duke of Grafton, Colonel of the First, or Grenadier, Guards, led in a contingent of infantry, which included the Second Foot under Lt-Colonel Kirke. Churchill also arrived with some of the Horse, and four regiments of Militia were not far off. On Saturday, the 27th, Lord Feversham paraded and reviewed his troops. He had sent scouts to ascertain if Monmouth was still at Philip's Norton or had marched on, and whither. When they returned, saying that a countryman had assured them that Monmouth was still there though preparing to march, Feversham was wrathful at their accepting hearsay. They should, he said, have pressed on until they had been shot at; and he sent another party with those orders.

The rebels were preparing to march out of Philip's Norton, when, says John Coad, 'our[14] enemies, coming on us by surprize, attacked the north-

The George, Norton St Philip, where Monmouth spent the night before the 'Battle of Phillip's Norton.'

west entrance into the town, guarded only with two companies'. Feversham's scouting party (which Wade describes by the soldiers' grim joke as the 'forlorn hope') seems to have been 45 grenadiers under Captain Hawley. They had pressed eagerly into North Street, closely followed by Grafton himself and some dragoons. They came up against the barricade and the shooting[15] commenced. There John Coad was shot through his left wrist and under the left breast, and fell bleeding excessively, and lay under foot throughout the action.

Wade says that 'the forlorn hope of the King's army advanced through the lane up to the barricade', which suggests that the barricade was at or towards the south end of North Street, perhaps at its junction with Bell Hill, and directly protecting Monmouth's headquarters at the George Inn. The Duke

> caused his own regiment of foot [Wade's Red Regiment] to march through the gentleman's court up to the side of the lane, and attack them [the forlorn hope] on the flank, which was done, and the regiment being much superior in number, we fell with a good part of them [Red Regiment] upon their rear, so that they were surrounded on all hands save the left flank, by which way through the hedge many of them escaped.

Wade had recorded that 'Just by the barricade was a little byway which led into the back part of the town through a gentleman's court, near which court the Foot were encamped in two fields'. If the gentleman's court was part of the manor outbuildings, the little byway would be Bell Hill, and the Red Regiment, moving up outside the west hedge of North Street would trap the royal grenadiers where Chivers Lane crossed the north end of North Street. Some of Monmouth's Horse seem to have come up Chivers Lane to help encircle the Royalists. Monmouth sent Colonel Holmes with the Green Regiment to attack the left flank of the royal troops and close the trap. The Green Regiment, suffering casualties, advanced from hedge to hedge, which separated small paddocks in Blood Close, until they had driven the Grenadiers beyond the furthermost hedge near the field, the then open land north-east of Chivers Lane. In the trap meanwhile the forlorn hope behaved valiantly, as reported in Feversham's despatch. Grafton seems to have had his horse killed, and the Quartermaster of the Blues who had distinguished himself at Ashill, promptly offered his mount to the Duke. Grafton declined the offer, but caught and mounted a wounded horse. The Grenadiers were ordered to fix bayonets, and fought their way out of North Street, Churchill having brought up enough troops to drive off Monmouth's Horse and part of the Red Regiment from the mouth of the lane.

During this action Feversham drew up his main body 'about 500 paces away' as they arrived from Bath; first the Horse, then the Militia of Somerset, Dorset, and Oxfordshire under Lord Fitzharding, Sir William Portman, Colonel Strangridge and Captain Barton; and lastly the few guns that had got through the foul ways. Then Churchill was ordered to bring off the Foot and Dragoons, and the royal army was posted as for a general action. The rebels, jubilant at the withdrawal of the royal troops, discussed cutting gaps in the hedges to enable their Foot to debouch to engage the enemy, but contented themselves with bringing up their four guns and firing them. Feversham described them as 'two very little[16] pieces', two-pounders he thought, and later two others, a little better but still inconsiderable. The royal guns replied, and apparently neither side did much damage. Then the rain came and drenched both armies, making musketry all but impossible, certainly for matchlocks. Feversham had thought of bivouacking on the ground but his colonels, having no tents, advised against it, and Feversham sent his Quartermaster General, Captain Coliford, to Bradford-on-Avon to arrange quarters for the troops, who were glad enough to get into shelter. As the royal army moved off, Captain Parker noticed the Duke of Monmouth riding a white horse, watching the army retreat.

Feversham's despatch, written the next day at Bradford, reported a trifling loss of seven or eight killed and about 30 wounded, but Barillon, the French ambassador in London, wrote[17] to his master, 'The royalists' loss has been greater than was said in the engagement at Philip's Norton: there were full 100 men killed at the spot where the Duke of Grafton advanced'. Captain Dummer[18] of the Artillery estimated 50 killed, beside the wounded. The rebels also had their losses. The anonymous account (? Venner's) estimated 30 royalists and 10 rebels killed on the spot, one rebel and 'some hundreds' of royalists killed during the cannonade, which can be dismissed as wishful thinking. Wade computed the royal loss at 80, the rebels' loss at 18, including Captain Patchall, Captain Holmes, the Colonel's son, and Lieutenant Blake, all of the Green Regiment, and Captain Chadwick of the Horse, accidentally killed by his own men and much regretted as a well-liked officer. Colonel Holmes was wounded in the arm. Tradition has it that he himself cut off the dangling stump, but at his interrogation he merely said 'wounded in the arm', and as eight days after his wound he led the Green Regiment into action at Sedgemoor, the tradition seems doubtful.[19]

John Coad, 'the fight being over, was taken up alive ... but my wounds being judged mortal, and wondering I was not dead, the chirurgions refused to dress my wounds; but the same evening ... I was cast on a waggon with few clothes about me. The shaking of the waggon made my wounds bleed afresh'.

An interesting letter survives from Lord Dumblane[20] to his father, the Earl of Danby, written shortly after the battle:

June the 27th:85.
My Lord,
This day we have joyn'd battell with the Rebells within halfe a mile of

fillipsnorton, where we found them so well posted, that for two hours wee had very hott worke; but then itt rain'd so fast that wee could do nothing on neither side but fire our cannon, and my Lord Feversham finding the raine very likely to continue, withdrew his armie into a towne close by him to quarter, till further orders, and hee has just now ordred mee out with a partie of 20 horse after Colonall Oglethrop, (who is gone with a partie of 100 horse to meet my Lord Pembrook att Troobridge) with orders to him, that hee should joyne my partie to his and go round the Ennimies Camp and bring him what news of them hee could. I humnly beg you will forgive this scrole; for I have not been in bed for four nights.

He hoped to be home within a week.

The rebel army spent a miserable night trudging on through heavy rain and deep mud to Frome. Wade did not see any need to retreat from Philip's Norton that night, and blamed Venner for persuading the Duke, who after the brief elation of directing the battle had sunk back into deep depression.

A story has crept into print of a French soldier of fortune named Chevalier being shot in the back by his own side. In the telling the officer has been transferred from the royal to the rebel army, and his wound, which was mortal, from Sedgemoor to Philip's Norton. He was buried in the nave of Middlezoy Church, where a small brass plate records his name and death. 'Here lyes the body of Louis Chevaleir de Misiers a French gentleman who behaved himself with great courage and gallantry 18 yeares in the English services and was unfortunately slaine on ye 6th of July 1685 at the battel of Weston where he behaved himself with all the courage imaginable against the kings enemies commanded by ye rebel Duke of Munmouth'. He was commissioned as 'Second Adjutant to the First Regiment of Foot Guards commanded by the Duke of Grafton' on June 18, 1685. (S.P.D. Entry Book 164, p.202, quoted in S & D N & Q, vol. 24, pp. 97-8.)

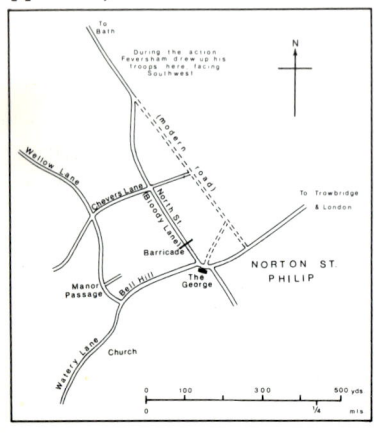

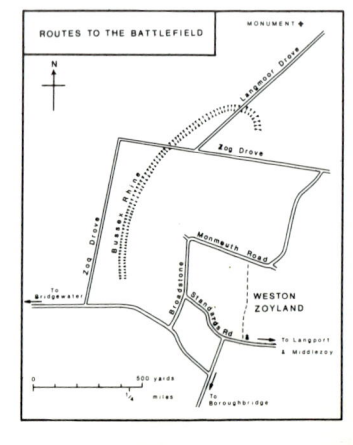

7

Retreat

That night march would have depressed anyone. The rebels were thankful to be able to dry their clothes and their weapons on the Sunday and Monday, while the royal troops were drying theirs at Bradford. Oglethorpe's patrol picked up the information that the rebels would be marching to Warminster; and to block that way to London Feversham moved to Westbury, where his main artillery joined him accompanied by Lord Dumbarton's Royal Scots and a regiment of Hampshire militia. From Westbury Feversham[1] wrote another despatch to King James.

A rebel cavalry patrol had visited Frome on Wednesday, 24 June, and the Constable had read the proclamation of King Monmouth and posted it up. The following day Lord Pembroke had arrived with Colonel Wyndham's regiment of the Wiltshire militia. The proclamation was torn down and replaced by King James's proclamation, denouncing Monmouth as a rebel and traitor. The militia searched for arms and took away all they could find, and carried the Constable as a prisoner to Trowbridge. Afterwards 19 men of Frome were presented 'For a Ryott and (being) amongst the Clubmen[2] the 25th June'; that is, for opposing Pembroke and the militia.

Monmouth was wishing he had never embarked on this adventure, relying on so many promises that had not been fulfilled. It was here at Frome that the news of Argyll's defeat and capture reached the Duke, and certainly for the moment he despaired of success. He called a Council of War on the Monday, and explained that as the Scottish rising had failed, and neither London nor Chesire had provided a diversion, nor had the promised Wiltshire Horse come in; nor had there been the promised desertions from King James's army, the rebellion 'must of necessity come to ruin, and therefore he thought it advisable to leave his army and repair with his officers to some seaport town and make his escape with them beyond sea'. So Wade[3] reported. The anonymous[4] account specifies Poole as the point of departure, mentions the seizing of a ship, and that 'we that came with the Duke' would accompany him to Holland, 'leaving our infantry at the mercy of the country'. Colonel Venner thought this was a splendid idea and that ' 'twas at last agreed on', but Lord Grey told Monmouth to pull himself together and that the suggestion was 'so base that it could never be[5] forgiven', nor the Duke trusted again, if it was carried out.

There is a very tragic irony in this, for had the rebel chiefs known, King James had just promised a pardon to rebels who laid down their arms within four days of the local publication of this offer and got a suitable certificate from a magistrate. Moreover a letter from Sunderland[6] to Feversham said 'If you think it may be of any service to His Majesty to give poor people who have been deluded, more time to come in, he leaves it to you to prolong the term limited, and what you promise, he will make good'. During the Bloody Assizes 53 rebels produced such certificates[7] and were released.

Monmouth recovered sufficiently to give orders for the army to march on Tuesday to Warminster. But Venner and Major Parsons (of the Green Regiment) took the Duke's suggestion as agreed, and departed en route to the continent. Richard Goodenough[8] said later that Colonel John Speke also departed. Lest desertion should become infectious, it was given out that Venner and Parsons had been sent to Holland to buy more arms. This was reported (and believed) by Captain Tellier, and was accepted by George Roberts, the great pioneer historian of the rebellion, but it was only propaganda, for there was neither cash nor credit to buy arms.

There were others who left the army about this time. In the Constables' Presentments Maurice Firth or Frith, gentleman of Wincanton, was listed[9] as 'in Armes in the Rebellion, [but] returned from Norton fight'. Mr Towgood, the Pastor of the Axminster Congregationalists, felt that he should return to his church; and Thomas Lane, the Ruling Elder, accompanied him. They reached Axminster safely, whereas John Ashwood, son of the former Pastor, and Thomas Smith, 'a very pious Christian and usefull Member, were[10] apprehended and imprisoned'. The Rev. Nathaniel Hook, Monmouth's own chaplain, had already been sent to London to urge the immediate need for a rising there.

On the Tuesday morning before the troops moved off, two pieces of news came in: first, that Feversham had moved to Westbury and blocked the road to London; second, that help was waiting for the Duke near Axbridge. A Quaker, 'whose name', says Wade, 'I know not', came to tell the Duke that 10,000 Clubmen were waiting to join him. During the Civil War Somerset men of the farming community had banded themselves together, armed with clubs, to resist the foraging parties of both armies, and had been formidable enough for both the Prince of Wales and Fairfax to speak them fair. This Quaker had revived the idea, and Monmouth agreed to march towards the Clubmen, naming Shepton Mallet as his immediate destination.

The Rev. Thomas Axe[11] mentions the Quaker in his account of the rebellion, and gives him a name which George Roberts read as Thomas Pheere, but which looks more like Thomas Phooce, which Mr Bryan Little[12] has modernised to Phooks. Quaker records know neither name, but almost certainly the leader of the Clubmen, 160 strong rather than 10,000, was Thomas Plaice[13] of Edington, who was disowned by the Society of Friends at their Quarterly Meeting[14] at Merston on the 24th of the 7th[15] mo. [Sept] 1685':

> The said Tho: Plaice did appear very active and conversant in the late Duke of Monmouth's Army (as we are Credibly informed altho not in Armes) . . . Now on consideration thereof, we do (on the behalf of the people called quakers) testifie and declare That we utterly disowne the aforesaid practises of the said Tho: Plaice . . .

A letter from Friends at Ilchester[16] to Friends in London, dated 1.6.(Aug) '85, specifically links Plaice with the Clubmen. No Pheere, Phooce or Phooks was presented or prosecuted for his part in the rebellion, but Thomas Plaice was presented as 'out in the Rebellion and att large'. He was eventually arrested in London and sent to Wells for the Spring Assize of 1687 (having been excepted from the General Pardon). There he was condemned to be hanged, but King James sent a stay of execution, and subsequently a pardon[17].

So to Shepton Mallet the rebels marched, 'where we came that night and were quartered in houses. Here I suppose we were at free quarters, money being[18] short'. The stop at Shepton Mallet gave time for Mr Hardy, the apothecary from Lyme, to attend[19] to John Coad's wound. He cut away the congealed bloody clothes, located the bullet in Coad's back and cut it out, but orders to march prevented him from putting on a proper dressing.

The army marched on to Wells and captured some waggons left behind with an inadequate guard by the royal troops. Some of the rebels got lead from the Cathedral roof to make bullets; some stabled their horses in the cathedral. Lest sacrilege should be attempted, Lord Grey posted himself with his sword drawn in front[20] of the altar. Some men got out of hand and there was some plundering.

On the Thursday the rebels marched towards Bridgwater, meeting the 'Club Army' of 160, and sleeping in the moor. On Friday they marched into Bridgwater, the Duke good-naturedly riding at the head of the Clubmen, whose banner was a white apron.

The only plan in Monmouth's mind was to make another attempt to reach Bristol; and to deceive the enemy a show was made of preparing Bridgwater to stand a siege. On 2 July Richard Goodenough[21] signed an order to the High Constable of Whitleigh to summon all the carpenters within the hundred and 190 labourers, with spades, wheelbarrows, etc. to Bridgwater to be employed on 'his Majesty's' business. Also to summon the inhabitants of the said hundred to bring in 'with all speed imajonable' such corn, provisions and cattle 'as can be spared at a reasonable price without present destruction and ruine to the inhabitants of the said hundred . . . upon pain of being treated as enemies'.

So short was money that at Wells Monmouth's Commissary, Captain Storey, had blackmailed a canon's wife into paying £20 'protection money', and Richard Goodenough attempted to get a forced loan from William Clarke of Sandford, near Bridgwater. William wrote an account to his cousin, Edward Clarke, M.P.

My house was . . . searched by the rebells, and at last by them plundered of all the *edimenta* and *bibamenta**; sadles, bridles and armes went at first, but at length Dick Goodenough would have made mee a usurer against my will, and most uniustly threatned to plunder mee of all I had left, if I would not lend his king £200, but *nec Lex, nec Arma cogunt impossibilia.*† I had not the mony, nor could not borrow, soe the paymaster left me in great Fury, and the next morning I must expect the utmost a beggarly enragd Enimy could doe: but before that time came they were . . beaten[22] and dispers'd.

The royal army was following the rebels from place to place. On 29 June (Monday), while the rebels rested at Frome, Feversham had marched to Westbury; on the 30th to Frome where, having tents, he rested his men on the Wednesday. That same day Lord Dumblane wrote again to his father[23] from Frome, which he described as

ever a most factious Towne. Upon the rebells comeing to itt, they had gott a paper sett up in the Markett place in which they proclaimed Munmouth to be thire true King, and the King to bee a traitor to his Country, and usurper of the Crowne; butt since our comming to itt, they have had great reason to repent them of thire villany, for our Soldiers have pritty well plunder'd them, though contrary to thire officers commands.

Dumblane, recently appointed A.D.C. to Feversham, expected the rebels would be brought to battle at Bridgwater 'and that Monmouth (whilst his Armie gives us battle) will stele privately away'.

On 2 July Feversham moved to Shepton Mallet, and on the third through Glastonbury to Somerton. Spies sent to Bridgwater returned with

---
*Eatables and drinkables.
†Neither law nor arms can produce the impossible.

an account of the rebels' preparation for the defence of the place. Two parties of Horse were sent out scouting and Feversham himself rode into the moor to choose camping places. On Sunday, 5 July, he cantoned his army in and around Weston Zoyland.

The badge that gave Colonel Kirke's regiment their nickname

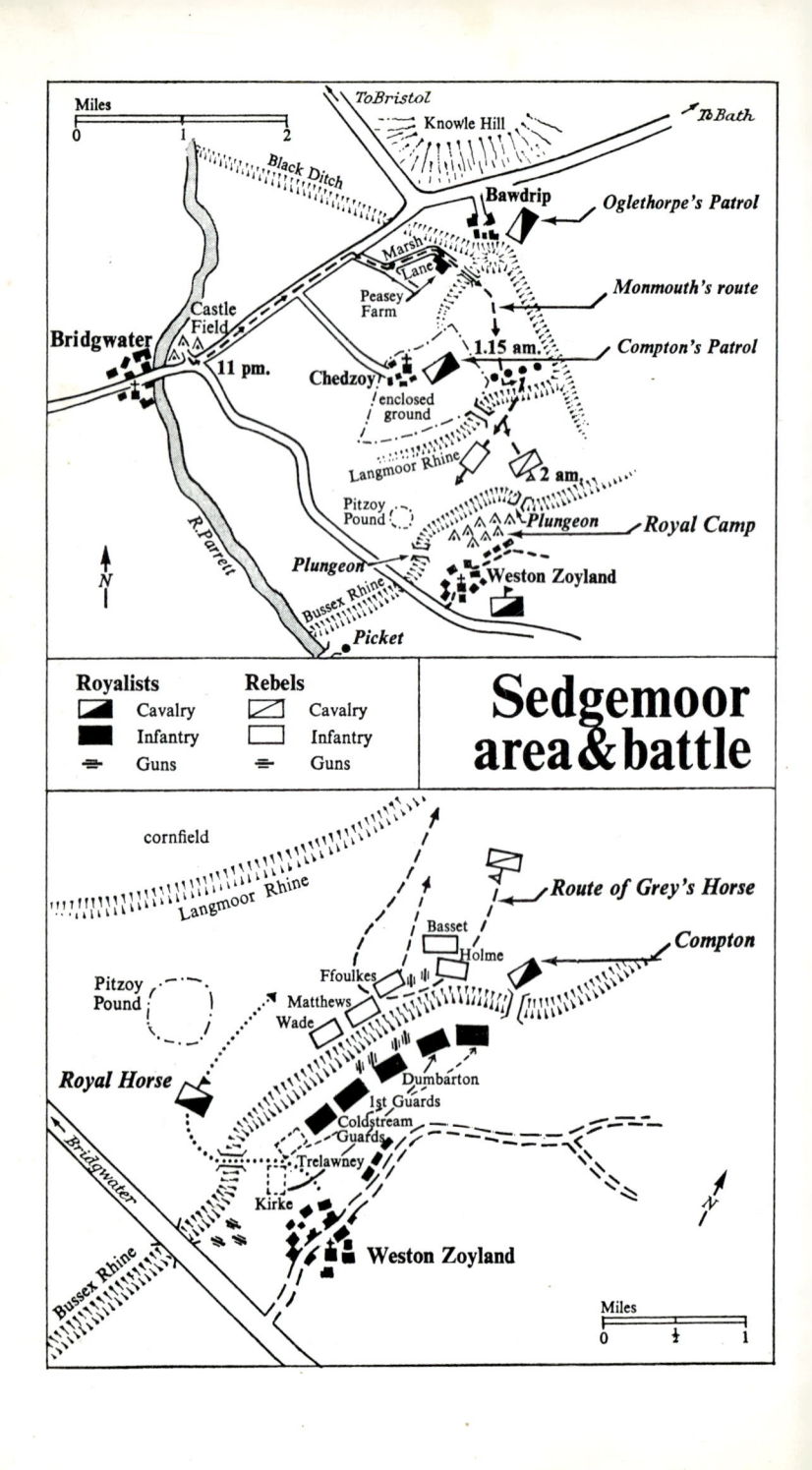

Sedgemoor area & battle

Royalists
- Cavalry
- Infantry
- Guns

Rebels
- Cavalry
- Infantry
- Guns

8

Sedgemoor

The anonymous historian[1] of Feversham's campaign estimated Monmouth's army as 'above 7000 rebels', and the royal army, not counting the militia, as '700 horse and 1900 foot'. His estimate of the rebel numbers was accepted by the Rev. Thomas Axe, who wrote not long after the battle, and subsequently by King James, but Monmouth's officers would not have agreed. At their interrogations[2] Williams, the Duke's steward, thought they were 'about 6000 when they fought'; Richard Goodenough, the Paymaster, said 'never 6000 fighting men'; Colonel Holmes 'beleaves the rebells att the fight by Bridgwater were not above 5000 men'; while Wade said 'The rebells were never 4000 when they fought, but 2600 foot and 600 horse'.

We can make two calculations of the size of Monmouth's army. As he lay wounded after being captured, Major Wade was questioned about the strength of the regiments at Sedgemoor, and he gave[3] these figures:

The Horse 600; Blue Regiment 600; White Regiment 400; Red Regiment 800; Green Regiment 600; Yellow Regiment 500; Independent Co. from Lyme Regis 80: which add up to 3580. To that number must be added those killed in the skirmishes in June: at Bridport 7, at Ashill 4, at Keynsham 14, elsewhere 3, at Philip's Norton 18; making at least 46. Then 57 are recorded as laying down their arms[4] before Sedgemoor, and we can name half-a-dozen deserters. There may have been many more, but adding only the figures we have, the total would be 3689.

The other sum is the addition of the names we have, plus an estimate for some missing names. There came with Monmouth from Holland 82; there rode down from London 12; presented by Dorset Constables[5] 295; by Devon Constables 494; by Somerset Constables 1832; Sentenced at Wells[6] 536; Bound over at Wells 140; in the Goal Delivery though not Presented by the Constables 918; Estimate of those presented[7] at Wells but not there to be tried, say 250. Total 4559.

To get the size of the rebel army at Sedgemoor, we should have to make a number of deductions: 46 killed; perhaps as many wounded; 32 presented not as rebels but as harbouring rebels or aiding and abetting; the 57 known to have laid down their arms, plus some deserters; the drivers of 42 wagons and one gun; two troops of Horse sent to Minehead; at least three messengers; some non-combatants, nine Quakers[8], five doctors, a minister or two, the Duke's servants; altogether something over 300. If the number of deserters was substantial, Wade's figure 'never 4000 when they fought' would be about right.

Feversham quartered his cavalry in the village of Weston Zoyland. His infantry pitched their tents in front of the village and 'behind a convenient ditch that runs from Weston into the moor', wrote one[9] of the royalists, 'which they did in one lyne, leaving room between their tents and the ditch to draw up'. The guns, with a guard of 40 Horse, were stationed at the left of the infantry, covering the road from Bridgwater to Weston lest the rebels should come by that obvious route. The horses and their civilian drivers were dispersed in the village. The Wiltshire militia were quartered in Middlezoy two miles away, and more militia in Othery. Colonel Oglethorpe was given charge of scouting on the Bridgwater to Bristol road, and Major Sir Francis Compton was sent with 100 of the Blues and 50 Dragoons to watch the moor around Chedzoy. An infantry picket of 50 musketeers was placed in Pitzoy Pound, slightly in front of the Lower Plungeon (or crossing) on the Bussex Rhine.

The infantry were aligned with the Royal Scots, the 1st Foot, on the right, just south of the Upper Plungeon. They are usually mentioned as Dumbarton's after their Colonel, though in the battle they were commanded by Lt-Col. Douglas. Next came the 1st Guards, the Grenadiers, under the Duke of Grafton; then the Coldstream Guards under Colonel Sackville. Beyond them were the two Tangier[10] regiments, the 2nd and 4th Foot, Kirke's and Trelawney's, the latter battalion being commanded at Sedgemoor by Lt-Col. Charles Churchill, John's younger brother. Only one of the infantry officers prepared for a night attack: Captain Macintosh[11] of Dumbarton's pegged tapes between his tents and the rhine on the line where his company should fall-in.

Having posted his troops and visited the outlying pickets and their vedettes, Feversham went to bed, leaving John Churchill in command.

One other royalist deserves mention. Dr Peter Mews, Bishop of Winchester, recently translated from Bath and Wells, had come back to his former diocese to see if he could help the royal cause. He had held King Charles' commission in the Civil War, and he had an eye for a military situation. He found a lodging near the church.

In Bridgwater the rebels made the most of their brief respite. Many were given short leave to visit their homes and families, and most of them had returned by Sunday evening. Ferguson enjoyed another opportunity to preach. That morning Monmouth despatched Major Manley and his son to London to get the promised rising started.

Wade[12] tells us that the Duke intended to set off in the evening, 'to march all night to Axbridge, and from thence passing Keynsham bridge to Gloucester, and so passing the Severn' to Cheshire. 'Our carriages were loaded in order to it', but about three o'clock in the afternoon a farm labourer came in from Chedzoy, sent by his master, William Sparke, to tell the Duke that the royal troops were carelessly cantoned around Weston and 'that we might march upon them another way and avoid their cannon'. The Duke called his senior officers together and climbed the tower beneath the spire of St Mary's Church, from which he examined the position of the royal troops through his 'perspective glass'. They debated the chances of a surprise night attack. Were the royal infantry entrenched? The messenger (who answered to either of two names: Benjamin Newton or Godfrey, his parents apparently not being married) went to investigate, and returned to report that the enemy were not entrenched, but he 'took no notice of the ditch that lay in the way of our march'. The field officers all agreed that it was 'advisable to fight if we could surprise them in the night'. Colonel Matthews ventured to suggest[13] that the Duke should divide the Horse into two, leaving Lord Grey in command of one half, and giving command of the other to a more experienced soldier. Characteristically the Duke replied that he would not affront my Lord Grey, and that what he had given him in charge was easy to be effected.

The rebels marched out of Bridgwater about 11 p.m. Young John Oldmixon, then 11 years old, 'saw the Duke of Monmouth ride out, attended by his Life-Guard of Horse; and though then but a boy, observed an alteration in his look, which I did not like ... I ran down with the stream, and was one of its [14] well-wishers'.

The Foot led the march until they reached the moor, so that the Horse should not get too far ahead. The vanguard were the Red Regiment, and the orders were that the march must be silent. They marched up the Bristol road for about two miles 'in great silence' and turned off down Bradney Lane and into Marsh Lane and round Peasey Farm. 'Then', says Wade, 'we made a halt for the Horse to pass by, and received our orders'. The Horse were to advance first and push into the royal camp, preventing the royal troops from forming or their guns being brought into action. The rebels' guns were to follow, and the Foot, when they approached the enemy's position, were to form in one line and advance. The wagons and one gun[15] were left near Peasey farm.

The rebels had given Oglethorpe the slip, and when he moved down from Bawdrip to the Bristol road he detected no sign of movement by them and sent a despatch to that effect to Feversham. Then he ventured down the road as far as Bridgwater and discovered that the rebels had gone. Full credit must be given to Monmouth's army for this achievement. They had had barely three-and-a-half weeks' training, and managed a silent night march in column to within a mile of the royal camp before they were detected. Oglethorpe attempted to repair his mistake by taking the direct route from Bridgwater to Weston.

On the moor Godfrey led the rebels roughly parallel to the Black Ditch until he came to the Langmoor Rhine (or royn, as William Clarke[16] spelt it). The crossing was marked by the Langmoor Stone, but that was hidden by a ground mist, and there was a delay while Godfrey scouted round to find the stone. Suddenly there was a shot fired, a pistol shot, so close that the rebels presumed it must have been fired by one of them. When Daniel Defoe came to write his[17] account, he said the shot was fired 'either by accident or by treachery'. Many of the rebels who survived were sure it was treachery, and named the culprit as Captain Hucker, who had been Monmouth's host in Taunton. They invented reasons to account for his treachery. After his death his son went to considerable pains to clear his father's name.

It is now generally agreed that the shot was fired[18] by the vedette posted by Sir Francis Compton. When he (the vedette) realised the approach of the rebels, he fired his pistol, galloped near enough to his picket to shout the alarm to them, and then galloped straight on to rouse the infantry, shouting to them 'Beat your drums; beat your drums; the enemy has come'. Monmouth made the best of the situation. Sending the cavalry ahead, he himself, carrying an infantry officer's half-pike, led the Foot and set a pace 'exceeding swift'.

It is not easy to be precise about the cavalry action that followed. Ferguson who says[19] he rode with the Horse, makes the almost incredible assertion that Grey dismissed the guide; more probably Godfrey on foot could not keep up with Grey's Horse. Certainly Grey missed finding the Upper Plungeon. After the alarm Compton fell back from Chedzoy to defend the Plungeon, the northern crossing of the Bussex Rhine. There seem to have been two clashes with Grey's Horse en route, in which both Compton and Captain Sands, who succeeded to the command, were[20] wounded. When the rebel Horse reached the rhine, Captain Jones turned to the left, Lord Grey to the right, followed by the majority of his troopers. Captain Jones and his troop fought a fierce little action with Compton's Blues for control of the Plungeon, but the training, skill, and discipline of the regulars was too much for Jones's enthusiastic amateurs, who were eventually driven off.

Grey's main body, riding alongside the rhine looking for a crossing, came under fire from the Guards, and disintegrated, some galloping across the front of Wade's Red Regiment, and some fleeing by the way they had come and causing panic among the drivers of the wagons, who fled leaving the wagons to be plundered. Others made for Bridgwater, where, after the battle, Wade 'met with two or three full troops of Horse that had run away out of the field without striking stroke'. One of these troops was that commanded by Captain Hucker, whose lieutenant, William Savage[21] of Taunton, tried in vain to take it back to support the infantry.

Grey implied[22] that, riding alongside the rhine looking for a crossing, he had got amongst the tents of Kirke's Foot, when Oglethorpe's Horse arrived from their reconnoitring of Bridgwater and forced him to draw off. Ferguson[19] is a most unreliable witness, but he also wrote of 'our horse standing scattered and disunited, flying upon every approach of a squadron of theirs commanded by Oglethorpe'. He praised the courage of Captain Jones and the two troops he led, though he did not name Jones and did not realise how fierce a fight they had. He asserts

> I not only struck at several troopers who had forsaken their station, but upbraided divers of the captains for being wanting in their duty. I spake with great warmth to my Lord Grey, and conjured him to charge and not suffer the victory which our foot had in a manner taken hold of, to be ravished from us.

He goes on to say that if the Duke had had but 200 reliable and well-led cavalry 'he could not have failed of being victorious'. He stated as a fact that Captain Hucker fired a pistol 'Within view of their camp . . . to give them notice of our approach' and went on to invent what Jeffreys said at Hucker's trial.

As Monmouth approached the Bussex Rhine, he left Wade in command of the vanguard and went to help Buyse site the three small guns they had brought with them. They chose a place just north of the right of the Royalist line, from which the gunners fired diagonally on the Scots and the Guards. Wade led the Red Regiment to within 30 or 40 paces of the ditch and wheeled to the right, bringing the column along parallel to the royalist line. A 'halt' and 'left turn' should have turned the column into line, but the rapidity of the march over the moor had disordered his men and it took a little time to arrange the line. Wade intended to lead his men across the ditch, which was then, says Mr Paschall[23] (the vicar of Chedzoy), dry enough for the foot to have got over. Wade meant to charge the royal infantry, but the Yellow Regiment following the Red, opened fire, and Wade's men then also started to shoot, and he could not get them a step further. Dumbarton's Scots were armed with match-locks, which were then going out of fashion and which showed the enemy at night just where the musketeers were standing. They shot it out for an hour and a half, and the rebels were then short of ammunition, no provision having been made to bring fresh supplies from the wagons. People who were not present[24] asserted that Monmouth's inexperienced musketeers aimed too high and inflicted casualties on the rear ranks of the Royal Scots and the Guards, instead of the front ranks. It may well be that Lt-Colonel Douglas had ordered his front rank to kneel with their bayonets fixed in case rebel cavalry appeared through the smoke. Until the invention of the bayonet infantry had needed a substantial number of pikemen, at one time, a half, but latterly a third, to protect them from a cavalry charge while the musketeers were re-loading. Bayonets had been issued to British regiments[25] in 1673, though largely withdrawn shortly after, to be re-issued after Sedgemoor. Monmouth had not muskets for all his men, and they had improvised pikes by fixing scythe blades to straight poles, which were described by some of the royal troops as 'murderous weapons'.

Realising that the action was being fought on the royalists' right, Churchill marched the two Tangiers regiments across from the left to the right behind the Guards and the Scots, posting them to the right of Dumbarton's Foot. The royal guns were also out of action, and, as their horses and drivers were not with them, Bishop Mews brought his coach-horses and got his coachman and groom to harness them to the guns and draw them into action. Three were posted[26] to the right of Dumbarton's, and another three were brought into the gaps between the infantry battalions. The first three did severe damage to the rebels, the Green and the White Regiments, perhaps still in column, suffering [27] especially.

Feversham, having been asleep, was 'late on parade', but approved Churchill's dispositions. Riding to the left he met Oglethorpe's cavalry returning from Bridgwater, led them across behind the infantry, and launched them against the rebels' left flank. He gave orders that none of the Foot should cross the ditch until he gave the word. As daylight broke, he sent in the cavalry on both flanks.

Lord Grey returned, seeking Monmouth, to tell him it was time to seek safety. Discarding their breastplates they rode off with Anton Buyse and young Dr Oliver,[28] through Chedzoy and up the Poldens.

'It being pretty light', recorded Wade,

I perceived all the battalions on the left running (who, as I since understood, were broken by the King's Horse of the left wing), and finding my own men not inclinable to stand, I caused them to face about and made a kind of disorderly retreat to a ditch a great way behind us, where we were charged by a party of

The Bussex Rhyne in flood—it was almost dry at the time of the battle. (An old photograph taken before the rhyne was filled in)

Horse and Dragoons, and routed. About 150 getting over the ditch, I marched with them on foot to Bridgwater'.

Feversham gave the order for a general advance. The Battle of Sedgemoor was over, but not the slaughter. One royalist officer was writing a letter by 7 a.m., adding 'Our men are still killing them in the corne and hedges and ditches[29] whither they are crept'. Lord Dumblane also wrote[30] shortly after the battle, dating his letter from the 'Duke of Grafton's tent in Sedgemoor, July 6: 85:

My Lord,
    I do not doubt but that before this comes to your Lordship's hands you will receive a more perfect account of what has this day past in the batle, from some of my Lord Feversham's expresses . . . This is therefore only to lett your Lordship and my Lady know (because possibly you may heare that I am wounded in this scermidge) that my wound is so slite, that I am only asshamed I do not give your Lordship the account of this day's worke my selfe in my owne hand, butt my Chirergion (Mr. Hobbs) will not give mee leave to write so much . . : Your Lordship's most dutiful and obedient sonn,
                      Dumblan.

For a Guide to the Battlefield, *see* p. 127.

Captain Dummer of the royal Artillery[31] wrote a brief but interesting account:

July 5. We marched into the Levell . . . Rebels said (to be) in their march towards Bristoll . . . We securely went to sleep, the Foot in camp, and the Horse in Quarters at Weston and Midlesea, saving some Outguards of Horse upon our Right and Left. July 6. At 2 A Clock this morning (securely sleeping) our Camp was Rous'd by the near approach of the Rebells; a dark night and thick Fogg covering the Moon; supiness and a preposterous Confidence of ourselves with the Undervaluing of the Rebells . . . had put us into the worst circumstances of surprize . . . Thus we rec'd the Alarme from Sir Francis Compton . . . with his single Party of 150 Horse and Dragoons . . . From this Alarme there seems to be 2 minutes distance to a Volley of Small Shott from the Body of the Rebells Foot, consisting of about 6000 (but All came not up to Battell) upon the Right of our Camp, followed by 2 or 3 Rounds from Three Pieces of Cannon brought up within 116 Paces of the Ditch Ranging our Battallions. Our Artillery was near 500 Paces distant, and the Horses Drivers not easily found through confusion and darkness. Yet such was the extraordinary cheerfulness of our Army, that they were allmost as readily drawn up to receive them, as a prae-informed expectation could have posted them, tho' upon so short and so dangerous a warning. Six of our nearest Gunns were with the greatest diligence imaginable advanced, three upon the Right of the Scotts, and three in front of the King's first Battalion; and did very considerable execution upon the Enemies. They stood near an hour and a halfe with great shouting and courage, briskly fyring; and then throwing down their Armes, fell into Route and confusion. The number of the Slaine with about 300 taken, according to the most modest computation might make up 1000, we losing but 27 on the spott and having about 200 wounded. A victory very considerable where Providence was absolutely a greater Friend than our own conduct. The Dead in the Moor we buried and the Country people took care for the interment of those slain in the Corne Fields.

POSTSCRIPT

The author of the Epistle to the Hebrews added to the first part of his Roll of Honour the comment 'These all died in faith, not having received the promises' (xi.13.) This epitaph might well be applied to those 300 who survived Sedgemoor for only three months, and died on the gallows. Several of the 'dying speeches' expressed a confident hope that in God's good time the cause for which they were laying down their lives would triumph. Few could have expected so speedy a fulfilment, but three years and seven months after Sedgemoor there was a Protestant king on the throne, and before four years had passed since the battle, the Toleration Act[1] was on the Statute Book, granting freedom of worship to almost all Nonconformists.

9

The Next Few Days

Monmouth, Grey, Buyse and Dr Oliver galloped away over the Poldens, and when they stopped further north Oliver advised the Duke to make for Uphill, just south of Weston-super-mare, where there is a sheltered creek from which they could get a 'passage boat' to Wales. There Monmouth would be safe until he could contrive to retire elsewhere. Oliver in after years told the story[1] to Oldmixon. He thought the Duke inclined to hearken to him, but Lord Grey dismissed the advice as foolish, and persuaded the Duke to make for Edward Strode's house at Downside near Shepton Mallet and hence towards the Dorset coast. Oliver, who was clearly fond of the Duke, had tears in his eyes after Grey's crushing remarks, as he said to Monmouth 'God bless you. Sir. I fear I shall never see you again'. Instead of riding to Uphill, Oliver rode to Bristol, where no one had yet heard of the battle, and found refuge in the house of a friend who did not know that he had been with Monmouth.

Monmouth has been severely criticised for deserting his men on the battlefield, but his grandfather, King Charles I, left his troops at Naseby; his father, Charles II escaped from the Worcester fight; and Bonnie Prince Charlie, his first-cousin-once-removed, left his followers at Culloden—all without incurring the censure that has fallen on the Duke.

John Oldmixon[2] recorded,

About 4 a-clock on Monday morning the run-aways began to come to Bridgwater, and I saw many of them so wounded that I wondered how they could reach so far. One fellow, particularly, had scarce lain himself down on a bulk, when he dyed away of his wounds ... I was upon the spot before the dead were buried, and young as I was, observed the slain to be more on the King's part than on the Duke's ... Not above 300 of the Duke's men were killed in the action, and about 400 of the King's'.

Oldmixon's estimates are surprising, but he was obviously judging by the centre of the fighting rather than the line of flight, and the royalist dead in red coats would be more conspicuous than the rebels in 'country clothes'.

Adam Wheeler[3] was a drummer in Colonel Wyndham's regiment of the Wiltshire Militia, and was very proud of being the first drummer to beat the Alarm when the news reached Middlezoy that 'the Enemy is Engaged'. The regiment fell in and marched to Weston Zoyland, where some of the men asked leave 'to get such pillage in the feild as they could finde', which the Colonel strictly forbade. Lord Feversham came to thank Colonel Wyndham and the regiment for their readiness. The militiamen then began to collect prisoners and bring them, mostly tied together, to Weston Zoyland Church, where Adam Wheeler sat writing the numbers on his drumhead; the first batch numbered 55, the second 32. Then came two wounded rebels crawling on hands and knees, and another who had been stripped down to his drawers, and another running with two horse-men belabouring him. Altogether Wheeler listed 284, of whom the militiamen brought in 238. 'Such of them', he admits, 'as had a good coat or anything worth the piling were fairly stripped of it'. The last prisoner he recorded, with admiration, had been shot through the shoulder and the belly, had been stripped naked and left in the scorching hot sun. Some soldiers abused him as a 'Monmouth dog', but one of them gave him a pair of drawers, and the men around tried to let him get more air. At last he struggled to his feet and 'having a long stick in his hand, he walked feebly to Weston Church'. He was one of five who died of wounds in the church that night.

Richard Alford, churchwarden of Weston Zoyland, is thought to have been the author of a brief account of the 'Ingagement' found in the church register. After recording the Christian burial of 16 King's soldiers, five in the church and 11 in the churchyard, he continues

One hundred or more of the King's souldiers wounded; of which wounds many died, of which we have no certaine account. There was killed of the Rebels upon the spott aboute 300; hanged with us 22 of which 4 were hanged in gemmasses. About 500 prisoners brought into our church, of which there was 79 wounded and 5 of them died of there wounds in our church.

One of those hanged was Monmouth's faithful and efficient Dutch gunner; another was 'a yellow coat soldier' (a militiaman) 'that ran out of his Majesty's army to Monmouth'. A third was the Wiltshireman, Captain Adlam[4], so badly wounded that he was not expected to last through the night, so they hanged him at once, and he was one of the four hanged in irons. Local family tradition[5] has it that after dark the church-warden and his daughter, though keen royalists, carried into the church buckets of water for the prisoners.

Among the prisoners was the Quaker, Francis Scott, whose brother-in-law, John Whiting, tells[6] this story:

Eighteenth-century engraving of Weston Zoyland church, in which 500 rebels were imprisoned after the battle.

As to brother Scott in particular, he was wonderfully preserved, being taken and put into Weston steeple-house with many more the night after the fight, in order to be hanged next day, as many were; but he got out at the little north-door, while the watch was asleep, and so escaped with his life; lying in corn-fields by day, and going by night till he got home, and so lay about till the general pardon'.

Some have found a difficulty in Whiting's phrase 'the little north-door'. Presumably he meant the door from the chancel to the present vestry, the outer wall of which has been rebuilt since that time. The churchwardens' account-book (which is preserved in the church safe[7]) contains several interesting entries dated 1685, among them 'Paid Andrew Newman for mending of ye Clocke and righting of the Key of ye North Dore ... £0-1-9'. Whether Francis Scott broke the lock, or was able to escape because the lock was already broken, we cannot tell.

We do not know how many days the prisoners were kept in the church, without sanitation, but two more entries in the account-book will cause little surprise. 'Paid John Jones and Andrew Elroy for cleansing the Church 0-10-6'; and 'Paid for Franckenssence and peivey and resson and other things to burn in the Church after ye prissoners was gon out 0-5-8'. Peivey might be saltpetre or peat.

Villagers from Weston Zoyland were commandeered to bury the slain.

As numbers increased, religious ceremony decreased. Adam Wheeler saw 174 bodies in one pile before they were put in a big pit, and he heard that the villagers had reported to the vicar and churchwardens that they had buried 1384. They believed there were many more dead, unfound in the corn. The graves were shallow and the covering mostly sand. It was not long before there were compliants that the covering was inadequate. Colonel Kirke sent an order[8] to 'Goodman Philipps', Tithing man of Chedzoy,

Whereas complaints have been made to me by the inhabitants . . . that the rebels lately buried are not sufficiently covered, and that they have been at great charge to build gallowses and gibbets, and to make chains to hang up the rebels: these are in His Majesty's name to require you . . . to press ploughs and men to come to the said place where the rebels are buried, that there may be a mount erected on them.

The number of the slaine, wrote Captain Dummer, 'according to the most modest computation might make up 1000'. It is very difficult to identify the rebel casualities, but almost certainly among those killed at Sedgemoor were Captain Francis Goodenough[9] of the White Regiment, Lieutenants Dalby, Lillington, Mitchell and Taylor, Ensigns Babbington, John Cragg and Sanford, all of the Red Regiment; Mr Rose of the Artillery; 'Young Chamberlain' and Mr Walters, who came with the Duke; Clement Bovett[10] and John Rugg of Wellington; William Harvey senior, William Loring, and Nicholas Mitchell, of Membury.

On Tuesday, 7 July, Colonel Wyndham's regiment of the Wilts militia set off to march home. At Glastonbury they hanged six rebel prisoners, one of them a lieutenant, from the sign of the White Hart Inn. They were stripped naked and left hanging when the militia marched on. This was recorded by both Adam Wheeler[11] and Wadham Wyndham. The regiment halted at Wells for a church parade at which Bishop Mews preached to them and their rebel prisoners, of whom they hanged five after the service, before marching on to Philip's Norton. Marching in the opposite direction, Colonel Kirke and 'the Lambs' proceeded through Bridgwater to Taunton, where Kirke ordered the hanging of 19 rebels without trial. Presumably they were taken with their weapons as evidence. The vicar of St Mary Magdalene buried ten of them, recorded them in the register merely as 'rebel soldiers'. The vicar of St James, with more humanity, entered the nine names in his register[12] under the dates July 9 and 10: John Gotrell, John Borges, John Grinslade, William Sharpe, Simon Sayer, Richard Barton, Abraham Pinney, William Bowne, and James Besson, 'executed for treason against his majesty.'

When Kirke and his men reached Taunton, they erected their tents in a district that is still known as Tangier. Kirke reduced his numbers by discharging temporary recruits, among them Daniel Manning, the blacksmith's apprentice. Fortunately for him his company commander, Captain Thomas St John, gave him a certificate[13] of his service in the king's forces, which twice saved him from arrest as a rebel:

Whereas by his Majesties Order of the 16th Inst. all foote Campanyes Except the Guards are reduced to the Number of Sixty Souldiers each, And that the Bearer Daniell Manning hath been SuperNumerrary in my Company in the Queen Dowager's Regiment under the Command of the Honn[ble] Coll. Piercy Kirke, These are to desire all whome it may Concerne to suffer and permit the said Manning to pass and travill about his owne Lawfull occasions without any Impediment.
    Given at Taunton the 20th July 1685
                      Tho[s] St. John.

The Constable of Stoke St Mary presented[14] him as 'Absent from his habitation at the time of the Rebellion', and he would have been arrested but for this certificate. He returned to his master, who said he dared not re-employ him, so Daniel set off to seek employment in London, and there we shall find him after the Bloody Assizes. Two other 'Lambs' made their way home by way of Crewkerne, where the Churchwardens (as Overseers of the Poor) entered in their accounts[15]

to 4 poor seamen that lay here	1-0
to others of Kerkes souldiers disbanded	0-6
to a souldier going to the Army	0-3

Apparently the men had 1d for supper, 1d for a bed, and 1d for breakfast.

Dr Pitman set off to ride home to Sandford Orcas, but was captured by soldiers or militiamen, who took his coat and purse, and lodged him[16] in Ilchester gaol. Wounded John Coad and Quaker John Whiting both thought they would be safer in Ilchester goal than waiting to be arrested by Lord Stawel's militiamen. Whiting[17] had been staying at Long Sutton and records that Sir Edward Phelips came to Sarah Hurd's house there

and sat and slept in her chair, while his men went a-hunting about the fields to take men; and several were brought to my friend's door and sent to prison in droves . . . And soon after, seeing that prison was the safest place as things were, I thought it better to go than be sent thither, or sent for; and so returned to Ivelchester, where the keepers began to look after their prisoners again, and to inquire for us . . . They shut us up in the ward, where we lay fourteen of us in one room, mostly on the floor, as close as we could lie one by another.

When the Quaker prisoners refused to pay rent, the same rent they had paid when they were 'boarded out', the under-gaoler put them in handcuffs in the 'inward ward amonst Monmouth's men, where at night . . . there was no room for us to lie down'.

John Coad[18] found his wife at Middlezoy, and 'being disabled as to any further service' intended to take advantage of 'the 4 days Act of Pardon', but a violent fever prevented him. The midwife at Long Sutton dressed his wound, but news of Sedgemoor brought trouble. Militiamen found him, gloated over him and robbed him. They reported him to Lord Stawel, who vowed to hang him. Hearing of this Coad

> instantly sent my wife to unkle Thomas Knight to desire him to go to Sir Edward Phelips, to desire him to crave the Lord's leave that I might be brought before him; which being granted, the messenger was sent to Lord Stawel to acquaint him that I was one of his (Phelips') soldiers, and he desired I might be referred to him; this also was granted . . . and I had this benefit of a few days liberty, till I could get a horse-litter to transfer myself from thence to Ilchester; and committed myself to the keeper of the prison for security and safety from other enemies; and although it was a hard shift, yet then I had some rest, and Sir Edward Phelips ordered a chirurgion[19] to take care, if possible he could, to save my life, though to an evil purpose.

Even in these early days there were some escapes. John Swain of Shapwick made his way home after the battle but was sought out by soldiers or militiamen, who marched him off towards Bridgwater, followed by his wife and children. As they reached the Bridgwater road, near Loxley Wood, Swain begged that he might be allowed to show his children his prowess as a long-jumper, that they might have that as a memory of him. The militiamen agreed, but were astounded[20] when Swain made not one, but a triple jump, and disappeared into the wood to make good his escape. Stones still mark 'Swain's Leaps', which measure about 13ft 8in., 13ft 3in., and 14ft.

Richard Cogan of Coaxdon Hall near Axminster got as far as the Green Dragon in Axminster and begged for shelter. Elizabeth Gray, the daughter of the house, took him upstairs, got him to lie face downwards on the bed sacking, covered him with the feather-mattress, and arranged the bedclothes 'so deftly' that though the soldiers following Cogan searched the room twice and looked under the bed, they did not find[21] him. After the General Pardon had been issued in the Spring of 1686, Cogan came back to marry the girl.

A strong and persistent family tradition takes Hugh Aldersey from Sedgemoor to Yorkshire. His family gave out that he had been killed in the battle to stop people looking for him. He settled in Lothersdale, married in 1686, and is the ancestor of numerous progeny, who preserved his name[22] and story.

After reaching Bridgwater with his 150 men, Major Wade[23] got his horses and with about 20 officers and others, amongst which was Ferguson, I went westward to meet 2 troops of Horse who were gone to Minehead to fetch up 6 pieces of cannon, being Captain Hewling's and Captain Cary's troops. With part of them, amounting in all to near 50, we went to Ilfordcombe and seized on a vessel, which we victualled and put to sea, but were forced ashore by 2 frigates cruising on the coast, after which we dispersed and fled into the woods. I for my part was alone from that time.

Wade was found, haggard and exhausted, in the Valley of the Rocks by a countrywoman called Grace Howe, and by her guided to Farley Farm in Brendon Parish, where John Birch took him in and looked after him and two other Monmouth men at the risk of his life. The Rector of Brendon, the Rev. Richard Powell, suspected that his parishioners had a secret[24] that he was not sharing. He asked questions at the inn, where he found that the best beer was 'bespoke' and someone came daily to collect it. So Powell, arming himself and a friend and disguising their route by a detour, rode off to get the help of John Whichehalse, J.P., who brought along a mounted and armed servant. Then they made for John Birch's farm, and stationed two near the front door and two near the back. Powell then knocked at the front door. After a slight delay both doors were opened and while someone greeted the Rector, Wade and the two Monmouth men made a dash from the back door. Powell's friend and Whichehalse's servant both fired and Wade was severely wounded in the back. The other two made good their escape, and Wade never revealed their names.

Magistrates questioned the wounded man, who replied briefly. The principal information he gave them was the size of the various rebel[25] regiments. Wade was wearing rough country clothes, but Powell pulled open his coat and said that the good holland shirt below did not match the disguise. At first Wade gave his name as John Lane, using his mother's maiden name which he had used as an alias in Holland; but the next day he apologised to Powell and gave his own name, promising an account of his own part in the rising, when he was less weak.

The capture of such an inportant officer was at once reported to Lord Sunderland, who ordered that Wade should be sent to the Tower of London as soon as he could be[26] moved. He was given to understand that his life depended on a written confession with plenty of names in it. Wade was allowed to send his washing out of the Tower, and with it he smuggled out a letter to some friend or relation, begging for the names of those known to have been killed at Sedgemoor, or known to have escaped abroad. The names came back concealed in the pleats[27] of his shirts. King James came to the Tower to interrogate the prisoner, and family tradition has it that he said 'Your friends, Mr Wade, seem to be among the dead'.

He was sufficiently interested to have Wade moved to Windsor where, in October, Wade dictated in two instalments to two different amanuenses his account of the rebellion, which is far and away the best contemporary account we have. In this account Wade says 'All the persons I can positively charge to have been concerned in it are either outlawed, dead, or executed', and it is probably true that no one suffered through Wade's 'confession'.

The villagers at Brendon had known without disapproval that John Birch was sheltering fugitive rebels, and did their best to keep their secret from the Rector, whose rebel-hunting they detested. The Treasury Books record Richard Powell's application for £100 as reward for the capture[28] of Wade. Powell moved away from Brendon in 1686. John Birch did not wait for the Lord Chief Justice to hang him; he preferred to hang himself. Wade did not mention Grace Howe in his narrative, while Jeffreys might seek to punish her, but he had not forgotten his debt to her and bequeathed her an annuity[29] in his will.

As an officer who had come from Holland with the Duke, Wade was excluded from the General Pardon; but that is not the end of his story.

THE CAPTURE OF MONMOUTH AND GREY

Early on 7 July Monmouth, Grey and Buyse set out from Downside, riding south-east. They crossed into Dorset near Gillingham, and somewhere thereabouts they picked up Richard Holyday to guide them towards Poole. Going east-south-east, near or through Berwick St John, they came to Woodyates Inn, near which Monmouth changed clothes with a shepherd, and Grey and Buyse seem also to have acquired country clothes. Their route turned due south, and when they had passed Wimborne St Giles, where Monmouth had stayed with Shaftesbury, they unsaddled the horses they had ridden nearly 40 miles that morning, hid the saddles and bridles, and turned the horses loose. They were hardly old friends, as they had owned them barely three weeks. Proceeding on foot, they soon separated, Grey and Holyday making the better pace. They had walked about six miles, and were only eight short of their destination, Poole, when they were seen and captured by Sussex militiamen, who had been authorised to cross into Hampshire to join in the search for rebels.

Monmouth and Buyse had only managed half the distance before they separated somewhere in the parish of Horton to hide separately. An old cottager, Amy Farrant, watched them disappear into a thicket. Monmouth laid himself down in a ditch, endeavouring to conceal himself with leaves. He had gathered a few pea-pods to lessen his hunger, and he had a few peas left in his pocket in the morning. As Sussex militiamen came near, Amy

Farrant told them what she had seen. Buyse was found first early on the 8th, and when questioned, admitted that he had been with the Duke 'some hours ago'. When Militiaman Parkin found the gaunt, unshaven stranger, he was so unlike the handsome Duke that his captors were doubtful about his identity. Lord Lumley, their Commanding Officer, was soon on the spot, with Sir William Portman of the Somerset militia. The captive was searched, and they found his 'lesser George', the badge of the Order of the Garter (his 'greater George' had been pawned in Holland). That and his pocket-book established his identity.

The King had promised £5000 reward for the capture of Monmouth. Lord Lumley insisted it should be shared among the Sussex militia; Amy Farrant was awarded £50 for her share.

Lumley and Portman took their prisoner to the nearest magistrate, Anthony Ettrick of Holt Lodge, and sent messengers to inform the King. They all spent the nights of July 8 and 9 at Ringwood, waiting for instructions. Monmouth used the enforced leisure to write[31] to the King, expressing his remorse for 'the wrong I have done you', and pleading 'My misfortune was such as to meet with some horrid people that made me believe things of your Majesty, and gave me so many false arguments, that I was fully led away'. He begged for an interview, not to

excuse anything I have done . . . I hope, Sir, God Almighty will strike your heart with mercy and compassion for me, as He has done mine with the abhorrence of what I have done. Wherefore, Sir, I hope I may live to show you how zealous I shall ever be for your service.

In this and subsequent letters Monmouth implied that he had something to reveal of such significance that he dare not put in a letter which others would read. It has been thought that he planned to reveal the double-dealing of James's Secretary of State, the Earl of Sunderland, who apparently had secretly bargained to serve Monmouth as Secretary of State, if Monmouth gained the crown. This was plainly told, five years later, by Ferguson to the Earl of Ailesbury, and is recorded[32] in Ailesbury's Memoirs.

Monmouth also wrote the next day to the Queen Dowager[33], who had always shown him friendship, and to Lord Rochester, the King's brother-in-law, begging them to help him get an interview with the King.

On 10 July Lumley and Portman took their prisoner to Winchester; on the 11th to Farnham Castle, where Bishop Mews lived; and on the 12th to Guildford, where they lodged him in the tower of Archbishop Abbot's Hospital, in a room which may still be seen. The next day, as Lord Ailesbury[34] relates, the Duke was conducted to Lambeth by a party of horse, and from thence brought over by water to the privy stairs at Whitehall; and I, coming from the city by water, unfortunately landed at the same moment, and saw him led up the other stairs on Westminster side, lean and pale, and with a disconsolate physiognomy, with soldiers with pistols in their hands. The Yeomen of the Guard were posted, and I got behind one of them that he should not perceive me, and I wished heartily and often since that I had not seen him, for I could never get him out of my mind for years, I loved him so personally. He was charming both as to his person and engaging behaviour, a fine courtier, but of a most poor understanding as to cabinet and politics, (who) gave himself wholly up to flatterers and knaves by consequence . . . I abhored the Duke's presumption [in claiming the crown] but loved him so much as my King's natural son . . . who was ever to us both a noble and good friend'.

'Us both' included Lord Ailesbury's father. He refers to Monmouth as 'the poor misguided Duke', who was however, 'a brave and good officer', an opinion confirmed by another keen royalist and soldier, Sir John Reresby. 'The Duke of Monmouth', Reresby[35] wrote, 'had from the very beginning of this desperate attempt behaved with the conduct of a great captain, as was allowed even by the king who, in my hearing, said he had not made one false step'.

Monmouth got his interview with the King, and begged for his life unworthily, being still shattered by his defeat and capture. His uncle had heard Monmouth's protestations of undying loyalty and service before, after the Rye House Plot, and was not impressed. The Quality of mercy was not conspicuous in him, though Lord Ailesbury[36] thought that he had been moved to pity but was warned against showing mercy by Lord Sunderland. As Monmouth had been attainted by Act of Parliament, no trial was necessary, and on 14 July he was informed by Bishop Turner of Ely and Bishop Ken of Bath and Wells that he was to be executed the following day.

Monmouth recovered his dignity and his courage before his death. His wife and their three surviving children had been lodged in the Tower on 9 July. The Duke saw them and said goodbye. He admitted in a written statement that his father had always insisted that he had not been married[37] to Monmouth's mother. To the bishops he expressed his regret for all the suffering he had caused his followers, but he was determined not to admit any sin in his living with Lady Henrietta Wentworth. He asked for Dr Tenison, the Vicar of St Martin's-in-the-Fields (and subsequently Archbishop of Canterbury), to help him prepare for death, and when Tenison suggested repentance for this sin, the Duke[38] replied 'he had heard it was lawful to have one wife in the eye of the law, and another before God'. Of Monmouth and Henrietta Lord Ailesbury[39] wrote 'They were both as infatuated, and imagined themselves man and wife . . . I respect her memory. I greatly esteemed and loved her, one of the best friends I ever had'. In his younger days as Lord Bruce he had hoped to marry Lady Henrietta himself, and he retained his affection for her. When she returned to England after Monmouth's execution, Lord Ailesbury[40] went to see her, and found her 'in a most lamentable condition of health'. If ever a girl died of a broken heart, that was the cause of Henrietta Wentworth's death in April 1686.

Monmouth met his death with courage, enduring five blows from the axe before the executioner completed his task. He was buried in front of the altar in the Tower Chapel of St Peter ad vincula.

All James Scott's titles were forfeited by the Act of Attainder, but his wife retained her Scottish titles as Duchess of Buccleuch, and so their elder surviving son James remained Earl of Dalkeith, though he lost his English title as Earl of Doncaster. He died before his mother, but his son became Duke of Buccleuch when Duchess Anne died in 1732, and in 1743 Parliament restored him to his grandfather's second title as Earl of Doncaster. All the Dukes of Buccleuch have been direct descendants of the Duke of Monmouth. The younger son, Henry, was created Earl of Deloraine in 1706, and rose to be a [41] Major-General. Monmouth's small daughter, Lady Anne Scott, was ten when her father died, and falling ill in the Tower, she survived him by less than a month; by the King's permission she was buried in Westminster Abbey. Three years later Duchess Anne married again, becoming the second wife of Lord Cornwallis.

Monmouth told Dr Tenison that there were no children of his liaison with Lady Henrietta, but a man who called himself[42] R. Wentworth Smyth-Stuart claimed to be their son. He perished on the Stuart side in 1746.

10

The Bloody Assizes

WINCHESTER, SALISBURY, DORCHESTER, EXETER

John Oldmixon mentioned a long range of gibbets[1] alongside the road from Weston to Bridgwater on which rebels had been hanged after the battle. There is a story that the Bishop of Bath and Wells warned Feversham 'My Lord, you do not know what you do. This is murder in the Law . . . Now the Battel is over, these poor Rogues must be tried before they can be put to death'. Of this Macaulay[2] wrote 'I should be very glad if I could give credit to the popular story that Ken, immediately after the battle of Sedgemoor, represented to the chiefs of the royal army the illegality of military executions'; and went on to explain that Bishop Ken was in London in the House of Lords on the Thursday before the battle, and with Monmouth in the Tower on the Monday after—he could hardly have attempted the long journeys to and from Somerset in between. Mr. Maurice Page in his lively and valuable book[3] on the Battle of Sedgemoor has suggested that the original writer of the story meant Bishop Peter Mews, who had been Bishop of Bath and Wells until the previous year, was present at the battle, and was known to Lord Feversham. Though transplanted to Winchester, he had returned to his former diocese in case he could help the royal cause.

Be that as it may, putting the poor rogues on trial presented the government with a serious problem. An order was issued requiring the Constables of the Hundreds in Somerset, Dorset and Devon to make a return of all the men in their Hundred who were 'absent from their homes (or habitations) during the rebellion[4] of James Scott, late Duke of Monmouth'; and Commissioners were appointed 'to assist them', which meant, to ensure that they did make their returns. In Holwell Poor Accounts in Dorset Record Office[5] is an item: 'Paid for a Presentment at Bruten to satisfy the Commitioners what men was out in Monmouth's Army'.

There is a similar payment in the accounts of the Church-wardens at Poyntington; and at Kilton (near Kilve)[6] they 'paid at the Commission concerning the rebels 10/-'.

We are fortunate in having a fair copy[4] of most of the Constables' returns, 47 large quarto sheets, written on both sides, which were offered in a miscellaneous lot at the auction of a library in Dorchester in 1875. They were bought by Mr. W. Bowles Barrett[7], who recognised their importance and sent them to the British Museum. There are photostat copies in Somerset Record Office. The returns name 295 men in Dorset, 494 in Devon, and 1832 in Somerset, most of them accused of absence from home during the rebellion. A few are listed as rebels, but the Constables preferred to be guarded and qualified their accusations as 'Absent . . . and supposed to be in James Scott's Army'. Others are said to have been 'In the late rebellion and not come home', or ' . . . and not taken'; a few are reported 'In prison'. The men of Taunton were all presented as 'Assisting, aiding and abetting the rebellion of James Scott, late Duke of Monmouth'.

Unfortunately the Presentment Roll for the Assize at Wells is missing. We have the Gaol Delivery Book[8] for the Wells Assize, and Jeffreys' report[9] to King James, but there must have been two or three hundred presented by the Constables but not at Wells for trial, either because they were killed and buried at Sedgemoor, or because they managed to conceal themselves until the King issued his General Pardon to the survivors (with a long list of those excepted) in March 1686. Had we the Wells Presentment Roll, we should find on it the name of John Hellier[10] of Mark, a Quaker 'who took up Arms in the late Insurrection contrary to the principle of trueth'; and we might find there the names of the Mendip miners who, John Evelyn[11] was told, 'did great execution with their tools, and sold their lives dearly',

About 1500 rebels were crowded into the available West Country prisons. Some had been sent to London for interrogation, where some were lodged in Newgate[12], some in The Gatehouse, Westminster, some in the Marshalsea. The reports of their interrogations are in the Lansdowne MSS[13] in the British Library; few of them add materially to our knowledge. It had been hoped that the rebels would incriminate some of their wealthier neighbours, such as Edmund Prideaux of Ford Abbey. Some few did escape the gallows, 'having made a discovery'.

To parade evidence against 1500 rebels would have taken untold time. Those responsible for preparing for the Autumn Assizes agreed that the prisoners should be interrogated in prison and as many as possible persuaded to plead guilty, which would obviate the need to produce evidence and enable the judges to proceed directly to sentence. We have two clear eye-witness accounts of the procedure. John Whiting the Quaker, who shared his imprisonment in Ilchester gaol with numbers of Monmouth rebels, wrote this account in his autobiography,[14] telling us that he wrote it on 3 September 1685:

I cannot forbear to mention what I observed passed at Ivelchester while I was a prisoner in the ward. There came David Trimm of Wells and took account of the prisoners, (which perhaps was his place as county-clerk to do), with the causes of their commitment; but not only so, but wheedled them to confess how far they were concerned; pretending, if they would confess, they would do them all the kindness they could at the assizes; so drew out of them what they could, under hopes of favour, and then went in and writ down their examinations; which I was an eye-witness of . . . The like they did at the common goal . . . It was such a piece of treachery to betray them out of their lives . . . Some were terrified to confess in hopes of pardon, and then hanged, whom otherwise they could have had little against . . . Some hanged for a little hay, or letting them have a little victuals, which perhaps was not in their power to hinder.

The other account comes in Dr Henry Pitman's *Relation*, which was printed[15] in 1689. At Ilchester, he says, the agents

extorted confessions from us by sending certain persons to the prisons . . . who called us forth one after another, and told us that the King was very gracious and merciful, and would cause none to be executed but such as had been officers, or otherwise capital offenders; and therefore, if we would render ourselves fit objects of the King's grace and favour, our only way was to give them an account where we went into the Duke's army, and in what capacity we served him, etc. otherwise we must expect no mercy or favour from the king . . . By which means they drew us into an acknowledgment of our guilt, and our examinations and confessions were written and sent to the King, before the Lord Chief Justice came to try us.

Further evidence comes from Lord Ailesbury, who wrote[16] in his Memoirs, of Andrew Loder, an attorney of Dorchester 'whom I knew well to be a very rascal. This fellow, by Mr Pollexfen's orders, went into the prisons, and made the poor people believe that they had nothing [to do] to save their lives, but by pleading guilty.'

They did not bother to interrogate John (or Thomas) Coad. As a deserter from the militia he was foredoomed to the gallows and could expect no mercy. In general King James decided that there would be no mercy for those who came with the Duke from Holland, nor for those in England who had prior knowledge of the Duke's coming, nor for those who had accepted commissions in the rebel army. The rest might be hanged or transported to the West Indies to be sold as slaves and not return to this country for ten years. At the auctions they were sold for four years, but were not then released. It is clear that King James and his Lord Chief Justice had some discussion about the selection of rebels for hanging.

To conduct the Autumn Assizes in the West the King issued his commissions[17] of *Oyer* and *Terminer* (to hear and determine the cases) and General Gaol Delivery (to empty the prisons) to the Rt Hon. George, Lord Jeffreys, Lord Chief Justice of England; the Hon. William Mountagu, Lord Chief Baron of H.M. Court of Exchequer; Sir Cresswell Levinz, Knight, one of H.M. Justices of the Court of Common Pleas; Sir Francis Wythens, Knight, of the Court of King's Bench; and Sir Robert Wright, Knight, one of the Barons of H.M. Court of Exchequer. The other four judges played singularly little part in the trials, though Wright came again in the Spring of 1686 and Wythens in March 1687 to try further batches of rebels. By naming Henry Pollexfen as prosecuting counsel, an appointment he could hardly refuse, the government deprived those to be accused of the one defence counsel who had shown (at the trial[18] of Richard Baxter) that he could stand up to the Lord Chief Justice without being crushed.

George Jeffreys had been born in 1644[19] (not as many books state in 1648), and after a year or two at Cambridge had entered the Inner Temple in 1663, and been called to the bar. He was a very clever rather than a learned lawyer, and soon showed great skill in cross-examination and in bullying witnesses. He sought the favour of the Court Party and in 1677 was appointed Solicitor General to James, then Duke of York. In 1683 he became Lord Chief Justice of the King's Bench. Fair play did not interest Jeffreys. As a judge he was as keen that the King's cause should triumph, as he had been when prosecuting counsel. No one can read the accounts of the trials of Algernon Sidney or William Penn[20] or Richard Baxter and maintain that Jeffreys gave the accused a fair chance. He did his utmost to prejudice a jury against the accused; he could hardly pronounce the word Presbyterian without adding the epithet 'snivelling'; he joined in the cross-examination as if he was still counsel for the prosecution. The cruelty of his jests at the expense of an old man supported by parish relief, and of a young woman who begged the life of her sweetheart[21], confirm the unbiassed contemporary opinion of him as 'the cruel judge'. Months before the Bloody Assizes began Samuel Storey, who had lived in London, had told members of Taunton Corporation[22] that 'Justice Jeffreys is as great a rogue as ever the nation bore'. It cannot be argued that all Stuart period judges were alike. After the imprisonment of John Bunyan, Sir Matthew Hale had explained to Mrs Bunyan[23] what steps she could take to secure her husband's release.

For Jeffreys it must in fairness be said that he suffered agonising pain from a stone, for which his only remedy was brandy, which did his temper no good. It is also recorded that in 1684 he saved the life of a West Country

Quaker, Richard Vickris, who having been convicted of constantly attending unlawful conventicles, and having failed to abjure the Realm, was liable to the death penalty. Pollexfen argued a Writ of Error before Jeffreys and, as John Whiting records, Vickris 'was cleared of the sentence on the 35th of Elizabeth, by Sir George Jeffreys, Lord Chief Justice, though so severe a judge otherwise, (few so bad but they may do some good acts) and so was legally[24] discharged'. Jeffreys opened the Assize at Winchester on 26 August and on the 27th came the trial of Dame Alice Lisle, who was 'Indicted for harbouring John Hickes, a Rebel'. Dame Alice was the octogenarian widow of John Lisle, who had sat as one of the judges of Charles I. She had disapproved of the execution of the king, and had no sympathy with Monmouth's rebellion. John Hickes she knew as a dissenting minister, and she gave him a night's lodging at Moyles Court, thinking his preaching was his only offence. She knew nothing of his companion, Richard Nelthorpe, and steadfastly maintained that she had no idea that Hickes had been with Monmouth's Army. 'I tell you', said Jeffreys, 'that there is not one of those lying, snivelling Presbyterian Rascals but one way or other had a hand in the late horrid conspiracy'. The jury found a difficulty in that John Hickes had not been tried and proved to be a rebel, but Jeffreys assured them that it did not matter whether Hickes had been tried or not. Reluctantly the jury found Dame Alice guilty, and the next morning Jeffreys, commending their verdict, said, 'Had she been my own mother, I would have found her guilty'. He then sentenced her to be drawn to the stake and burnt by fire[25] until her death: it was the sentence prescribed by law for a woman found guilty of treason. With some difficulty Jeffreys was persuaded to grant a respite of five days, which were used to make several appeals to the King who ultimately commuted the sentence to beheading, and on 2 September Dame Alice Lisle was beheaded.

After sentencing six folk at Salisbury to be fined and whipped, five for 'seditious words' and one for spreading false news, the judges moved on to Dorchester, and opened the Assize there on 5 September. The Gaol Delivery produced 320 men accused of 'Levying Warr against the King', and 15 men and two women accused of speaking seditious words or some comparable offence; one of them Richard Holyday 'for conducting the Lord Grey from Gillingham to Ringwood after the fight at Weston'. Some of those presented had been shipped from London to be tried at Dorchester.

Very little survives of what was said at the Assizes, except for the trial of Dame Alice Lisle. The Lord Chief Justice made an opening[26] address 'That if we would acknowledge our crimes by pleading Guilty to our

Indictment, the King, who was almost all mercy, would be as ready to forgive us, as we were to rebel against him; yea, as ready to pardon us as we would be to ask it of him'. Those arranging the trials had picked him out for the first batch 34 who insisted on pleading Not guilty, against whom they had evidence. Of them 29 were found guilty and sentenced that Saturday afternoon to be hanged on Monday. The rest were cowed into pleading Guilty.

Jeffreys reported to King James[27] that he had hanged 74, nearly a quarter of the rebels he tried at Dorchester. They included Colonel Holmes, Ensign Askew, Lieutenant William Hewling, Dr Temple, Captain Hayes, Sir John Kidd (formerly Keeper at Longleat, the only knight Monmouth dubbed), Captain Marders (Constable of Crewkerne), Sampson Larke (Baptist Minister, who lived at Combe Raleigh), Christopher Battiscombe (described as 'gentleman', whose sweetheart begged his life unavailingly), and Samuel Glisson, a Baptist of Yeovil and one of John Whiting's brothers-in-law. It was Captain Marders who was described in court as 'a good Protestant', which provoked Jeffreys' well-known retort, 'You mean Presbyterian. I'll hold you a wager of it. I can smell a Presbyterian forty miles off'. Jeffreys told young Hewling, then 19. 'You have a grandfather who deserves to be hanged as richly[28] as you'. Hewling's grandfather was William Kiffin, a much respected City merchant and a leader among the Baptists.

Glisson was hanged at Sherborne on 15 September; the others here listed were hanged at Lyme Regis[29] on 12 September, on the spot where several of them had landed with the Duke. Friends were allowed to bury William Hewling in the churchyard at Lyme. His memorial stone was still decipherable when George Roberts[30] was writing his great book about Monmouth at the beginning of Queen Victoria's reign.

Transportation was the sentence of 175, and King James 'gave' them in large numbers to folk he wished to reward, like Sir Jerome Nipho, the Queen's Italian secretary; or to men who could dispose of the transportees overseas, Sir Philip Howard, Governor of Jamaica, Sir William Stapleton, Governor of the Leeward Islands, Sir Christopher Musgrave and Sir William Booth. From the Dorchester Assize Booth got 100 and Nipho 59, all sent to[31] Barbados; Musgrave got 16 of whom some went to Jamaica.

Certificates that they had laid down their arms in time to qualify for the King's pardon were produced by 27 rebels. One ran 'William White of this place (Lyme Regis), latterly in the camp of James Scott, late Duke of Monmouth, hath laid down his arms[32] and is returned to his obedience, and craves the liberty of his Majesty's most gracious pardon'. His certificate was allowed. The judges recommended another 28 'humbly proposed for his Majesty's gracious pardon'. They left 15 prisoners in custody, nine of them 'not indicted'; and they discharged 15 'for want of evidence'. Richard Holyday, Grey's guide, was 'to be whipt twice, fined a Marke, and to find suretyes for the good behaviour of a year.'

The 74 sentenced to be hanged were distributed around the county of Dorset to spread the grim warning against rebellion. At Dorchester 13 were hanged; at Lyme Regis, at Sherborne, and at Weymouth[29] or Melcombe Regis a dozen each; at Poole 11; at Bridport 9; and at Wareham 5. Weymouth and Melcombe Regis, once separate boroughs, are now virtually the same town, divided by the river Wey. Heads and limbs, treated with salt and pitch to prevent decay, were scattered further afield.

Melcombe Regis Corporation archives[33] contained an

Order for a gallowes to be erected whereon 12 were to be executed and their quarters and heads distributed at several places:

To Upway	4 Quarters and	1 head
Sutton Points	2	1
Osmington	4	1
Preston	2	
Weeke	2	
Winfrith	4	1
Broadmaine	2	1
Radipol	2	
Winterborne St Martin	2	
Puddletowne	4	1
Bincombe	2	
	32	6
		[actually 30 and 6]

The rest in Waymouth and Melcombe Regis

At the grand Piere	6 Quarters and	1 Head
Waymouth town's end	2	
Neere the Windmill	4	1
Waymouth Towne Hall	2	
On the Bridge	1	2
Melcombe Towne hall	1	2
	16	6

'Burning and Boyling the Rebells executed att this town' cost the borough £16-4-8. Some of the quarters must have been moved subsequently. Bishops Caundle Overseers' accounts for 1685 include an entry of 17/9 'Allowed to Trevillion for his Expenses about fetching from Sherborn and hanging up the Quarter of the Traitour att the towns end'. On 22 September the Mayor of Poole sent some quarters on to Lytchett Matravers to be set up 'on poles or spykes in the most notable and convenient plaices'. Occasionally poles were blown over and the town archives show a payment on 20 November 'for new setting up a post with the quarters of the Rebells att Waymouth Towne-End'.

John Whiting[34] wrote,

There were eight executed, quartered, and their bowels burnt on the market-place before our prison window. I went out of the way because I would not see it, but the fire was not out when I returned; and they forced poor men to hale about men's quarters, like horse-flesh or carrion, to boil and hang them up as monuments of their cruelty and inhumanity, for the terror of others, which lost King James the heart of many; and it had been well he had shewed mercy when it was in his power.

A not entirely accurate broadsheet[35] printed in 1686 records that Thomas Tyler, who was to be hanged at Wareham, was repreived, but he is not listed so on Jeffrey's report to King James.

From Dorchester the judges moved on to Exeter, where they opened the Assize on 14 September. Although the Constables had presented 494 as suspected rebels, the Gaol Delivery[36] produced only 28 to stand trial for treason, 11 or 12 for 'seditious words', and two others for 'Wilfully suffering George Legg to escape'. George Legg came from Sidmouth, and the two accused of letting him escape pleaded, and were found, Not guilty.

The first two accused of Levying war against the King, John Foweracres and Robert Drower, and Thomas Hobbes, accused of 'Proclaiming James Scott, late Duke of Monmouth, King', pleaded Not guilty, but were found guilty and condemned[37] to die the same day, John at Exeter and Thomas at Crediton, while Robert was reprieved and later transported. Of the 24 who pleaded guilty, ten were sentenced to be hanged, four at Honiton, two at Ottery St Mary, two at Colyton, and two at Axminster. Five others were reprieved. Seven were given to Nipho to transport to Barbados but one of them, Walter Teape, was replaced later by someone from the Wells Assize and he was reprieved[38] and pardoned. Lewis James, for proclaiming Monmouth king, and William Andridge, for 'assisting Roger Bryant to make his escape', were fined and whipped, as were eleven others for speaking seditious words.

After the record of these sentences there is a list of 343 'persons who are indicted for high treason and are at large'. The names are in the same order as the Constables' presentments, and were not checked with much care, for the list includes eight men who had been hanged after the assize at Dorchester, one already reported 'slain[39] in the service', another already reported 'in prison'; and two of the men just sentenced at Exeter to transportation.

A letter dated 1 October from Thomas Northmore, Assistant Deputy

Sheriff of Devon, mentions[40] the 'Places where quarters and heads of rebels are to be sent: Honiton, Axminster, Colliton, Ottery, Crediton, Bideford, Barnestable, Torrington, Tiverton, Plymouth, Dartmouth and Totness'.

TAUNTON AND WELLS

The Assize at Taunton, which opened on Friday, 18 September, was considerably larger than those at Dorchester and Exeter together. The Gaol Delivery[41] produced 514 prisoners, almost all accused of Levying war against the King. Four of them made bold to plead Not Guilty, and were promptly sentenced to be hanged on the following Monday, though Jeffreys reprieved one of them. The others duly pleaded Guilty. All told, Jeffreys sentenced 146—over a quarter—to be hanged, and subsequently reprieved only two of them. The clerk who kept the Gaol Book marked the first four with great stars, indicating 'for execution'. No more stars were added, and some historians deduced from this that only these four (or only three of them) were executed after the Taunton Assize, and that the figures usually accepted for the Bloody Assizes have been greatly exaggerated. One historian[42] went so far as to state, 'The best opinion seems to be that about 150 persons suffered death'. It is impossible to justify this low estimate. The clerk of the Gaol Book could not add more stars because Jeffreys delayed deciding which of the rebels tried at Taunton were to be hanged and which transported. He may well have sent an express to consult the King. He had moved on to Wells before he sent to Edward Hobbes, the Sheriff, the definitive[43] list, which is dated 26 September, and the rest of those executed at Taunton were hanged on 30 September. Almost all the 144 sentenced to death were hanged. The hangings were ordered by Jeffreys for two dozen places: Taunton 3+19; Chard, Ilminister, and Ilchester 12 each; Keynsham 11; Crewkerne 10; Bridgwater 9; Yeovil 8; Somerton 7; Minehead 6; South Petherton, Castle Cary, Langport, Nether Stowey, Stogumber, Dunster, Dulverton, Wiveliscombe and Wellington 3 each; Chewton Mendip, Milborne Port, Stogursey, Porlock and Cothelstone 2 each. We know that a few died in prison of smallpox or gaol fever before they could be hanged. John Whiting[44] assures us that only eight were hanged at Ilchester. A Newsletter[45] mentions three hanged at Minehead, instead of six; and two each instead of three at Dunster and Dulverton.

Those sentenced to transportation[46] numbered 284, of whom 84 were given to Sir Christopher Musgrave, 27 going to Jamaica and 57 to Barbados. The Queen was given 100 (and asked for more[47]). Of these, 67 were shipped[48] at Bristol on the *Jamaica Merchant* and, except for one who died at sea, were landed at Barbados. Sir William Booth was given 100, destined for Barbados on the 'John Frigget' (perhaps the Frigate *John*) from Bristol. Of them 13 died, one at Bristol, eleven at sea, and one on shore before the sale. Of Booth's 100, 56 had been imprisoned in Taunton Bridewell, 33 at Bridgwater, and 11 at Exeter. Musgrave's batch travelled from Weymouth on a later voyage of the *Jamaica Merchant*, and three died at sea. The captains' reports on arrival stated that so many 'died at sea and were thrown overboard', but on the official report this was amended to 'buried at sea'.

Some of the lists state the villages from which the men came. The list of the Queen's transportees gives the ages and occupations of 66 of the 68 shipped for Barbados. One man was 40, seven were 30 or over, 29 were between 21 and 29, 13 were 20; six were 19 and six, 18; two were 17, one was 16 and one 15. Their occupations show 16 'plowmen' and one husbandman; 9 weavers, 5 sergeweavers, and one ribbon-weaver; 9 combers and 4 woolcombers; 4 clothiers, 2 taylors and a mercer, a hatter, a glover and a tanner; 3 butchers, 2 carpenters, 2 masons, 2 shoemakers, a soapboiler and a carrier.

The Lord Chief Justice added five[37] other lists. Twenty accused rebels produced magistrates' certificates[49] that they had laid down their arms within the time-limit to qualify for pardons. Twenty-two were 'humbly proposed to his Majesty for his gracious pardon'. Then came 15 'Prisoners in Goale omitted in the Warrant for Execution altho designed to be executed'; and 33 'Prisoners remayning in Goale till further order'; and lastly two prisoners bailed at Taunton. These lists add up to 522, eight more than those named in the gaol Delivery. Of those 'omitted', seven and of those 'remayning' 24, were subsequently shipped for Jamaica on the *Constant Richard* by Thomas Heywood and Sir Richard White. Three others were left behind: Samuel Dare was 'sick of the smallpox'; John Chappell was allotted to Sir William Booth; and James Indoe (or Judes) had 'run away'.

What was the significance of the omission of the 15 originally designed for execution from the warrant? A clue is provided in a newsletter[50] which reports that John Parry escaped from prison in Taunton one morning and returned in the evening, having then more trouble getting back into prison than he had in getting out in the morning. No John Parry was listed in the Gaol Delivery, but John Pacey was, and anyone familiar with the Stuart period handwriting would agree that one of these names, not well written, might easily be misread as the other. If John Pacey got out of prison and returned, and was subsequently omitted from the warrant for execution, the inference is clear that he used his day's liberty to make it worth

The archway at the entrance to Cothelstone Manor, Lord Stowel's home, from which Col. Bovet and Thomas Blackmore were hanged on Judge Jeffrey's order.

somebody's while to omit his name from the warrant. He had been presented as of West Monkton[51] and was granted a pardon under the Privy Seal in December.

One of those to be hanged at Taunton was Benjamin Hewling, elder brother of William, who had been hanged at Lyme Regis after the Dorchester Assize. His sister Hannah begged an audience with the King to plead for Benjamin's life, and Lord Churchill agreed to present her to the King. As they were waiting in an anteroom, Churchill[52] said to her 'I wish well to your suit with all my heart, but do not flatter yourself with hopes', and placing his hands on the mantlepiece, added 'This marble is not harder than the King's heart'. Benjamin was duly hanged on 30 September, but his body was not quartered. At a high price Hannah obtained his body for burial in St Mary's graveyard.

Also tried at Taunton were Richard Bovet, Colonel of the Blue

Regiment, probably of Bishop's Hull, and Bernard or Barnaby Thatcher of Stoke St Gregory, who sheltered and attempted to conceal Bovet. Thatcher was hanged at Yeovil. Bovet was one of two rebels hanged from the archway at the entrance to Cothelstone Manor, the home of Lord Stawell. Lord Stawell was a zealous royalist, who had vowed to hang Coad[53] as a deserter, but resented this 'pleasantry' of the Lord Chief Justice. During the Interregnum Bovet had been the sequestrator of part of Stawell's estate, so Jeffreys thought it fitting to have him hanged there.

The Gaol Delivery for the Assize at Wells is dated 22 September. It provided 518 accused of levying war against the King; nine of 'Aydeing and assisting the Rebells'. Six were accused of seditious words; and ten were pardoned by proclamation.

We have two accounts of Jeffreys' address to the prisoners, one from Dr Henry Pitman, quoted on page 86, and the other from John Burd of Beckington in a letter[54] to John Dunton the publisher:

The judge made a speech, telling us how merciful the King was, and how he was ready to show mercy to the worst of us . . . Nay, says he, (and thumps the cushion) I had almost said, the King is more ready to forgive than you were to rebel.

The one man bold enough to plead Not Guilty[41] on the first day was William Mangell, said to be Colonel Matthews' servant, and he was hanged the same day at Wells. Later in the Assize John Holloway and John Richards pleaded Not Guilty and were so found by the jury.

At Wells Jeffreys sentenced 99 to be hanged, and reprieved one of them, Roger Hoare. The hangings[43] were to be nine at Wells; 12 each at Philip's Norton, Frome, Pensford and Shepton Mallet; six each at Bath, Bristol, Axbridge and Wincanton; five at Glastonbury, and three each at Bruton and Wrington; one at Ilminister, and five elsewhere. The man to be hanged at Ilminster was Charles Spake of Whitelackington and London, who had shaken hands with Monmouth as he passed through Ilminster square. This was construed as 'Aiding and assisting' and Jeffreys duly sentenced him to death. It is credibly reported[55] that a Major of the Guards inquired if Jeffreys really meant to hang Speke, and that Jeffreys replied, 'His brother escaped. The family owe us a life'. The word 'Reprieved' has been written beside Charles Speke's name on Jeffreys' report to the King, but if a reprieve was issued it arrived too late: there is no doubt that Charles Speke was hanged in Ilminster Square.

Another found guilty of 'Aiding and assisting' was the Rev. John Hickes, guest for one night of Dame Alice Lisle. Born in 1633, he took his degree at Trinity College, Dublin, and was Curate of Saltash, Cornwall, from 1657 until he was ejected in 1661. He was licensed as a preacher under Charles II's Declaration of Indulgence in 1672, and was minister of High Street Meeting, Portsmouth, before the licences were cancelled in 1675. Jeffreys condemned him to death and he was hanged in Glastonbury.

Sir William Stapleton[46] was allotted 100 transportees to be sent to Nevis or St Christophers (St Kitts). Sir Philip Howard was to have 200, and complained bitterly that 25 of them 'made their escape[56] from the Guards betwixt Wells and Sherburn', and three more escaped 'out of prison at Sherburn'. Sir Jerome Nipho had 33 to make up his hundred, and they were shipped to Barbados on the *Betty*, two dying at sea. A further 50 were given to William Bridgeman, and transported by Sir Richard White to Jamaica.

In Jeffreys' report[37] to King James there follow seven short lists and one enormous list. Six prisoners produced allowable certificates; 26 were recommended for the King's pardon; five designed for execution had been omitted from the warrant; 10 prisoners remained in custody, but five of them were later transported by Captain Heywood; another seven remained in custody for want of evidence. Five were whipped for speaking treasonable words, and one was fined £100 for that offence. Fourteen were left in custody as witnesses for the King. The long list gives the names of 140 prisoners who were bound over in £100 each, and each for the other, for their appearance at the next Assizes and for their good behaviour.

There had been no rebels to be tried at Bristol, and the judges returned to London, where the King rewarded the Lord Chief Justice by making him Lord Chancellor, and 'giving' him Edmund Prideaux of Ford Abbey, to extract from him as much as he could by fine or blackmail. Jeffreys' clerk had travelled from Bristol to London by coach. On that same coach[57] travelled William Oliver, known to the rebels as Dr. Oliver. Jeffreys' clerk did not suspect that his fellow traveller was a fugitive rebel, and Oliver managed to cross to Holland, from whence he returned in due course with Prince William of Orange.

The bloodshed was continued in London after the return of the judges. Richard Nelthorpe, the companion of the Rev. John Hickes when they were sheltered by Dame Alice Lisle, was examined at Windsor on 9 August, but gave nothing away. He was sent to Newgate. He could have bought his pardon but refused to ruin his children's patrimony. As he had been outlawed after the Rye House Plot no trial was necessary, and being a barrister Nelthorpe[58] was hanged before the gate of Gray's Inn.

Two others who suffered were Elizabeth Gaunt and John Fernley. Each of them had sheltered[59] James Burton, Elizabeth when he was wanted after the Rye House Plot, Fernley after he had escaped from Sedgemoor.

East Gate, Langport, above which is the 'hanging chapel'. It may well be that it was from the parapet of this arch that Humphry Pierce, Nicholas Venting and John Sellwood were hanged in October, 1685.

The King regarded the harbouring of rebels as unpardonable. Burton bought his pardon by denouncing and giving evidence against the two who had risked their lives by giving him refuge in their homes. The King had no mercy for them. Fernley was hanged; Elizabeth Gaunt burnt at the stake.

From Somerset that October Colonel Sir Charles Lyttleton wrote[60] to Lord Hatton:

I cannot but believe we shall hear more of this when parliament meets; and of the execution of so many of the traitors here, 18 in one lump, and all quartered, and more every day in other parts of the country, which will be to the number of near 300; and most of their quarters are and will be set up in the towns and highways, so that the country looks, as one passes, already like a shambles.

11

Prison, Transportation, and Escape

Not unnaturally we have few descriptions of life in prison between Sedgemoor and the trials. Overcrowding was inevitable. John Tutchin mentions 19 young men in one room[1] in Dorchester gaol, all under 21, and 18 of them subsequently hanged. He also mentions several deaths from smallpox.

John Burd[2] of Beckington was captured about 20 miles from the battlefield, gave his captors the slip but was captured again and lodged in the Lower Church in Wells, presumably St Cuthbert's. Thence he was moved to the Common Gaol in Bath, and lay there for 14 weeks, confined with 27 others in a little room. Some of them slept on the floor-boards; others had with difficulty obtained straw to lie on. Two of his companions were aged 60 and 70, and both were hanged. At or after their trial Burd and Jacob Tripp, aged about 21, were 'hand-bolted' together. Both caught gaol fever (typhus), 'a very malignant infectious feaver', and were dangerously ill. A reprieve arrived for Burd, who was 'given to a pardon-monger, who made his market upon me'. Tripp was so ill that the doctors said he could not live another 24 hours. Although he was unconscious, they carried him away to be hanged in Wells Market Place, although Jeffreys had ordered his execution at Axbridge.

John Whiting[3] also mentions being hand-bolted and put 'into the inward ward amongst Monmouth's men, where there was no room for us to lie down when the beds were spread over the room'. His hand-cuffs were left on for five weeks and three days. Smallpox spread among the prisoners, and the Quaker prisoners were then separated from the rebels.

The grimmest account of prison conditions comes in the petition of Joseph Winter[4] of Ilchester, surgeon, for the payment due to him. He was the surgeon sent by Sir Edward Phelips to look after John (or Thomas) Coad. Winter speaks of some hundreds of rebels committed to Ilchester gaol, 'many of them being dangerously wounded, which for want of looking after and due dressing, began to be very offensive, and their putrid soars were very probable to have bred such infectious diseases'. He mentions the 'numerous concourse of friends and relations; and officers and ministers of justice to take their examinations and confessions'.

First on Winter's bill was Richard Masters of Taunton who, on his way to Lyme to join the rebels, was taken by King's men, taken to 'Burport' (Bridport) and there wounded in the cheek and jawbone. Winter removed several pieces of bone 'and cured him sound and well', after which Masters went to the Duke's army and 'is since transported' . . . 'I honestly deserve £2-10-0'. Next Richard Cox of Combe near Lyme, was shot at Norton with a brace of bullets that broke his hand to pieces. Winter 'reduced [=set] the bones and cured him with a great care for which I deserve £2'.

John Dods was also shot at Norton, but gaps in the torn manuscript prevent our knowing the particulars. He was brought to prison in a 'Lamitable Condition, but I cured him and he was transported. Care at the Lowest Rate is worth £3'.

Thomas Coat [gap] Youill, at Norton was shot [gap] parte of his Lungs was sha[ttered]. Judged by all the Chirurgons that [gap] Mortell. He was also shot through the hand and Broake the bones to many pieces. He was brought to prison on a Horse Litter in a dieing Condition. He promised me a large gratuity which made me very diligent, sparing Noe Cost. I cured him and made him a sound man, but before he was quite hole, the soldiers at Yeuill took all that he had and left him very poor. He is since Transported and his Wife and Children exseeding poore. The Cure as it now stands is Honestly worth £10.

Winter charged £5 for curing Robert Sandy of Cullington (Colyton) whose skull was badly cut by two sabre blows at Norton; and £3 each for mending the arms of Joseph Phelps of Whitechurch Canonicorum and John Parsons of Ilminster.

John and William Slade of Ilminster, father and son,

were taken for spies at Wincanton. The soldiers, to make them confess, Burnd their Hands to the Bones, soe that the flesh did Mortifie and fall away in pieces; but with a greate deale of trouble and Cost I (cured) them. They are poore and not able to p(ay any)thing. The Cure is justly (worth) £2-10-0'.

This cruelty looks like the work of Kirke's Lambs, and is perhaps our only documented example.

Two more patients have lost half their surnames in tears and cannot be identified. They bring Dr Winter's bill[5] up to £35-10-0. Masters, Dodds and Sandy went to Barbados; Coad, to Jamaica. John Parsons 'is yet in prison', and Richard Cox was left in gaol till further orders, while Joseph Phelps was recommended for the King's pardon.

John or Thomas Coad[6] gives us a glimpse of prisoners, and a clearer

A Memorandum of the Wonderful Providences of God to a poor unworthy Creature,

during

the time of the Duke of Monmouth's Rebellion and to the Revolution in 1688.

BY JOHN COAD,
one of the Sufferers.

LONDON:
LONGMAN, BROWN, GREEN, & LONGMANS,
PATERNOSTER ROW.
1849.

The title-page of Coad's narrative. Official records all call him Thomas Coad; perhaps his second wife called him John after their son Thomas was born.

description of transportation than we get from anyone else. His *Memorandum of the Wonderful Providences of God to a poor unworthy creature* was kept as a family manuscript until it was printed in 1849. It has been mentioned rather than quoted in previous books. Quotations have had to be abridged, but for the sake of the reader omission dots have been omitted. After 10 or 11 weeks in Ilchester gaol, his wounds 'much mended yet still open', Coad was

drawn in a wain to Wells, where we had a church for our prison, a board for my bed, and something more than the shadow of death for my comfort; for a neighbour came and told me that I might expect nothing but death, for evidence was prepared, and the aggravations were that I was a deserter, and ran from my colours to the Duke. Less than which was argument enough to make the Lion's Whelp George Jefferies to roar against, yea, to damn me, if it lay in his power; for being arraigned and pleading Guilty, I was condemned to be hanged and quartered, together with 600 and more, my name set on the dead list to be executed at Wells a few dayes after. Yet may I say, the Lord hath helped me; even when I stood before that bloody Nero, George Jefferies, I found such inward support and comfort that I could not say that I feared any evil: but when above 600 condemned men fell on their knees, and most dolorously cried for mercy, I could not bow a knee or speake a word for mercy, for God was my hope, my help. A few days later while I was at prayer with many others, in a morning came my sister and told me there was an Officer come into the cloister to call out 200 men for Jamaica. She much pressed me to endeavour to get amongst them, she being much troubled that morning by an information that she had, that my flesh was to be hung up before my dore. I seeing her in so sorrowful a plight, did go with her to the Officer, and privately told him the circumstances I was under, and offered him a fee to take me into his list, which he refused, but told me that when he called a man that did not answer, I might answer to his name and step in. To deny my name I was cautious of, and stood by while many others under my circumstances went in, for I judge there was near 30 men saved by so doing. I seeing the list full went away; but such was the wonderful providence of God, there stood a poor woman of Charde, a stranger to me, who observed one of the company unwilling to be transported, came after me and pulling me to the man, he hastily shifted himself out of the string and put me in his place, and told me if I was called, his name[7] was Jo Hawker. Thus the Lord sent from above; he delivered me from my strong enemies.

The first night we lay at Shepton Mallet. The next day, going to Castel-carye, the Sheriff's men overtook us and seized one Mr. Shepphard[8] for execution. The next night we lay at Sherborn, where I was known by many, particularly the constable, who being an adversary to our cause, demanded of the officer that was our convoy, whether my name was on his list. No other answer would satisfie him but he would see it, for he said I ought not to be there. Having seen the list he went away, but by the good providence of God I heard no more of him. Doubtless the same hand that shut up the mouths of the Lions from devouring Daniel, shut up his mouth and restrained him from doing me the intended hurt. Though I lay in the town two nights, contrary to my expectations and beyond hope I was delivered thence, and setting forward for Weymouth was known by several on the roade;

notwithstanding went safe to Weymouth, where I lay one night. Next morning I went aboard the ship for Jamaica, and took my leave of my native country.

The next day being sabbath day, our ship-master being ashore, the sheriff's men came aboard our ship and took one of our men, and discoursed of me also; on which our Ship-master, though a bad man, fearing he should lose his passengers, ordered to weigh anchor and hoist sail immediately. So that by the hand of my God I was delivered as a bird out of the snare of the fowlers; the snare was broken and I[9] escaped; for the next day they came to Weymouth hunting for me. The master of the ship shut 99 of us under deck in a very small room, where we could not lay ourselves down without lying one upon another. The hatchway being guarded with a continual watch with blunderbusses and hangers, we were not suffered to go above deck for air or easement, but a vessel was set in the midst to receive the excrement, by which means the ship was soon infected with grievous and contagious diseases, as the smallpox, fever, calenture[10], and the plague, with frightful blotches. Of each of these diseases several died, for we lost of our company 22 men. This was the straitest prison that ever I was in, full of crying and dying. Though we were shut down in the dark as in a dungeon, yet we did pray and sing praises to our God. Eventually the well were separated from the sick and allowed above deck, but they suffered from short rations and shortage of water.

After a voyage of 6 weeks and 3 days I arrived in Jamaica, 24 November 1685, and we were put on shore at Port Royal. People took pity on us when they saw us almost starved, and provided what they could get ready soonest: bisket and butter, and fresh fish fried, and fresh water. We were put together in a stable for ten days, but had liberty to walk out in the town in the day time. Mr Robert Speere, a Nonconforming Minister, was a great comfort to us in advising and directing us. Mr Christopher Hicks, a Merchant to whom we were consigned to be sold, made supply to our necessities and sent us a Physitian, and some to wash our clothes and cleanse us from vermin. He appointed me the best place he could think of in the Iland, to serve one colonel Bach, but to follow the law of the country, I must return with the rest of my fellow captives to the ship, and at the fire of a gun the Market begins. I was sent to my service, about 40 miles from Port Royal, by water, when I had about 5 miles to go by land to the Plantation.

Coad was far more fortunate than most of the transportees. Finding no religious servce at all in the neighbourhood, he started 'Family Prayers' with the six other servants. Hearing of this, Lieut. Garbrand, on the next plantation, urged Coad to conduct Sunday services at his house. After some hesitation Coad accepted this call, and he includes in his narrative the gist of some of his sermons. Being needed as a carpenter, Coad was superseded as Overseer by a drunken bully, and he and the other servants had a bad time until the bully's premature death. 'When we had served full four years, the time for which we were sold, divers of us went to Port Royal and carried evidence to a Justice of the Peace that we were sold for no longer time of servitude. But our suit was rejected, and we were sent to our former service. And now the thoughts of ten years' servitude being a law made particularly for us by[11] King James's order, to us seemed very hard'. With amazing faith and courage Coad took as his text for his next sermon 'The God whom we serve is able to deliver us, and he will deliver us' (Daniel 3, 17.) Coad and his friends saw the arrival of William of Orange and the flight of James II as the direct intervention of God, and found expression of their feelings in Psalm

126, 'Then was our mouth filled with laughter and our tongues with singing . . . The Lord hath done great things for us, whereof we are glad.

A new Governor, the Earl of Inchiquin, arrived in May 1690, and though the first applicants for freedom were rebuffed, Coad plucked up courage to try to see the Governor, persuading Gideon Dare to go with him. Dare, once a husbandman of Luppitt in Devon, had been sentenced to be hanged, but his name had been omitted from the warrant and he had been transported instead. Coad found Dare very depressed, saying 'we should never see our wives and children any more', and at first he flatly refused to accompany Coad to the Governor. The next morning, however, Coad drafted a petition for their release, based on the suffering of their wives and children bereft of their support. Dare reluctantly went with Coad, and they handed their petition to the guard:

We went in before him, [the Governor] who received us very kindly, with the compliment of a small bow. His answer was I have received an order to set you all free, and the King hath given orders for your coming home; go, and pay your respects to your masters, and in two or three days your business shall be accomplished. I humbly thanked his Excellency, and wished him a happy Government, and withdrew.

'The tidings went thro' the Town like lightening', and Coad had difficulty in restraining the celebration his fellow transportees suggested. Some of the masters got together to petition the King and Parliament for an Act to retain the transportees, though free men, in the land of their captivity, and managed to delay the sailing of a convoy in hopes of preventing the return of some of the released captives.

Colonel Bach wrote from London that his 'servants' were to be paid full wages as soon as their four years were completed. Through the cheating of his agent, Coad received £10 instead of the £36 due to him, but this was enough to pay his fare home. 'Mr Dare and I and a few more got a passage in a merchant ship, the better to avoid the rude rabble in the Man-of-War'. They sailed on 9 September, and three weeks later rounded the Florida Cape. They ran into contrary winds, which damaged the rigging of some of the 32 ships in the convoy. A later storm broke the tiller of the rudder, and Coad, the only carpenter aboard, had much ado to replace it. Another storm caused great distress aboard, but drove the dreaded French privateers into their harbours so that they reached Plymouth safely, though separated from the convoy. Eight men from a Man-of-War came aboard 'to press our seamen', but these managed to hide, and the Pressgang had to help with the sails. 'The day we arrived was the 24th November, 1690'—five years to the day since they had anchored in Jamaica in 1685. 'Dec. 4th', Coad concludes his narrative, 'Got home, and found my Wife and 3 Sons living, but in a poor low condition'.

Coad's reference to 'the rude rabble in the Man-of-War' implies that a good many of the rebels who had been transported to Jamaica, were able to come home. When the Earl of Inchiquin received orders delaying the return of the transportees, he replied that half had already returned.

TWO MORE ESCAPES

Azariah Pinney left no account of his adventures in and out of Monmouth's army, but in family letters[12] we have a unique record of the alternating hopes and fears of a rebel's father and sisters. Azariah was born in 1661, the youngest son of the Rev. John Pinney, who in Cromwell's time was the ordained Presbyterian vicar of Broadwindsor, Dorset, a gifted preacher and so well-liked that his parishioners petitioned for him to stay after the Restoration. He was ejected in 1662. After farming his estate of Bettiscombe Manor for several years, he was called to be Minister of Cooke Street Presbyterian Church in Dublin. The Rev. John, his son and daughters had developed a thriving business in lace, made in Devon and Dorset and sold in London and Dublin.

Azariash is described in the Presentment of the Rebels as a yeoman and of Axminster. When he was in Dublin selling lace, he had married an impecunious Scots servant girl called Mary, who became a great trial to the family. In 1685 she was still in Dublin, but Azariah had returned to Axminster and there joined Monmouth's army, with whom he marched to Sedgemoor. His father had heard with some anxiety that Azariah had joined the rebels. Then he heard of Sedgemoor, and for the next fortnight he did not know whether his son was alive or dead. He was too distraught to study; he wept and prayed day and night. Three weeks after the battle he received a letter from his ablest and favourite daughter, Hester, telling him that Azariah was alive and had reached London, where Hester lived. We do not know how he got there, except that 'someone befriended him'. The Reverend John hastened to reply to her 'sorrowful letter', saying

> I would not omit any cost or care for Az to preserve him. His wife will goe hence in the first ship that goeth for England. God almighty shew us mercy. The bearer hereof is his wife. Helpe her to goe to him to see him er he dye. Supply the bearer hereof with what money she shall need, and you shall have a bill from me presently to repay it.

The 'sorrowful letter' and the haste 'to see him ere he die' suggest that Azariah had been wounded, as the judicial hangings had not then begun. In another letter John fears 'I shall never see that poor soule more in this world. With sorrow shall I goe to the grave. I have sent Az wife to see how it is, though I despaire that he shall live till she come'. In August John wrote to his daughter Rachel, 'I am comforted in the preserv(ation) and recovery of life, for God hath heard my prayer. I shall be glad to see Azariah[13] here if possible and prudent. His last letter was life to me from the dead'. To Azariah he wrote

God hath heard prayer. Wednesday and fryday we kept a fast, Aug. 5th and 7th, and your letter came to me in the end of the fast, fryday last. Every post I expected to heare of death and trembled to open this letter. I hope your Mary came safe to London. God, even your father's God, open a way for you and restore you to life and liberty, that you may come hither againe, whiles I ame living

John then asks his son to write an anonymous third-person account of his journey from Sedgemoor to London. He resumes, 'Since the writing of this I received yours dated August the 4th, which was a comfort to me on many accounts, being glad the Girle came so providentially. God preserve and direct you, to whom I commit you'.

The mention of liberty not yet restored implies that Azariah had been arrested. He was sent from London to Dorchester for the Assize, where both he and Robert Pinney, who was no relation, were condemned to be hanged. Robert had pleaded[14] Not guilty, and was hanged at Dorchester[15] on 7 September, two days after trial. Azariah was to have been hanged at Bridport[16] on 12 September. Muddiman's Newsletter duly reported the hanging of Robert Pinney and others at Dorchester. Reading this, and not knowing of any Robert Pinney, John presumed it was Azariah, and that the reporter had got the Christian name wrong. No letter survives to show John's grief. He saw himself alternately as Job, when the news was bad, and as Jacob, if there was any hope. So with Job he would be trying to say 'The Lord gave and the Lord hath taken away. Blessed be the name of the lord'. But Hester was nearer at hand and very efficient. Gathering her savings together, £65, she offered them as a ransom for her brother. Whoever took the bribe first got Azariah transferred from the hanging list to Nipho's list of transportees and to George Penne's agency. Getting the bribe, Penne acquiesced in the moving of Azariah to Bristol, and his transportation as a fare-paying passenger. Not until 26 September did John hear that Azariah was still alive. On the 30th he wrote to Hester acknowledging her letter, and mentioning one from Azariah

from Dorchester, which I little expected, concluding [he had] bin dead by the public papers [in which he is missnamed]. But [God hath] spared him. I thank you (to whom he is so much obliged for his life) for your care, love and paines. For the cost it shall bee mine to repay you. I have here £100 by me which shall be returned to you speedily (if a pardon can be gott for him). I hope he may yet live to be a comfort to ua all.

On 21 October George Penne completed his report[17] on 'Mr Nepho's Account of Prisoners', mentioning 65 from Dorchester, a wounded man in Exeter gaol, and 33 from Ilchester, 'besides Azarias Pinney who was sent in custody to Bristoll to be transported, who, it will be made to appear upon the Return of my Express sent for that purpose, hath been shipped for some one of his Majestes Plantations'. Before Azariah was shipped, his elder brother Nathanial had come to the rescue, and equipped him for the voyage and the start of his new life. Nathaniel[18] sent his father a bill for £100 for his expenses, and sent a supplementary account in January:

Bristoll, September 1685
Mr John Pinney is Debitor to money paid Geo. Penne, Esq. for the Ransume of my Brother Aza, August 1685   65- -
To my jorney for 10 dayes and horse hyre   2-10-
To 6 gallons Sack for his voiage   1-16-
To Botles for the same   - 5-
To 4 gallons Brandey   -16-
To Botles for the same   - 3-
To two Cheeses   - 6-
To his horse hyre to Bristol and expenses   -10-
To 10 dayes dyet and Lodgeing in Bristol   -17-
To 3 pair thread hose   - 7-6
To 4 pairs worsted   -14-
To 2 pair shooes   - 8-
To a hatt   - 8-6
To shifts and handcerchiffs etc.   -14-
To Tobbaco and pipes   - 9-
To the Mate and Boston for their kindness   - 7-6
To Boate hyre to King roade   - 6-6
To a Bed, Boulster and rugg   2- 9-6
To his passadge to Nevis   5- -
To 2 Trunks   -10-
To a bible and other bookes   - 6-6
To Sugger, Spice, etc.   - 4-6
To money given him   15- -
To money given Mr Coope for Makeing bond   -10-
To Given his Man   - 1-6
                                                                       £100- -

Mr. John Pinney Debitor More owing Brothers account, January 1685 (i.e. 1686)
To money paid for him and Lent him in   1- 5-
To carriage his Cloathes from London and Freight to Nevis   -10-6
To makeing affidavit of his transportation   - 8-
To Swordbelt, Rasor, Shooes, Buttons, etc. and
    Sword sent with his cloathes   3- 4-

His passage was in the *Rose*, a pink, with Captain Wogan. Azariah had been granted 'a pardon of his life and a grant of his goods and chattels from King James, on condition that he went to the Caribbean and did not return within ten years'. Hester was upset that her bribe had not secured a free pardon. Her father wrote to her on 29 October:

I ame concerned from my very soule for Az. and could cheerfully have gon with him. Azariah owes his life to you, my dear daughter, who have ben as tender as a mother to him, and don more for him than his mother could have don. The charges I will reimburse to you, and bless God that raised you up for him, prospered you in saving him. My deare Daughter, murmur not at God's dispensation; bless God he is saved. I hope to see him again with Comfort, whose life hath bin so oft saved by wonderful providence. How I wish I knew in what condition A. went and to what place. The Lord bless and preserve you. Your loving and thankfull father, Jo Pinney.
P.S. Read this to A. wife, Mrs Mary. Be not offended at this admirable providence of God. Bless God as I doe it is no worse. My son's life is preserved beyond my expectation. He is removed for a tyme. His youthfull afflictions will be recompensed with future comforts. He may be a Joseph, sent away, not as a slave but as a purveyor, to prepare a place for us all. God will goe with him. If you please to come hither you shall be welcome.

As there was no mention in the pardon of a sale as an indentured servant, Azariah was able to set up as a Factor, selling the lace and other goods Nathaniel sent him, and returning Nathaniel's share of the profit in sugar. His trade and his income[19] increased, and having shown himself a shrewd and reliable businessman, Azariah was employed by neighbours as an attorney, a guardian of orphans, and as a tax-assessor. He became a planter, a landed proprietor, a Lieutenant in the Defence Force, and in 1696 a member of the House of Assembly, and shortly after was elected Treasurer of the island. He held that post for ten years, and was never accused of waste or dishonesty. He was appointed to the Council of Nevis, and the Governor, General Christopher Codrington, described Azariah as one of the 'two best men of the island'.

In England in May 1686 Azariah's young wife bore him a son, who was christened John, and who must been conceived during their brief reunion in the August after Sedgemoor. Mary Pinney took the boy out to Nevis, but found the climate intolerable, and returned to England. John entered Pembroke College, Oxford, and later the Middle Temple, where he acquired enough legal knowledge to function as Chief Justice of Nevis, where he lived from 1715 until his early death in 1720.

Azariah visited England in 1706 and 1719, and died in London a few months before his son's death. His grandson, John Frederick Pinney, was

M.P. for Bridport from 1747 to 1761. Memorial tablets to him and other members of the family are to be seen in Wayford Church, not far from Crewkerne.

Dr Henry Pitman[20] was much less fortunate than Coad. At Wells he and his brother William were ordered to be transported to 'the Caribe Islands', given to 'Jeremiah Nepho' and

> by him sold to George Penne a needy Papist, that wanted money to pay for our transportation, and therefore was very importunate with my relations to purchase mine and my brother's freedom. With threats on the one hand and promises of particular favour on the other, he prevailed with our relations to give him threescore pounds, upon condition that we should be free when we came to Barbadoes, only owning some person as a titular master.

The brothers were marched to Weymouth and put on board[21] the *Betty*, which took about five weeks to reach Barbados.

> We were consigned to Charles Thomas and his Company, who compelled us to live with one Robert Bishop, pretending that they had not absolutely sold us to him, but afterwards, when we were constrained by the great unkindness of our master to address ourselves unto them to remove us, we found they had positively sold us, and also given it in on their oaths at the Secretary's Office.

Bishop expected Pitman to practise as a doctor and surgeon at Bishop's profit, but fed and housed him as a slave. 'Our diet was very mean: 5 lbs of salt Irish beef, or salt fish, a week, for each man: and Indian or Guinea corn ground on a stone and made into dumplings instead of bread'. The fare upset Pitman, and when he asked for better treatment, Bishop beat him with a cane on his head, arms and back until the cane split in pieces. Then he put Pitman in the stocks, where he was exposed to the scorching heat of the sun for about 12 hours. Fortunately for Pitman Bishop ran into debt and could not pay the instalments on his purchase of the brothers, who had to be returned after 15 months' service. They remained in the merchants' hands as 'goods unsold'. William Pitman died, and Henry resolved to attempt to escape from the island. He met a debtor, John Nuthall, who wanted money for his release. Henry's relations had sent a consignment of goods to a friend in the island, who sold them and held the money for Henry's use. He gave Nuthall £7 to pay off his debt, and £12 to buy a boat, though helping a rebel convict to escape was a very serious offence. Nuthall reported that magistrates had become very inquisitive about the boat, although he had assured them that it was for his own use. Pitman told him to sink the boat, which saved Nuthall from further questions and the boat from confiscation.

Unobtrusively Pitman and Nuthall began to enlist a crew, and to assemble stores in a friend's cellar, not far from the waterside. They gathered bread, cheese, water, some wine and beer; a compass, a quadrant, a chart, a tarpaulin, and some carpenter's tools. For crew Pitman chose John Whicker and Peter Bagwell, both from Colyton[22]; John Cooke, probably from Chard (or else from Wookey), who had all come with Pitman in the *Betty*; Thomas Austin and William Woodcock, who were[23] respectively 27 and 19 when shipped in the *Jamaica Merchant*; and Jeremiah Atkins of Taunton who had been shipped in the *John Frigget*. To these Nuthall added a friend, Thomas Waker, who had not been a rebel.

For a date Pitman chose the evening when the Governor of Nevis was being entertained by the Governor of Barbados, and the troops were likely to be celebrating. Nuthall employed 'two lusty blacks' to raise and empty the boat, which was then brought round near to the storehouse, of which John Whicker had been custodian. They were loading their stores when their sentry gave warning that the Watch was approaching. 'We all', says Pitman, 'of an instant betook ourselves to our heels'. Pitman was near despair, but one of his friends found him and assured him that the Watch had passed by without noticing the boat. Thomas Austin was so shaken that he refused to go any further, but the rest embarked. The negroes were given three half-pieces-of-eight, and told to stay in the cellar till morning.

The boat dropped down the harbour, past the fort and a man-of-war, and then the crew dared to raise the mast and hoist the sail. The boat leaked atrociously and kept two men busy baling the water out with a tub and a large wooden[24] bowl. Pitman had to be navigator and helmsman, and steered south-west as well as he could judge by the stars, as it was too dark to read the compass. They hoped to reach the Dutch island of Curaçoa, as they might be arrested if they landed on any English island. Most of the crew were miserably seasick, and one of them dropped the wooden bowl overboard, which made them realise that they must be more careful with the tub.

The next day the rudder split and they had to steer with an oar until one of the crew managed to mend it; they kept much water out by nailing their tarpaulin along the gunwales. After three days they weathered Grenada and continued westward, nearly splitting their boat on rocks when they hoped to land for fresh water:

The sea heaved us so fast in, that we could not possibly have avoided being split on the rocks, had I not leaped into the sea to fend her off, which whilst I laboured to do with my feet against the rock till I was almost spent, my companions with their two oars rowed her off. At which our hearts were filled with joy and our mouths with praises to the Lord, who had so wonderfully preserved us from being cast away on this island.'

They were convinced that the inhabitants whom they had seen lighting a fire were cannibals.

From the west end of this island we directed our course for Saltatudos; but about nine at night a dreadful storm arose, which made us despair of ever seeing the morning sun. We brought our boat to with her head against the sea, but the wind and sea still increasing, we were forced to bear up before it, with only sail sufficient to give her steerage way. But the Omnipotent (who is never unmindful of the cries of his people in distress) heard our prayers; so that when all our hopes were given over, and we had resigned ourselves into his hands, expecting every moment when the wide gaping sea would devour and swallow us up, God, of his infinite mercy and unspeakable goodness, commanded the violence of the winds to cease, and allayed the fury of the raging waves.

On 16 May at break of day they sighted the island of Saltatudos, which the Spaniards called Tortuga. It lies about 270 miles WSW of Grenada, and the voyage from Barbados would be about 450 miles: they had been at sea for a week. On the island they found a crew of pirates, who treated them kindly until they found that Pitman's crew had no intention of joining them. Then the pirates burned Pitman's boat and took his sails, but

I continued my resolution, and chose rather to trust Divine Providence on that desolate and uninhabitable island than to partake or be anyways concerned with them in their piracy: having confidence in myself that God, who so wonderfully and miraculously preserved us on the sea and brought us to this island, would in like manner deliver us hence, if we continued faithful to Him.

The pirates departed, leaving Pitman's crew marooned. Before they sailed, Pitman gave them 30 pieces-of-eight for an Indian whom they had kidnapped, thinking he would be useful in helping them to fish. For three months the party lived on turtle, turtles' eggs, fish, young birds, and wild vegetables, and were very grateful for Pitman's medical skill in coping with their indigestion with opium pills. The men made themselves huts, which they thatched with grass, and extracting fibre from long leaves they managed to mend their badly worn clothes.

At length a man-of-war steered in toward the shore, and proved to be an English privateer. Pitman went on board to try to negotiate passages for his crew to any English port or passing ship. The captain consulted his crew, who voted to keep the doctor, but refused to take the other rebels. They did, however, give them a cask of wine, some bread and cheese, a gammon of bacon, some cloth, needles and thread.

The privateer steered north, passing between Porto Rico and Hispaniola (or Haiti) and after some to-ing and fro-ing landed Pitman in New York, from which he got a passage in a vessel bound for Amsterdam. About five weeks later Pitman landed at Cowes and crossed to Southampton. 'I

A RELATION OF THE Great Sufferings AND 𝔖trange 𝔄dventures

Of *HENRY PITMAN*,

Chyrurgion to the late Duke of *Monmouth*, containing an Account;

1. Of the occasion of his being engaged in the Duke's Service. 2. Of his Tryal, Condemnation, and Transportation to *Barbadoes*, with the most severe and Unchristian Acts made against him and his Fellow-sufferers, by the Governour and General Assembly of that Island. 3. How he made his escape in a small open Boat with some of his fellow Captives, namely, *Jo. Whicker*, *Peter Bagwell*, *William Woodcock*, *Jo. Cooke*, *Jeremiah Atkins*, &c. And how miraculously they were preserved on the Sea. 4. How they went ashore on a uninhabitable Island, where they met with some *Privateers* that burnt their Boat, and left them on that desolate place to shift for themselves. 5. After what manner they lived there for about three Moneths, until the said *Henry Pitman* was taken aboard a *Privateer*, and at length arrived late in *England*. 6. How his Companions were received aboard another *Privateer* that was afterwards taken by the *Spaniards*, and they all made Slaves; And how after six Moneths Captivity they were delivered, and returned to *England* also.

Licensed, June 13th, 1689.

London, Printed by *Andrew Sowle*: And are to be Sold by *John Taylor*, at the sign of the *Ship* in *Paul's Church-Yard*, 1689.

Title-page of Dr Pitman's exciting account of his escape from Barbados

returned', he wrote, 'in a disguise to my relations who, before this time, unknown to me, had procured[25] my pardon; and joyfully received me, as one risen from the dead'.

Pitman's account finishes with a paragraph of thanksgiving to God 'who miraculously preserved me on the deep waters, and delivered me when appointed to die'. He dated his narrative 'From my lodging, at the sign of the Ship, in Paul's Churchyard, London. June the 10th, 1689'.

Appended to Pitman's account is a long letter he received from John Whicker, who had assumed the leadership of the crew. Shortly after the doctor's departure from the island, the two debtors, Nuthall and Waker, took themselves off in a small boat the privateers had left. They were never heard of again. Then another small privateer arrived at the east end of the island, and remained at first unknown to Whicker's party. Three of the pirates schemed to take command, and took three others prisoner but one escaped, and seeking water and food came across Whicker's camp. With his help Whicker's men ambushed the hostile pirates, tied them up, and took possession of the ship. Leaving the three pirates marooned, but with some food, they set sail northwards, making for the passage between Porto Rico and Hispaniola. Their pilot mistook his position, missed the strait, and sailed along the south coast of Hispaniola, looking for a creek where they might get fresh water. They missed the fresh-water creek of which the pilot had read, and ran far up the wrong creek. Landing, they decided they must dig a well, and found fresh water about five feet down. 'Lying ashore all night', Whicker continues, 'to take up the water as it sprang, we were almost stung to death with a sort of flies called Musquitoes. By next morning we had got about forty gallons of water aboard, with which we put to sea again'. Before long they sighted a ship they took to be a Jamaica sloop 'for she had our King's Jack', but when they anchored alongside her, Spaniards 'all armed as pirates' overcame them. They 'carried us aboard their sloop, stripped us naked, and put us down in their hold'. Fed on short rations, the Englishmen were taken to St Jago, a Spanish town on Cuba. They were kept as slaves for more than six months sometimes at sea, sometimes ashore. Not unaturally they all went down with malaria which they called the ague, and Jeremish Atkins died of it.

After various piracies the Spanish crew returned to port with their prizes. The Governor was informed that the Duke of Albemarle had arrived in Jamaica, and he hastened to order the release of all English prisoners, who were to be sent to Jamaica. And so, wrote Whicker,

We embarked once again free men together, by God's grace, bound for Jamaica, where we arrived safely about the latter end of March. So, separating ourselves, we endeavoured in the best manner we could, to get passage for England, our native country, desiring God Almighty to deliver us, and all our dear countrymen Protestants from the barbarous cruelty of the Spaniards and Papists.

Pitman probably reached England late in 1687, and Whicker in the summer of 1688.

12

Social Consequences of Sedgemoor

The first and most obvious of the after-effects of the rebellion was the withdrawal of about 4000 of the labour force of the West Country. A thousand or more had fallen in the battles and the immediate pursuit. A thousand and more had suffered hanging or transportation. Something like 2000 kept out of sight until the General Pardon was issued in March 1686. Most of these would then as far as possible resume their former callings.

Immediate evidence is scanty, but the petition[1] of five Devon men for the recall of 41 former neighbours is relevant. It is dated 3 May 1689:

The petition of John Clapp, Joseph Pitts and John Gould of the parish of Colyton, co. Devon, and Daniel Cleveland and Nathaniel Smith of the parish of Honiton, shewing that the persons there-after mentioned, inhabitants of the said parishes and neighbourhood, men of sober and industrious lives, were, after the defeat of the Duke of Monmouth, taken into custody, some having joined in arms with him, some having supplied provisions, but others of them in nowise having assisted. That at the time they should have been tried, the Lord Chief Justice Jeffreys required them all to plead guilty, or else they should be immediately executed; which threat, having been made good upon one that put himself on trial, terrified the rest into a compliance, though several of them were innocent, and being thus attainted by a forced confession they were banished for ten years and sold as slaves into America. That by reason of the great number so banished, the country wants inhabitants, artificers and labourers. The petitioners pray that the said persons may return home to their wives and children.

The petition was authenticated by Sir Walter Yonge, who in 1690 persuaded King William to pardon and recall the Monmouth transportees. One of the 41 was Gideon Dare of Luppitt, who did come home from Jamaica in 1690. How many of the transportees returned it is impossible to say. We know that Coad and Dare came home and perhaps half the rebels from Jamaica, so did Dr Pitman and four of his crew. Few if any others returned from Barbados, where the transportees were made to complete[2] their ten years' exile, and then found no transport home. By grace, it is said, of a shipload of 'Poor House girls', sent out to be servants to the wealthy or wives to the poorer settlers, the little company of West Country exiles kept their community white. Many of them moved into a remote valley, vaguely reminiscent of the scenery of their homeland, and there they built cottages whose ruins still show a recognisable West Country style, unknown in the rest of the island. They also built dry-stone walls, either as boundaries or as wind-breaks to shelter their crops from the Atlantic gales. The reader will remember that Thomas Austin of Pitman's crew decided to stay, rather than risk capture or drowning. His descendants are still in the island. Some other surnames of recorded transportees still survive, mainly among the 'poor whites'. Somerset intonation and some Somerset words are still recognisable in their speech.

In the Treasury Books[3] for 1686 there is a list of 130 rebels whose small estates had been confiscated and granted to three commissioners to sell for the king's benefit. The location of their land is mentioned, most of it in Devon and Somerset but also seven estates in Dorset and four in Wiltshire; and the occupations of 118 of those named are given. As they had land, it is natural that more than half were engaged in agriculture, 41 being husbandmen, 18 yeomen, two gentlemen, two labourers, two blacksmiths, three millers, a maltster, a cheesemonger, a butcher, a two tanners. There were besides, three carpenters, two joiners, two shoemakers and five cordwainers, three tailors, nine clothiers, a bodice-maker, a mercer, a carrier, a tinker, a chandler, and a mason. There were five weavers and five combers, a cloth-worker and a dyer; and more surprisingly a chirurgeon (Robert Thatcher of Wedmore) and a Doctor in Physic (Richard Evans of Cotleigh). Andrew Loder of Dorchester and two of his friends were also selling rebels' land for the king, and were suitably rewarded.

The impoverishment of the families of rebels inevitably followed the loss of their breadwinner, the confiscation of his land, and the spending of savings for pardons or ransoms. A petition of the Company[4] of Weavers, dated March 1686, refers to 'the present deadness of trade occasioned by the late mourning and cursed rebellion'. Coad, who had lived comfortably, returned in 1690 to find his wife and sons 'in a poor low condition'. Thomas Place of Edington, Quaker and leader of the Clubmen, petitioned the King[5] for a remission of forfeiture. He had been disowned by the Quakers in September 1685 for being 'very active and conversant in the late Duke of Monmouth's army'. Excepted from the General Pardon, he had been arrested in London in the autumn of 1686, committed to Newgate, and sent to be tried at the Wells Assize in March 1687, where he was condemned to be hanged on 15 April for levying war against the King. The King sent a stay of execution and then a pardon. The Treasury Book records the 'petition of Thomas Pleas of Edington, sergemaker', returning

Cabin built by a Monmouth rebel—a time-expired transportee—beneath Pico Tenerife, north Barbados. It was originally thatched with coarse grass or Palm leaves. (Photo: A. E. Hughes)

Dry-stone walling in the valley beneath Pico Tenerife, Barbados. In the field behind was grown a crop of tobacco to provide the ex-rebels with a livelihood. (Photo: A. E. Hughes)

the King thanks for pardoning his life, and praying a remission of his forfeiture, 'his estate being most taken from him in the time of the late rebellion, and what is left being surveyed at 20 marks by the King's Commissioners in order to seizure, which will be the ruin of the petitioner'.

Another petition came from Walter Osborne[6] of Crewkerne, a dyer. Commissioners had seized a little spot of ground of his as forfeited, notwithstanding that he was included in a circuit pardon for County Dorset, by the words of which pardon he was freed from all penalties and forfeitures. He therefore prayed for restitution.

Widows were even harder hit. Mary Hallet[7] for example had five children to support. Her husband had been in the rebellion, was condemned at Dorchester to transportation but died in prison. His small holding, worth £8 a year, was seized into the king's hands. Mary prayed the king to remit the forfeiture and 'a fine of £44 set upon her goods'. She had not regained possession by June 1688, but maybe she got the land back then or in the next year. Her husband was Joseph Hallet of Marshwood, who was a husbandman.

An unusual petition came in March 1687 from Mary Collins[8] of Bath and her daughter Jane, widow of John Brome, rebel, who died before the date fixed for his execution. His estate of £18 per annum in Horton near Ilminster reverted to his mother, who died two days later. It was then 'enjoyed' by Thomas Brome, brother of the deceased John, who also had been in the rebel army, but absconded until the General Pardon was issued. Mary asked for a grant of the estate for the support of Jane and her four children, who had no maintenance, although one, either Mary or Jane, had appeared as King's Evidence.

Thomas Cox was another[9] petitioner. Long before the rebellion his brother Philip, of Colyton, had borrowed £300 for which Thomas had been bound. Philip, a rebel, had been transported and died at sea. Robert Cox, their father, had previously bought a small estate worth £30 per annum and settled it on Philip. This had been seized for the King, and Thomas, threatened with imprisonment for his brother's debt of £300, petitioned for a grant of the small estate to enable him to pay his brother's debt. But Philip's widow also petitioned for the estate, as she and her daughters had been forced to beg, and were heavily in debt. Her petition was granted, and she was given power to sell the estate to pay the debts.

Then there are petitions for rewards out of the fines paid or the lands forfeited. Henry Hodson[11] petitioned for the estates of Andrew Speedwell and John Gold, late rebels in the West, convicted at last Wells Assizes, in consideration of his losses 'that morning he received his wound at King's

Sedgemoor'. John Skinner[12] asked for a grant from the estate of William Cox worth £32 per annum, 'for dangerous services in the late rebellion'. (William Cox of Musbury, Devon, husbandman, had been hanged at Wareham in September 1685.) Edward Morgan[13] asked to be made Receiver of Rents of the Duchy of Cornwall for gathering intelligence for Lord Feversham 'which he faithfully performed by going several times privately into the rebel army', and had the Earl's certificate.

Two petitions[14] in the Treasury Books came from Christopher Penny, Constable of Shepton Mallet, for a share of the £1000 fine imposed on Hugh Green of Nether Compton for distributing Monmouth's Proclamation, and a share of the £2000 fine on George Speke of Whitelackington, he, C. Penny, being 'utterly damnified in his trade by the late rebels'.

Not all the fugitives from Sedgemoor were able to hide near enough to their homes for them to be fed by friends or relatives. There is a traditional story of a rebel called Gifford, thought to have come from Bishops Hull, who hid in a hollow tree and was fed with eggs by an old woman who lived near, until he could escape further afield. John Gifford of Kingsbury Episcopi and Simon Gifford of West Buckland were presented[15] by their Constables, but never brought to trial.

Some rebels had fled in groups and foraged together. A Newsletter[16] of 29 October 1685 reports

Letters from Lyme of the 24th that several of the rebels are still lurking about in parties. Some were at a widow woman's at Wolten, two miles thence; on notice whereof Captain Follier sent a small party to take them, but the rebels were too strong, wounding one very dangerously, and forcing the rest to march away, some of the inhabitants taking the rebels' parts . . . The night before about 20 other rebels went to Charmouth, a mile thence, wounding the tithing-men who opposed them and carried away a great deal of provision.

A note in the Privy Council Register[17] for 8 January 1686 records

Whereas severall of the rebells that were seized in the West of England, to the number of about three score, some time since did make their escape out of Ilchester gaol, to which they were committed in order to their tryal, by the neglect of those that had charge of them, since which time twenty-three of them being again apprehended, His Majesty is informed have been again suffered to escape.

An enquiry was ordered.

The sums exacted for ransoms or pardons cause surprise that poor folk could produce so much. The customary price of a pardon was £60, but Andrew Loder the attorney told various people that the pardon they sought would cost £200, £250, £300, or even £400.

John Gardner was a Nonconformist minister living in Martock. In June 1685 he was seen[18] in Neroche Forest with Monmouth's army, on horseback with sword and pistol, and a Martock friend spoke of him as a Captain. After Sedgemoor Sir Edward Phelips with soldiers had in vain searched John's house in Martock and his mother's house in Stoke St Mary. John was in fact concealed for seven or eight months in the house of Dorothy Jeans in Martock, and his friends kept the secret, George Bishop, a yeoman, visiting him daily with provisions, at the risk of his life. John's mother, aged 70, was terrified, and consulted a friend, John Coleby, who went to Loder, 'reputed to be a Pardon-monger'. Loder promised to get a pardon 'for life and estate' for £200. Some time later Coleby had a letter from Loder, saying that he would need £300 for the pardon, and showed the letter to John's mother. She 'was troubled that there was one hundred added to the first proposals, yet she did consent unto the payment of the said Three hundred pounds'. Arrangements were made to pay £200 in London, and two friends took the other £100 from John's wife to Mrs Loder in Dorchester. John came out of hiding and appeared before two magistrates who granted him bail. So, on 30 March 1686 at Wells Assize[19] John Gardner was called, appeared, and was discharged by the Proclamation of the General Pardon granted by the King. Had his well-meaning relatives and friends kept clear of Loder, John would have had his pardon free. After the Revolution he brought an action against Loder in the Court of the Exchequer, demanding restitution of the major part of the £300, Loder's nephew having admitted that the pardon had cost only £60. The astute lawyer had already safeguarded himself against such an action, for when he was appointed a commissioner to sell rebels' land for the King, he also got a grant[20] allowing him to keep 'all moneys which Andrew Loder received from various clients under colour of obtaining a pardon'.

George Bisse of Martock[21] was a friend of John Gardner and like him a Nonconformist preacher, who had been licensed as a 'General Teacher' in 1672. He was about 45 at the time of the rebellion. No one suggested that he had joined Monmouth's army, nor that he was absent from his home during the rebellion, but he was 'taken up' and imprisoned at Wells, accused of 'Aydeing and assisting the Rebells against the King'. In the Gaol Delivery Book Bisse's name stands next before that of the Rev. John Hickes. George regarded himself as innocent, and it was without his knowledge or consent that his wife approached Loder 'to be directed by him what course should be taken to preserve his life'. Loder insisted that George must plead guilty; and should he be condemned, Loder would procure a pardon for life and estate for £250. George at first refused to plead guilty, but his wife's anxiety and her insistance on his playing for safety persuaded him to plead guilty at the Wells Assize: he was duly sentenced to death for high treason. Mrs Bisse rode to Dorchester to see Loder, and returned to tell George that Loder said his pardon could not be obtained under £400. George's friends rallied round the the £400 was put together and paid to Loder's nominee, Symon Harcourt. Jeffreys' first report[22] on Wells Assize listed George Bisse among ten prisoners remaining in custody. His later report, dated 12 November 1685, has George Bisse in the list headed 'Prisoners reprieved and remaining in Gaol, humbly proposed for his Majesty's most gracious pardon'. George had to wait for this until 30 March 1686, when at the Wells Assize 132 rebels were released[23] by the King's General Pardon.

In January 1686 a query had been raised[24] at the Treasury, whether pardons restored forfeited lands, money and goods. The answer recorded was 'Pardons do not restore, but a grant of restitution does. If pardon preceded attainder, there would be no forfeiture'. Loder had seen to it that the attainder of George Bisse preceded his pardon. Later among the Treasury Papers is a Royal Warrant, dated 15 May 1688, granting the estate of certain rebels in the West to three gentlemen, of whom Andrew Loder was one, for their services in selling for the Crown estates forfeited by rebels. Among the lands[25] listed was 'The interest possessed by George Biss (lately attainted of high treason)' in various copyholds and tenancies of arable, meadow and pasture in Bower Hinton (which adjoins Martock). As these lands were held jointly by George and his sons, their interests would be saved. A similar grant safeguarded the money paid by George Bisse to Simon Harcourt 'under colour of obtaining the king's pardon', but it did restore the remainder of the real and personal estate of George Bisse to George Bisse.

Another instance of friends contributing to raise a ransom comes in the Book of Remembrance[26] of Axminster Congregational Church. One

of the Brethren, named John Spiring, being taken by the rude Souldiers after the Battle, was stripped of his rayment and barbarously used and imprisoned, and sentenced for banishment, and accordingly was carried captive into the Isle of Barbadoes, where he was sold as a slave once and again. Yet, after some time was past, a door was open for his Redemption by paying a sum of money; which was agreed unto, and the money being collected of Christian friends (who readily communicated to the same), was sent for his ransome. Now being redeemed from his bondage state, and returning home to his family and to the house of God, whilst he was on the seas, both the ship in which he sailed, with the persons and wares in it, were cast away and drowned.

A more expensive pardon was that ultimately granted to Edmund Prideaux of Ford Abbey, whose father had been Attorney General under the

Commonwealth and Protectorate. The younger Prideaux had welcomed and entertained Monmouth during his progress in 1680. In June 1685 Thomas Heywood Dare and Hugh Chamberlain had visited Ford Abbey after being landed at Chideock, and some at least of the 40 horses they brought to Lyme Regis came from Prideaux's stable. The government suspected that Prideaux had also supplied £500. Monmouth landed on 11 June, and the news reached the King on the 13th. That day the Earl of Sunderland, Secretary of State, issued a warrant[27] to Thomas Saywell to apprehend Prideaux and take him to London. Saywell arrived and arrested Prideaux on the 19th. In the meantime a party of rebels from Ilminster—Samuel Key, Joseph Standerwick and James Carrier, with George Stuckey of Whitelackington, and Joseph Holmes[28] also of Ilminster but not a rebel—visited 'Esquire Pridicks' and with his permission searched the house for arms, collecting five or six muskets, two carbines, two blunderbusses, some half-pikes, and two rapiers. Holmes took one of the rapiers to Taunton, left it there, and returned with his servant, whom he got discharged from the rebel army.

A week after Sedgemoor Prideaux's lawyer got him released on a Writ of Habeas Corpus. He seems to have remained in London, and two months later was re-arrested and committed to the Tower on a charge of high treason. A batch of rebels tried at Dorchester had been sentenced on 10 September to be hanged[29] on the 12th. One of them, Malachi Mallack, a clothier of Axminster, who was to have been hanged at Bridport, decided to save his life on the 11th by volunteering to act as King's Evidence[30] against Edmund Prideaux. He is thought to have been with Dare when the horses were collected at Ford Abbey, and so to be able to swear that Prideaux had aided and abetted the rebels. Malachi was 'humbly proposed to his Majesty for his most gracious pardon', and that was granted in October.

In a trial for treason, however, unless the accused pleaded guilty, the law demanded two witnesses, and as Dare was dead, the government had only Malachi Mallack. As the son of Cromwell's Attorney General, Prideaux was a marked man; and there is little doubt that Jeffreys coveted Ford Abbey for a country seat, especially as the King had 'given' Prideaux to Jeffreys. There was a search for a second witness. Charles Speke of Whitelackington, William Thomson, a rebel from London, Joseph Standerwick and Samuel Key of Ilminster, and James Butcher of Crewkerne[31] were in turn offered their lives if they would swear that Prideaux had sent horses or money or arms to the Duke. To their honour these all refused, and Charles Speke was actually hanged. Key and Standerwick were sought and arrested[32] in London in February 1686.

Thomson, Stuckey, Chamberlain, and Carrier were excluded from the General Pardon issued in March, the government hoping to find them and secure a second witness. Although Joseph Holmes had not marched with the rebels beyond Taunton, he had been presented by the Constables, and he was frightened into making a 'confession' about the searching of Ford Abbey for arms.

Prideaux was seriously ill[33] in December. His wife and his sisters, Lady Churchill (widow of Sir James) and Lady Tooker, all made appeals for clemency, release or pardon, and were all told that the King had given Mr Prideaux to Lord Jeffreys. Having secured a second witness (of sorts), Jeffreys fixed the date of Prideaux's trial for mid-March. Mrs Prideaux panicked, capitulated, and enquired what fine would be required for a pardon. Jeffreys stipulated for £15,000 but allowed a discount of £240 for a cash payment of the first instalment of £2400. Prideaux was released on 12 March, and his pardon[34] for 'all treasons, etc. committed before March 1st' was granted on 12 March. Key, Standerwick and Holmes were granted pardons[35] on 4 July 1686, but Carrier, who had had prior knowledge of Monmouth's coming, had to wait until 31 May 1687. With Prixeaux's £14,000-odd and other funds Jeffreys bought himself an estate in the Midlands. After the Revolution Prideaux petitioned Parliament to get him a refund from the Midland estate, Jeffreys being dead, but he seems to have been unlucky.

The Maids of Taunton were excluded from the General Pardon to give more time for the negotiation of their ransom. They had been given to the Queen's Maids of Honour, who hoped[36] to get £7000 but had to be content with about £2000, which meant an average of about £70 a maid.

The biggest fine or ransom was that exacted from Lord Grey, who had been given to the King's brother-in-law, Lord Rochester. Grey's northern estates had been sequestered to Rochester's use after the Rye House Plot, and Rochester is thought to have netted £16,000 from them. Grey's estates had been so cleverly entailed[37] that Rochester found it more profitable to keep Grey alive than have him executed. Having the usufruct of Grey's lands, Rochester is said to have made £40,000 from them in James II's reign. Grey was made to write a confession, which is known as *The Secret History of the Rye House Plot* and tells us much more about that than about Monmouth's rebellion. He told the King a good deal that the government already knew. He quoted a letter he had written to Lord Shaftesbuy, in which he said, 'Being trusted by the duke of Monmouth, I would not deceive him in anything'. He referred to Wade as a man of good understanding. He tells us nothing about Sedgemoor, but finishes, 'Two or three days after, God delivered us[38] into your Majesty's hands'.

A number of pardons granted to rebels in May and June 1686 and recorded in the State Papers Domestic, contains the proviso 'if they return from abroad with their goods within two calandar months'. This surprising condition is explained in Mr Peter Earle's valuable book *Monmouth's Rebels*, in which he shows that a group of rebels proposed to establish a manufacture of 'English Cloth' in the Low Countries. They secured premises, privileges, and advantageous contracts, until the English government was sufficiently frightened of the prospective competition to grant these conditional pardons, even including one to Joseph Tily who had read the proclamation of Monmouth as king. Some of those pardoned with the proviso were Christopher Cooke of Wilton, Somerset, clothier; William Cox, sergemaker, John Perry, worsted comber, and Peter Perry, mercer, George Burroughs, comber, and John Atkins, sergemaker, all of Taunton; John Shore of Ling, comber; and Hugh Crosse of Bishop's Hull, merchant[39]. Their manufactory was duly closed down.

13

Some Survivors

Some half dozen of Monmouth's officers, having escaped in 1685, returned to England in the army of William of Orange. One of them was young Dr Oliver, who came back as a combatant officer but completed his medical qualification as L.C.P. London, in 1692 and served throughout King William's reign as Physician to the Red Squadron of the Navy. He was elected an F.R.S. early in Queen Anne's reign, and later became Physician to the Chatham Hospital for Seamen, and then to the Royal Hospital at Greenwich. In 1716 he was buried in Bath[1] Abbey.

Colonel John Speke returned to civilian life and became a Whig M.P. for Taunton. Colonels Foulkes and Matthews commanded regiments in King William's service, Foulkes having Major Fox, once of Monmouth's Yellow Regiment, and Captain Joseph Tily of the Red Regiment under his command. In 1691 a Lieut-Colonel Samuel Venner was commissioned[2] in Colonel Dering's Regiment of Foot. He may have been Monmouth's Colonel Venner, but we cannot be sure.

Andrew Fletcher of Saltoun had an adventurous time[3] during his exile, escaping from a prison in Spain, collecting books for his library, and fighting in Hungary against the Turks. He had been tried *in absentia* at Edinburgh for treason. Anton Buyse and Captain Robert Bruce had been shipped[4] to Edinburgh to appear as King's Evidence against him. He was sentenced to death and his estate forfeited, but after he had returned with William, these judgments were reversed by the Scottish Parliament of 1690. Fletcher thereafter played a prominent part in Scottish affairs, and was a leader of the opposition to the Act of Union of 1707. To the end he remained upright, courageous and quarrelsome, having to be restrained from fighting duels with leaders on the government side.

Robert Ferguson[5] turned up again, accompanying William, someone said 'as a necessary evil'. He was conceited enough to think he deserved a bishopric; and was so disgruntled when he got nothing more than appointment as 'Housekeeper at the Excise' at £400 a year that he secretly changed sides, and began to plot for the exiled King James against King William. Even more surprisingly he became a Roman Catholic. He spent some time in prison and was deprived of his post at the Excise.

Another who turned Roman Catholic was Monmouth's other chaplain, the Rev. Nathaniel Hook. The Duke had sent him to London[6] to try to stir up Colonel Danvers and Major Wildman to start a 'second front'. As one who had come with Monmouth from Holland, he was excepted from the General Pardon, and went into hiding. In November 1687 he was seen in London, and a warrant[7] was issued for his arrest. This was followed in July 1688 by a pardon, and Hook entered the service of King James. He joined Dundee in Scotland the next year, then fought in the Battle of the Boyne, and entered the French army as an officer in the Irish Regiment of Galway. He was sent to Scotland on Jacobite missions in 1705 and 1707; fought against Marlborough at Ramillies and Malplaquet, by which time he was a Brigadier. In 1775 Dr Johnson[8] met Hook's great nephew, the Rev. Luke Joseph Hook, D.D., Librarian of the Mazarin Library at St. Cloud.

One who greeted the arrival of William with enthusiasm was Daniel Defoe, who joined the Prince at Henley, riding as a trooper[9] in a Volunteer Regiment. He claimed some personal friendship with King William, whom he admired wholeheartedly, and in whose support he wrote poems and pamphlets.

Defoe met Alexander Selkirk, the original of Robinson Crusoe, in the home of the daughter of a former comrade[10] in arms, Nathaniel Wade.

Wade had been taken to the Tower[11], and thence to Windsor, where he completed his narrative[12] of the Rebellion. He had been put in the witness-box at the trial of Lord Delamere for treason. All Wade could say was that Monmouth hoped Delamere would raise Cheshire in his support. As he had not done so, the House of Lords followed the lead of Lord Churchill, who as junior peer spoke first[13] and said 'Not guilty, upon my honour'.

Wade and King James began to have a real respect for each other, and in 1687 King James not only pardoned Wade but appointed him Town Clerk of Bristol, Wade's native city, and sent him to reform the corporation, bringing in Nonconformists as City Councillors. Though King James had lost the popularity he once enjoyed, he never lost the admiration and support of Samuel Pepys, his devoted Secretary of the Navy, and of William Penn the Quaker, who never doubted James's sincerity in seeking to establish freedom of worship for all Christians; Wade also seems to have accepted the King's sincerity in this. When Bristol gathered a cavalcade to welcome William of Orange, Wade, in gratitude for King James's kindness to him, declined to ride with them, though he had no hesitation in accepting William as king.

John Romsey, the Town Clerk displaced in 1687 was restored to his position, but begged to keep Wade as his deputy, which is a considerable tribute to Wade's ability. Wade married a young Quaker widow at a Friends' meeting, and lived happily with her and their daughters at Nailsea Court. He made his will in 1716, when he was 70, and died two years later.

The Rev. John Gardner of Martock probably served several village groups of Nonconformists, notably one at[14] Barrington; but after the Toleration Act had allowed them freedom of worship, his quarrel with the Church of England ceased to be acute. In 1692 he applied to Richard Kidder, D.D., the Bishop of Bath and Wells, for ordination. Kidder ordained Gardner and two other Nonconformist ministers, noting[15] in his autobiography 'I should be glad that many such might come into the church. I am sure they were all such as I could not fairly refuse'.

John (or Thomas) Coad, another Nonconformist, left us no record of his further activities after his return from Jamaica, but his wife died not long after. In due course he married again, and the one son of his second marriage grew up to become minister[16] of the Congregational Church in Dorking, Surrey.

Why Henry Pitman should return to Barbados remains a mystery, but return he did in 1691, and died there in 1693. A lawsuit about his property in England between his brother John and his married sisters was settled[17] in favour of the sisters.

Two of the Axminster Congregationalists, John Ashwood and Thomas Smith, had been arrested on their way home after the fight at Norton St. Philip, and both were at Wells sentenced to be hanged at Shepton Mallet. 'But', says the Axminster Book[18] of Remembrance, 'God so over-ruled this sentence, that by endeavours used, a Reprieve was granted him [John Ashwood] and afterwards a pardon procured', and he lived to become Minister of a church in Exeter. 'As for Thomas Smith, he was sentenced also to dye, and the time being come to be led forth of the prison house in order to his execution, another prisoner standing forth in his name was carried out of the prison in his stead'. Joseph Smith of Chard was also sentenced at Wells[19] to be hanged at Shepton Mallet, and it may be that he was counted twice. Francis Smith of Honiton and John Smith, who may have come from Chard or from Upottery, were also sentenced at Wells to be hanged, Francis at Frome, John at Norton St. Philip, and one of them might have 'stood forth' when Thomas Smith was called.

The said Thomas Smith continuing in the prison a little time longer, having a fitt opportunity, made his escape; but he being a man of a weak constitution of body, (though he had a prosperous soul) grew very weak. Afterwards being tost from place to place, he remained but a few weeks ere he dyed.

The 'endeavours used' on behalf of John Ashwood suggest a substantial bribe, but so far no record of his pardon has been found. Perhaps he had to be content with the General Pardon.

Another who reached Barbados was Daniel Manning, the blacksmith's apprentice, who gave Monmouth's army the slip and was discharged from Kirke's Lambs after they had marched[20] to Taunton. He needed his certificate of service both in Taunton and in London, where he was thought to be a fugitive rebel. On Tower Hill Manning met one John Peirceson, who pretended to be helping him to find a job 'four miles over the river', but when they got there, Manning found he was being kidnapped, and was physically bullied into making his mark on an indenture to serve a master for four years in Barbados. He was shipped with 22 others, not rebels, and some were sold in Barbados, while others went on to Nevis. When he reached Barbados, Manning appealed to the Lieut-Governor, Edward Stede, for release and repatriation. Stede forwarded Manning's statement and a certified copy of his certificate to the Lords of Trade and Plantations. There Manning disappears from history, but perhaps not entirely from tradition, for Barbadian folklore[21] has it that 'Manning co-habited with a negress', and maybe their descendants are there to this day. There was another transportee, a Monmouth rebel, named William Manning, but he, having been sold as a slave, was probably more straitly kept than was Daniel while awaiting the decision of the Lords of Trade and Plantations. Daniel certainly did not return to be married or buried at Stoke St. Mary. There are two families of Mannings in Barbados.

Richard Goodenough perhaps merits a paragraph. After leaving Bridgwater with Wade, whose little company dispersed near Ilfracombe, Goodenough was taken[22] by one of Captain Prideaux's troops' and sent to London for interrogation. As one who had come with Monmouth he was excepted from the General Pardon. He was imprisoned[23] in Newgate, but allowed to have access to pen, ink and paper. 'Having made a discovery' Goodenough was spared the death penalty, but was sent[24] to Elizabeth Castle, Jersey, 'for life'. Before he went to Jersey he had been used as King's Evidence against Alderman Cornish, Dr Charles Bateman, and Lord Delamere. Rather surprisingly his release was ordered[25] on 30 May 1687. Goodenough appears to have taken himself off to Ireland, and there practised as a lawyer.

Lord Grey had been present at Monmouth's last interview with King James, who on the next day wrote[26] to his nephew, William of Orange. 'Lord Gray', he said, 'apeared more resolut and engenius, and never so much as once asked for his life. His execution cannot be so soone by reason of some forms, which are requisite to be complyed with'. Grey was permitted to have a servant in the Tower, and was allowed[27] visitors: his brothers and sisters, his daughter Mary, the Countess of Berkeley, his mother-in-law, and his much-forgiving wife. He was at once provided with pens, ink, and paper, and understood that a written confession was required. In due course it was written, the major part being about the Rye House Plot. Finding it financially more profitable to keep Grey alive, the King granted him a[28] pardon, allowing the reversal of his outlawry, and restored his title as Lord Grey of Warke. He was made to appear as King's Evidence against Lord Brandon and Lord Delamere, but like Wade had only hearsay evidence to give.

Grey managed to avoid joining King James when he began his march against William of Orange, a fall from his horse[29] conviently incapacitating him. He quickly threw in his lot with the Convention Parliament. After Queen Mary's death in 1694 Grey began to take a much more active part[30] in the House of Lords, and was soon recognised as one of their most effective speakers. A year later King William revived for him the Earldom of Tankerville, once held by his ancestors. He was sworn of the Privy Council, and began to be employed as a commissioner for special cases and as chairman of special committees. After the discovery of the Assassination Plot in 1696, Grey led the House of Lords in approval of The Association in support of King William. He was made Deputy President of the Board of Trade, declined appointment as First Lord of the Admiralty, but accepted the post of Second Lord of the Treasury. In 1700 Grey was made[31] Lord Privy Seal, but he died the following year. There was more in Ford Grey than people had thought in 1685.

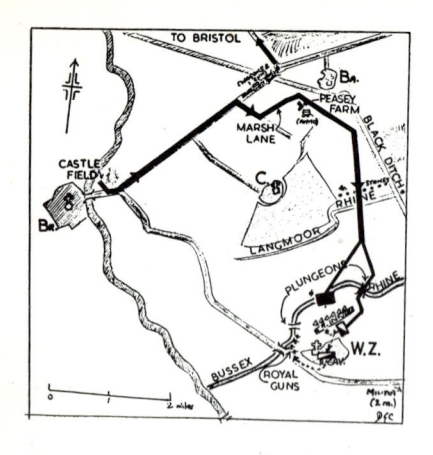

MONMOUTH'S PLAN

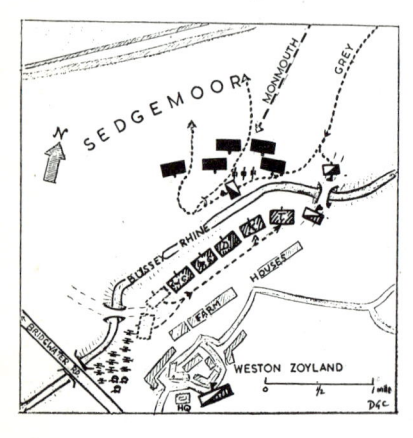

MONMOUTH'S ATTACK: 1.30 a.m.

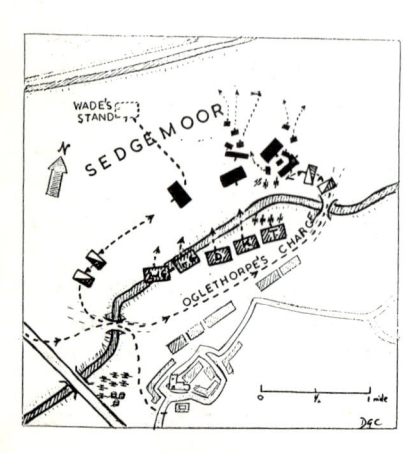

FEVERSHAM'S COUNTER-ATTACK

A Guide to the Battlefield of Sedgemoor

As the crow flies, Sedgemoor battlefield lies about three-quarters of a mile NNE of Weston Zoyland Church, but 1¼ miles by road and drove. The footpath runs from the west end of the Church to the middle of Monmouth Road. Cars should follow Standards Road (just beyond the Sedgemoor Inn and the Post Office), Broadstone, and Monmouth Road. Do not turn into Bussex Square, but continue along Monmouth Road, which turns left to Bussex Farm (at the junction with Liney Road). Here the route turns sharp left along Sugg or Zog Drove, a rough ride if you take the car. A quarter of a mile along this drove, Langmoor Drove turns off NE at an acute angle, and the monument is 300 yards along this on the left with Graveyard Field behind it, where about 1384 men were buried.

The Bussex Rhine, which can be traced only on an aerial map, ran westward from a point not quite halfway along the Langmoor Drove, and bent round south-west for half a mile or perhaps more, before it bent round again to the south. The Upper Plungeon (or crossing) must have been about a quarter of a mile SE of the monument, the two plungeons being at least three-quarters of a mile apart, with room for five battalions to be deployed in line. It must be emphasised that the droves and the present water-courses are modern, the Bussex Rhine having been filled in long ago. The Lower Plungeon must have been shortly after the Bussex turned south.

As you stand at the monument, Pendon Hill is due north, a mile-and-a-half away. Chedzoy Church is a mile-and-a-quarter to the NW. Monmouth led his army between these two points, and sited his three small guns about 200 yards east of the monument, to fire obliquely SW across at the Royal Scots (Dumbarton's Foot, commanded by Col. Douglas), the right of the Royal line. Beyond them were the First Guards (now the Grenadier Guards) under the Duke of Grafton, and the Coldstream Guards under Col. Sackville. When the battle started, Kirke's and Trelawney's regiments were out of action, away beyond the Coldstream, with no enemy

A veteran of Monmouth's infantry, armed with a pike made from a scythe-blade. He is wearing obsolete armour from the Civil War and carries a cavalry sword of that period. The regimental coat is of the type discarded by the Somerset Militia at Axminster. RIGHT One of the Grenadier Company of the Foot Guards. Recently formed, they were intended as shock troops and were armed with a satchell full of grenades and a musket (he is holding a plug bayonet). It is these troops that Monmouth trapped in the lanes of Philips Norton.

---

in front of them until Lord Churchill, newly promoted Major General, marched these two battalions behind the Guards and the Royal Scots, and aligned them further to the right of the royal line.

Major Sir Francis Compton of the Blues had fallen back from Chedzoy to guard the Upper Plungeon, having two collisions with Lord Grey's Horse on the way, and getting wounded. Resuming command, he fought a fierce and successful little action against Captain Jones's troop of rebel horse. The rest of Lord Grey's cavalry rode along the Bussex, looking in vain for a crossing, and riding off the field when struck by a volley or volleys from the royal infantry.

Major Wade led the rebel Red Regiment somewhere near the present monument, and wheeled right to deploy his column into line facing the

A musketeer of Dumbarton's Regiment with the matchlock musket which, by 1685, was rapidly becoming obsolete in the British Army, and he is struggling to keep alight the slow-burning fuse, or 'match'. The glow from these matches guided Monmouth's infantry to the right of the British Line, held by the Dumbartons. RIGHT Trooper from a British cavalry regiment threatens with his sword to enforce contributions to his foraging expedition. On his head he retains the iron lining ('skull') of his hat, and carries a short-barrelled musket on shoulder belts. In action he would probably wear armour over his regimental coat. (Drawings by Michael Dickinson)

Royal Scots. While he was getting his men into line, for the pace of their advance had disordered them, Col. Matthews' Yellow Regiment, following the Red, opened fire on the Scots, whose match-locks gave away their position in the dark. Wade's men, without orders, also opened fire, and Wade could not get them to make the charge he intended across the Bussex. The Scots and the Guards suffered casualties, probably more from the little guns than from the musket-fire.

The royal guns had been sited to command the road from Bridgwater to Weston Zoyland, which showed reasonable foresight, but as Monmouth did not come by that road the guns were at first useless. Bishop Mews, however, had his coach-horses harnessed to the guns and brought six of them up, posting them in pairs between the infantry battalions, whence

One of Monmouth's musketeers with a long-barrelled sporting gun, game bag and powder-flask. Typical of the professional man from one of the West-country towns deeply committed to the cause, he is searching for a relevant text in his bible. RIGHT A captain of Monmouth's cavalry at a council of war. He is wearing a fashionable wig and is dressed in a long buff coat and gentlemen's long leather riding boots. He would be armed with a sword (which lies on the table) and a pistol.

---

they caused severe casualties among the rebel Foot, whose rear battalions were probably still in column and therefore vulnerable to artillery fire.

As dawn broke, Feversham brought his cavalry into action across the two plungeons against the rebel flanks; the rear regiments broke and fled. Wade fell back, and tried to withstand cavalry charges on his flanks. Three quarters of his men were killed, wounded or missing, but he managed to march the remaining 150 men back to Bridgwater, whence they dispersed as best they could.

There is an alternative route to the battlefield for those coming from Bridgwater or Chedzoy. The other end of Zog Drove leaves the Bridgwater road (A 372) about 100 yards before you come to the first red brick house of Weston Zoyland, about 1½ miles from the monument, a level walk but a rough ride. The drove runs NNE for 1000 yds and then turns at right angles ESE, meeting the Langmoor Drove about 500 yds from the angle.

Opposite Weston Zoyland Church there is a square redbrick house whose doorway is framed with Hamstone uprights and lintel preserved from the house that stood there in 1685. The old house was the home of the Bridge family, on whom some of Kirke's ruffians were billeted. One of them so grossly insulted Mrs Bridge, that her infuriated 12-year-old daughter Mary snatched the offending officer's sword and stabbed him dead. Brought before Colonel Kirke, she explained the provocation and the Colonel, accepting the explanation, gave her the sword to keep and pass on to her descendants. They preserved it for two centuries, and it is now in the Monmouth Room in the Blake Museum in Bridgwater.

Two miles away to the SE is the village of Middlezoy (zoy = island), where the Wilts Militia had been camped in reserve. There the French-born Adjutant of the Guards, Louis de Misiers, was buried, 'slaine on the 6th of July 1685 at the Battle of Weston, where he behaved himself with all the courage imaginable against the king's enemies commanded by the rebel Duke of Monmouth'. The brass tablet recording this is in the middle of the main aisle, level with the third pew from the front.

The monument erected in 1933

Notes and References

INTRODUCTION
1. Fifth Monarchy Men. The 2nd and 7th chapters of Daniel contain symbolic references to 4 kingdoms preceding the coming of the Messiah: Chaldean Babylon, the Persians, the Medes (who always in Daniel come after the Persians), and Alexander with his Successors. The Puritans of the 17th century regarded the Medes and the Persians as one kingdom, and thought the Romans were the 4th kingdom. The Fifth Monarchy Men thought that in the Rule of the Saints they were establishing the Fifth Monarchy, the Reign of King Jesus.
2. The Commons' resolution and Coleman's letter are quoted from G. M. Trevelyan's '*England under the Stuarts*', pages 387-8.

Chapter 1
1. Hickes' last speech, quoted in Muddiman's The Bloody Assizes, p. 107.
2. The story of the marriage certificate circulated verbally, with variations, but was printed by Lt. Col. J. Benett-Stanford, who heard Lord Herbert Scott tell it, in a booklet called "Monmouth the Rebel", printed by C. A. Woodward, Devizes, no date.
3. "The Army of Charles II" by John Childs, Routledge, 1976, pp. 51, 65.
4. The letters of the Duchess of Lauderdale in "Elizabeth of the Sealed Knot" by Doreen Cripps, pp. 224-227.
5. Place-names in the Stuart period: Ivelchester was only just being shortened to Ilchester. All names ending with "minster" were almost invariably spelt "mister", as Ilmister. Yeovil sometimes became "Evil". "Saint" was usually omitted, Stoke St. Gregory becoming Gregory Stoke, Norton St. Philip, Philip's Norton.
6. John Whiting: "Persecution Exposed", 1st edition 1715; 2nd edition 1791.
7. Allan Fea: "King Monmouth", Appendix B, pp. 409-416.
8. Gay: The Beggar's Opera, Act 2 Scene 13.
9. L'Allegro, lines 85-6: "Of herbs, and other country messes,
   Which the neat-handed Phyllis dresses".
   Sedley: "Phyllis is my only joy . . . She never fails to please". In "Child and Maiden" Sedley addresses Chloris, which suggests that Monmouth copied the poem, misreading Chloris as Clovis.

Chapter 2
1. Grey's story is told in "Cold Caleb" by Cecil Price, Melrose, 1956. Cold

Caleb is mentioned in Dryden's "Absalom and Achitophel" as one of Absalom's friends, and has been thought to represent Lord Grey, though one hardly thinks of him as cold.
[2] D.N.B.
[3] The preparations for the rebellion are best described in Nathaniel Wade's narrative in the Harleian MSS 6845 fo.266 in the British Library. The date of Wade's birth is given in D.N.B. as 1666, which is clearly a slip for 1646. His will was made in 1716, when he was 70, and is quoted in 'The Book of Nailsea Court' by S. Hope Evans.
[4] Holmes is mentioned in Sir C. H. Firth's 'Cromwell's Army', p.52; and in D.N.B. His interrogation after Sedgemoor is in Lansdowne MSS 1152A fo.240 in the B.L.
[5 & 7] Lansdowne 1152A fo.237, under dates July 16 and August 16.
[6] Stopford-Sackville MSS. H.M.C. vol.1, p.23; and Fea, ch.1, n.7, pp.212-3.
[8] Louis Duras was made Lord Duras in 1673, and by special remainder succeeded his father-in-law as Earl of Feversham in 1677. It is interesting to find him reputedly so high in Charles II's favour. In 1685 he commanded the royal army against Monmouth.
[9] Both Grey and Wade mention Dare's activity in planning the rebellion.
[10] See 'The Army of Charles II', as ch.1, n.3.
[11] D.N.B. and C.S.P.D. J.II. vol.I. § 1445 and 1449.
[12] 'Ferguson the Plotter' by James Ferguson, and D.N.B. Dr Thomas Tenison's account of Monmouth's conversation before his execution. Tenison was then Vicar of St. Martin's-in-the-Fields, the church where Monmouth worshipped when he was in London. He became Arch-bishop of Canterbury in 1694.
[13] D.N.B. and ch.13 below.
[14] John and Phineas Showers, late of London, were pardoned in November 1686, C.S.P.D. J.II, vol.2, § 1119. Turner's pardon § 1230. Interrogations of Tellier, Burton, Jones, Kidd, and Ascue (who spelt his name Askew) are in Lansdowne MSS as n.4 above.

Chapter 3
[1] The story of William Way, the letter to James Carrier, the other letter, and the story of the horsemen are in the Axe Papers in Harleian MSS 6845, commencing fo.284.
[2] The Axminster Book of Remembrance, compiled in 1687. An article by the present writer, quoting the references to the rebellion is in 'Proceedings of Somerset Archaeological Society', vol.119 (1975).
[3] Dassell's account is in Harleian 6845, fo.252, and was printed in S&D N&Q Vol. XXVII (1961).
[4] Harleian 6845, fo.256. Printed in English Historical Documents, Vol.8.
[5] Names and occupations in "Presentment of the Rebels", B.L.Add.Mss 30077. Photostat copy in Somerset R.O.
[6] "The Dying Speeches" were first printed in 1689, reprinted several times, notably in Muddiman's "The Bloody Assizes".
[7] Whiting, as Ch.1 n.6, p.294.

Chapter 4
[1] Wade as Ch.2, n.3.
[2] A brass tablet in Bridport Church records the death of Lieut. Coker. There is a

photograph of this in B. Little's "Monmouth Episode". A stone in the chancel of Bradford Abbas Church records William Harvey, wounded at Bridport on June 14, died of wounds July 2 1685.

[3] Coad's book "A Memorandum of the Wonderful Providences of God to a poor unworthy creature (from 12th of June 1685 unto the 24th of November in the year 1690) in and after the Revolution between the Duke of Monmouth and King James" was printed in 1849. Official documents always call him Thomas Coad. Whether Th^o was misread as Jno or vice versa we cannot tell. Lord Macaulay saw Coad's manuscript (or a ms. copy) and he calls Coad John.

[4] Manning's story is in the Colonial Office Papers in the P.R.O. CO 1 59, fo 75-7. A shortened version is in C.S.P. COL. VOL 12 561.

Chapter 5

[1] The first edition was entitled "The Protestant Martyrs or the Bloody Assizes" and was printed in 1689. The second edition added the Dying Speeches. The fifth edition was The Western Martyrology or the Bloody Assizes". In Muddiman's edition, 1939, the anonymous narrative is on pp 164-170.

[2] Harleian mss 7006, fo.196. The names of the other Maids of Taunton may be found in their pardon, C.S.P.D. J.II, vol.2, 785 (and 750). Beside those already named the list runs Miss Musgrave, Sarah Langham, Anna Grove, Mary and Margaret Hucklebridge, Mary and Sarah Walter, Elizabeth Knash, Elizabeth Bidgood, Mary Smith, Mary Bird, Grace Germain, Elizabeth Waye, Mary Page, Elizabeth March, Hannah and Hester Whetham, Hannah and Sarah Stacey, all of Taunton, and Elizabeth Dyke of Dulverton.

[3] Information sent by Taunton Corporation to the Lord Chief Justice, printed in Stopford-Sackville MSS pp. 24-26.

[4] Harleian MSS 7006 fo.184; printed in Fea, p. 249.

[5] Several proclamations "in the King's name" as n.4 above, fo.186, 188, 190 and 191. Also Stopford-Sackville, p. 8.

[6] Presentment of the Rebels, as n.5 of ch. 3.

[7] Ferguson, as no.12 of ch.2.

Chapter 6

[1] Presentment as no.5 of ch.3.

[2] Manning as n.4 of ch.4.

[3] D.N.B. For better estimates of Feversham's military capacity see Lt-Col. A. H. Burne's "The Battlefields of England" and Brigadier Peter Young and John Adair's "Hastings to Culloden".

[4] The Rev. John Hickes, B.A. of Trinity College, Dublin, had been Curate of Saltash, Cornwall, but was ejected at the Restoration. He remained there as a Nonconformist preacher, but had moved to eastern England. It was for sheltering him that Lady Alice Lisle was executed. His younger brother was a Conformist and became Dean of Worcester, and subsequently a Nonjuring Bishop. John's "Dying Speech", printed in "The Bloody Assizes", pp. 104-112, was probably the paper he sent to his wife with his last letter to her, October 3rd 1685, printed on p.116.

[5] "Records of a Church of Christ in Bristol, 1640-87".

[6] Wade as n.2 of ch.2.

[7] The letter is or was in private hands, but was printed in S&D N&Q.

8 Feversham's reports to King James, written in French, are in Stopford-Sackville MSS, vol 1, pp. 4-22. Also there is a very valuable anonymous account, in English, of Feversham's movements from June 20 to July 6, on pp. 12-19.
9 Coad as n.3 of ch.4.
10 Gifford's grandson's account was written in the front of his copy of the "Western Martyrology", now in the library of Baptist College, Bristol. It is printed in the "Records" as n.5 above.
11 "Memoirs and Travels of Sir John Reresby, Bart.", p. 270 of the edition of 1904.
12 As n.8 of ch.6.
13 Wade, as n.3 of ch.2.
14 Coad, as n.3 of ch.4.
15 North Street is still known locally as Bloody Lane. Blood Close is now Lyde Green.
16 Monmouth's guns certainly were "very little pieces" to judge by such cannon balls as have been found at Sedgemoor. One, ploughed up with a skeleton in a field near Weston Zoyland almost certainly came from one of Monmouth's guns, and measured 2¼ inches in diameter, and weighed 1¾ lb. Its outer casing had rusted away, so its original measurements were probably those of the "Falcon's" shot, 2¾ inches and 2¼ lb. It was kindly lent to me by Mrs. Parkes, then of Drayton Court, near Langport.
17 Barillon's despatches to Louis XIV are printed in Charles James Fox's James II. Extracts have been printed in various books.
18 "A Journal of the Proceedings of the Duke of Monmouth . . . kept by Mr. Edward Dummer, then serving in the Train of Artillery Employed by his Majesty". The original is in the Pepysian Library at Magdalene College, Cambridge; there is a transcript in B.L. Add.MSS.31956.
19 The traditional story may be true, perhaps of an unknown soldier, transferred to one known to have been wounded in the arm.
20 Lord Dumblane's letter is in B.L. Add.MSS.28050, fo.47.

Chapter 7

1 Feversham, as n.8 of ch.6.
2 The Clubmen were presented with the rebels, as n.5 of ch.3. The Clubmen come into the story on pp. 58-9.
3 Wade, as n.3 of ch.2.
4 See n.1. of ch.5.
5 Wade.
6 C.S.P.D. J.11. Vol.I. § 1113, dated July 2.
7 An example is quoted below on p. 87.
8 The interrogations of Richard Goodenough and Captain Tellier are in Lansdowne 1152 A fo.242 and 269.
9 Presentment, as n5 of ch.3, sheet 38.
10 Ecclesiastica, as n.2 of ch.3.
11 The Axe Papers, as n.1 of ch.3.
12 "The Monmouth Episode", p.158.
13 My friend, Mr Stephen Morland, M.A. of Glastonbury, first identified Thomas Plaice as the leader of the Clubmen.

14. Friends' Quarterly Meeting Minutes are in Somerset R.O.DD/SFR
15. Quakers always used numbers for the months. Until 1751 the year began on March 25th, March being reckoned 1st month. 7th month would therefore be September.
16. Somerset R.O. DD/SFR 10/2 fo.50
17. Treasury Books, 1685-89, vol.8, part 2, p. 1684, Dec.20, 1686; Gaol Book, quoted by Inderwick, Sidelights on the Stuarts, p. 393. C.S.P.D. J.II, vol.2, § 1667, April 11, 1687 and § 1833, May 31, 1687.
18. Wade.
19. Coad.
20. Cold Caleb, p. 183.
21. Stopford-Sackville, p.12.
22. William Clarke's letter, Somerset R.O. DD/SF 3109.
23. Lord Dumblane's letter of July 1st was printed in S&D N&Q Vol.10, 296-7.

Chapter 8
1. N.8 of ch.6.
2. Lansdowne 1152 A fo. 237, 242, 240, and Wade under date Sept. 28.
3. Harleian 6845, fo.264.
4. In the Gaol Book their names are marked "Certificate allowed".
5. Presentment of Rebels, as n.5 of ch.3.
6. Jeffreys' report, B.L. Add.MSS 90337.
7. Either buried at Sedgemoor or safely in hiding.
8. Somerset R.O. contains "A faithful Testimony from the peaceable people called Quakers in the Counties of Somerset, Devon and Dorset, upon occasion of the late Insurrection and Rebellion ... utterly denying all plotting, sedition, contriving or Assisting in any Insurrection or Rebellion, or to use any force or violence whatsoever ... And if any ... reputed a Quaker ... have been overcome and join or Assist in the late ... rebellion, the same are wholly disowned ... as not being of us ..." (DD/SFR 10/2 fo.48) Letters between Friends in Ivelchester and Friends in London in August 1685 (in the same deposit of documents) have enabled Mr Morland to identify the 9 backsliding Quakers, in his edition of Quaker Minutes published by Somerset Record Society. Three of the Quaker rebels appear later in this story.
9. Stopford-Sackville p.16 n.8 of ch.6.
10. See above p. 48. The Queen's Regiment had become The Queen Dowager's Regiment. (They later became The Queen's Royal West Surrey Regiment.)
11. Account written by the Rev. Andrew Paschall, Rector of Chedzoy, in B.L. Add MSS 4162, fo.127.
12. Wade as n.3 of ch.2.
13. Ferguson's account contributed to Archdeacon Eachard's History, and quoted from there in "Ferguson the Plotter", n. 12 of ch. 2.
14. Oldmixon, History of England, p. 703.
15. Mr David Chandler, Deputy Head of War Studies at Sandhurst, has suggested that the gun was left behind because it had developed a squeaky wheel, that might betray the approach of the rebels.
16. See n.22 of ch.7.
17. Defoe: "Tour through England and Wales in 1724", vol. 1 p. 269 in the Everyman edition.

[18] Paschall's shorter account which was found in a box deposited at Hoare's Bank, London, in 1706, and not opened until the middle of this century. It was printed in S&D N&Q, Vol. 28 (1968).
[19] See n.13 above.
[20] Stopford-Sackville p.17.
[21] He was excepted from the General Pardon, but pardoned in 1687, C.S.P.D. J.II, vol.2. § 1833.
[22] Paschall, quoted in "Cold Caleb", p. 187.
[23] Shorter account.
[24] e.g. the anonymous account, n.1 of ch.5; and King James' account in Harleian 6845.
[25] Fortescue: History of the British Army, vol.1, p. 329.
[26] Dummer as n.18 of ch.6. Also anonymous royalist account, Stopford-Sackville p. 18.
[27] Stopford-Sackville p. 19.
[28] Oldmixon p. 704.
[29] Duke of Ormonde's MSS, quoted in Fea, p. 294.
[30] B.L. Add. MSS 28050. 48.
[31] See n.7 of ch.7.

Chapter 9

[1] Oldmixon p. 704.
[2] Oldmixon p. 704.
[3] Wheeler: Iter Bellicosum, printed in Camden Miscellany, xii, 1910.
[4] Oldmixon, p. 704; Adlam was probably a Nonconformist. Members of the family were members of Horningsham Congregational Chapel, the oldest Nonconformist chapel in England, built in 1566, originally Presbyterian.
[5] I am indebted to the Vicar, the Rev. C. E. E. Meredith, for this tradition and for showing me the churchwardens' account book.
[6] Whiting p. 302.
[7] See n.5 above.
[8] The MS is in the possession of J. Stevens Cox, Esq. of Guernsey. Dr Dunning kindly gave me a copy. Chedzoy's share of the wages bill was £2-4-1, the demand note is also in Mr Cox's possession.
[9] Those who came with the Duke from Holland were excluded from the General Pardon. If they were not named in that list, they were presumably already killed.
[10] Presentment of Rebels, fo.13 v :Clement Bovett of Yarcombe Slaine in ye Service; John Rugg dead; Wm. Harvey, sen mort; Wm. Loring killed; Nich Michell killed.
[11] Wheeler, as above n.3; W. Windham: Journal of the movements of the Regiment of Wiltshire Militia commanded by Col. Wyndham during Monmouth's Rebellion", quoted in the History of Devizes.
[12] Quoted in Toulmin's History of Taunton, 1874, p. 138.
[13] CO I 59 fo. 76.
[14] Presentment fo. 44v.
[15] Somerset R.O. D/P 4/1/1.
[16] "A Relation of the Great Sufferings and Strange Adventures of Henry Pitman, Chyrurgion to the late Duke of Monmouth", 1689.
[17] Whiting, 301-2.

[18] N.3. of ch.4.
[19] Joseph Winter of "Ivilchister". His bill is quoted on p. 97 below.
[20] Swain's story is traditional, with the stones as corroborative evidence. A John Swayne (probably a Dorset man) was captured after the Bloody Assizes, brought to the Spring Assize at Dorchester 1686 and pardoned by Royal Proclamation. Gaol Book quoted by Inderwick, as n.17 of ch.8.
[21] Traditional story accepted by Roberts, vol.2, p. 216, and Fea, p. 384n.
[22] Aldersey's story was told me independently by two of his descendants, Mrs Bower of Cheadle Hulme, and Miss M. Smith then of Taunton. The tradition is also recorded in Harry Speight's book Through Yorkshire from Goole to Halifax.
[23] Harleian 6845.
[24] Powell's Relation of the taking of Nathaniel Wade, Harleian, 6845, 260.
[25] Harleian 6845, fo. 264.
[26] C.S.P.D. J.II. Vol.I 1518.
[27] This family tradition was told me by Lt-Col. Newton Wade, a direct descendant of Nathaniel's elder brother, John.
[28] Treasury Books, 1685-89, Vol.8, Part 2, under date July 15, 1686.
[29] Book of Nailsea Court of S. Hope Evans.
[30] The route of Monmouth's flight has been described in many books, notably by George Roberts and Allan Fea.
[31] The letter is in the Bodleian. It was transcribed by Roberts, vol.2 pp. 112-3, and by Fea, 318-9.
[32] Memoirs of Thomas, Earl of Ailesbury, vol.1, p.117.
[33] See Fea pp. 320-1.
[34] Ailesbury p. 119, 83, 108, 21.
[35] Reresby as n.11 of ch.6, p. 270.
[36] Ailesbury p. 119.
[37] The document is in the Bodleian. There is a facsimile in the "Jackdaw" of the Monmouth Rebellion, and in Fea, p. 366. It is also printed in Stopford-Sackville, p. 22.
[38] Tenison's account, see n.12 of ch.2.
[39] Ailesbury, 76, 75.
[40] Ailesbury, 118.
[41] Encyclopaedia Britannica; Monmouth's eldest son by Eleanor Needham also became a Major-General, known as James Crofts.
[42] Fea, p. 359.

Chapter 10
[1] Oldmixon, p. 704.
[2] Macaulay, vol.I. p. 311, n.
[3] The Battle of Sedgemoor, 1932.
[4] Presentment of the Rebels, n.5 of ch.3.
[5] Overseers of the Poor Accounts, Holwell, Dorset.
[6] Somerset R.O. D/P/KLN 4/1/2.
[7] His article in vol.5 of Proceedings of Dorset Natural History and Archaeological Field Club, pp. 99-135.
[8] F. A. Inderwick printed the Gaol Book of the Western Circuit in his book, "Sidelights on the Stuarts" (2nd edition 1891) There is a photostat copy of the

original in Somerset R.O. It was written in a difficult Court Hand, which Mr. Inderwick's amanuensis did not always read correctly, always reading "Nic" for Nicholas as "Ric" for Richard, and once reading Elias as "Chas", an abbreviation never used in Stuart documents. The Gaol Book is in P.R.O. ASS1/23/3.

[9] B.L. Add.MSS 90337, photostat in Somerset R.O.
[10] Minute Book of the Western Division of Somerset, from 15 May 1676 to 10 Nov. 1718, now in Somerset R.O. Monthly Meeting at Taunton 12 April 1686: "That John Hellier of Marke be visited by friends, who tooke up Armes in ye late Insurrection contrary to ye principle of trueth . . . That Francis Scott be visited for his appearance in ye late Insurrection . . ." (P. 94.)
[11] Evelyn's Diary, under date July 8, 1685.
[12] C.S.P.D. JII, vol.I. § 1249, 1250; vol.2, 876; Treasury Books, 1685-89, Part 1, Dec. 5.
[13] Lansdowne 1152 A fo. 227 onwards.
[14] Whiting p. 322.
[15] Pitman as n.16 of ch.9.
[16] Ailesbury, vol.I. p. 122.
[17] Presentment of Rebels opening sheets. The Court of King's Bench tried cases Rex v. commoner: Common Pleas, commoner v. commoner: Court of Exchequer, cases concerning the King's revenue. Assizes were sittings (asseyez-vous) of the King's justices. Quarter Sessions were sittings of the County Magistrates.
[18] Autobiography of Richard Baxter, Everyman edition, pp. 259-263.
[19] The Burgess Roll of Shrewsbury for 1654, when John Jeffreys was admitted, lists his children and their ages. George, the future L.C.J., was born in 1644. M. C. Balfour in Times Lit. Supplement, Aug.1, 1929.
[20] In 1670 William Penn and William Mead, locked out of their Quaker Meeting House, held a meeting for Worship in the street. They were indicted for riotous assembly, Jeffreys prosecuting. The jury found them Not Guilty, but were fined 40 marks each. Edward Bushell, refusing to pay, was imprisoned. He sued out a Writ of Habeas Corpus, and L. C. J. Vaughan ruled it illegal to fine or imprison a juryman because of his verdict.
[21] The cruel jests are given in Locke's Western Rebellion. Macaulay printed one but held the other too horrible to reprint.
[22] Stopford-Sackville, p. 26.
[23] Grace Abounding, p. 127 in Everyman edition.
[24] Whiting, pp. 250-1.
[25] Macaulay, vol.1. 312-214 (Popular edition) followed the account in State Trials.
[26] The wording is given by Pitman for the Assize at Wells. It is clear that Jeffreys had said much the same at Dorchester.
[27] B.L. Ad.MSS 90337.
[28] Macaulay 1.316, following the Memoirs of William Kiffen, the young man's grandfather.
[29] Locke's Western Rebellion, and contemporary Broadsheet.
[30] Roberts: The Life, Progresses and Rebellion of James, Duke of Monmouth, 1844.

31. Jeffreys' Report (n, 27 above), Colonial Office Papers, CO 1 59, etc. and Hotten's Original Lists.
32. Dorset R.O. quoted in Mr. Chenevix Trench's 'Western Rising'.
33. J. Hutchins: History and Antiquities of the County of Dorset, vol.2 p. 448.
34. Whiting p. 323.
35. A List of the Names of the Rebels that were executed (at various places), London, Printed by E. Miller, next Door to Mr. Shipton's Coffee-House near Fleet-Bridge, 1686. The sheet is marked "This may be Printed, R.P. April the 1st, 1686." A re-print.
36. N.8 of ch.10.
37. Jeffreys' Report, Add.MSS 90337.
38. Jeffrey's duplicate report in Treasury Books, vol.8, Part 1. pp. 414-425.
39. Clement Bovett of Yarcombe. N.10 of ch.9.
40. H.M.C. quoted in Muddiman's Bloody Assizes, pp. 38-9.
41. Gaol Book, as n.8 above.
42. Sir G. N. Clark: The Later Stuarts, p. 120. He also says, on the same page, "Poverty and unemployment among the wage-earners were Monmouth's recruiting agents". In "England in the reigns of James II and William III" the late David Ogg says (p. 149) "It was the year 1686, not 1685, that was noted as a year of special hardship in the clothing industry . . . (The Levant Company, in difficulties, took less than its usual amount of west country cloth.) The majority of the rebels were peasants, not craftsmen . . . There was not a word about economic matters in the declaration of Lyme."
43. B.L. Add.MSS 34516, fo. 21-24, quoted in Muddiman's Bloody Assizes, pp. 226-231.
44. Whiting, p. 323.
45. Quoted in Muddiman, p. 40.
46. Jeffreys' report, CO papers and Hotten's Lists.
47. Postscript to Sunderland's letter to Jeffreys, Sept. 14. C.S.P.D. § 1629.
48. As n.46 above.
49. See pp. 58, 87 above.
50. Muddiman p. 32.
51. Presentment of Rebels, 39v.
52. Macaulay 1. 317, following the Memoirs of William Kiffen, the grandfather of Hannah and Benjamin.
53. Coad's narrative.
54. Quoted in Muddiman pp. 133-6.
55. Locke: Western Rebellion, p. 6; Also "Bloody Assizes", p. 172.
56. CO/I/58, fo. 285-6.
57. Oldmixon p. 704.
58. D.N.B.
59. Macaulay 1.326, and C.S.P.D. J.II, vol. 2, 292.
60. Quoted by Judge Parry: The Bloody Assize, from Correspondence of the Family of Hatton, Camden Society, 1878.

Chapter 11
1. Muddiman pp. 39 and 143.
2. Muddiman pp. 133-6.
3. Whiting pp. 303-4.

4   Somerset R.O. Phelips MSS DD/PH.
5   Vol. IV of the Register of Proceedings at Sessions: Brewton Sessions, Anno 3 James II, 1687. Petition of Jo. Winter, chyr^n for payment £36.10-0. (£1 more than his original bill.) "This Courte . . . doth allowe and approve of the same bill, and doeth hereby order and require the present Treasurers of the Hospittalls of either division of the county . . . to pay and reimburse unto the said petitioner, Jo. Winter, the aforementioned summe by equal porcions, each Treasurer to pay one moyety thereof".
6   Coad's Memorandum.
7   The printed text has "Haker", which led some to look for a J. Hacker. Only Jo. Hawker fits the requirements: Joseph; a man from Chard, tried at Wells, and "escaping in England". CO 1/58, fo. 285-6.
8   Probably John Shepherd of Crewkerne, who had been sentenced to be hanged at Wells.
9   Quoting Psalm 124.
10 A tropical fever or delirium, which often caused sailors to leap overboard.
11 King James instructed the colonial governors to get the colonial assemblies to pass a law to retain convicted rebels for ten years servitude. Pitman quotes the act of the Barbadian Assembly, which included fierce penalties for aiding the escape of a convicted rebel. C.S.P. J.II. Col. Vol 12. § 404, Oct. 11. 1685.
12 Letters of John Pinney, 1679-1699. There is an account of John Pinney in "Calamy Revised".
13 The full text is "If Nathaniel come to London, I shall be glad to see him here and Azariah allso if possible and prudent". For ease of reading I have not inserted omission dots.
14 Gaol Delivery Book.
15 Jeffreys' report and Broadsheet.
16 Broadsheet, n. 35 of ch.10.
17 CO 1/59 and 66. Also in Hotten's Lists, p. 320.
18 Nathaniel's account book, in Bristol University Library.
19 "A West India Fortune" by Richard Pares.
20 N.16 of ch.9.
21 CO 1/59 fo. 31, 82, 83, 150-1. Also in Hotten.
22 Presentment of the Rebels, 18v. 30v. 29.
23 Hotten, p. 315.
24 Probably a calabash.
25 C.S.P.D. J.II, vol.2. § 1833, dated May 31, 1687, a warrant for the pardon of Henry Pitman of Yeovell, William Pitman of Sandford Orcas, and 31 others, including Thomas Plase of Edington, Azarias Pinney of Axminster, James Carrier of Ilminster, William Way of Combe St. Nicholas, and Daniel Foe.

Chapter 12
1   C.S.P.D. W. III, 1689-90, April 3 and May 3.
2   I am indebted to my friends, Mr and Mrs Hughes, recently returned from Barbados, for this information about the Monmouth transportees in Barbados.
3   Treasury Books, vol.8, p. 2002-6.
4   C.S.P.D. J.II, vol.2, 345.
5   Treasury Book 8 (4) 1973. Friends' Quarterly Meeting Minutes for 24th of 7th

month, 1685. Newgate Calendar, December 1686. Treasury Book entry, Dec. 20th p. 1684. Wells Assize, Inderwick. Stay of Execution, C.S.P.D. § 1667, April 11; Pardon § 1833, May 31, 1687.
6. Treasury Book, 8. p. 1798.
7. Treasury Book, 8. p. 1973.
8. C.S.P.D. J.II, vol.2 § 1417; Treasury Book 8, part 2 p. 1253.
9. Treasury Book 8, part 2, p. 1618.
10. Treasury Book 8, part 2, p. 1820
11. Treasury Book 8, part 2, p. 919.
12. Treasury Book 8, part 2, p. 985.
13. Treasury Book 8, part 2, p. 1545.
14. Treasury Book 8, part 2, p. 985, Nov. 8 and Dec. 24.
15. Presentment of Rebels, 30 and 28v.
16. C.S.P.D. J.II Vol. I. § 1840.
17. Quoted in Muddiman p. 41.
18. Depositions sworn by witnesses in the action Gardner v. Loder early in King William's reign. Dr R. W. Dunning very kindly lent me photostat copies of the depositions.
19. Inderwick, Sidelights on the Stuarts, Gaol Book.
20. Treasury Book 8 p. 1894 and following pages.
21. Lyon Turner: Original Records of Early Nonconformity under Persecution and Indulgence, vol. 2, p. 1109. Depositions as in n.18. Treasury Book as n. 20.
22. B. L. Add. MSS 90337. Treasury Book 8, Part 1.
23. Gaol Book in Inderwick, as n.19.
24. Treasury Book 8, Part 2 under date January 18 (1686).
25. Treasury Book 8, as n.20.
26. Ecclesiastica, n.2 of ch.3.
27. C.S.P.D. J.II, vol.1 § 857.
28. Deposition of Joseph Holmes in the possession of J. Stevens Cox, Esq of St. Peter Port, Guernsey, who very kindly sent me a photostat.
29. Jeffreys' report and Locke.
30. C.S.P.D. J.II, vol.I § 1629.
31. Journal of the House of Commons, vol.x, pp. 113-6: examination of petition of Edmund Prideaux for restitution of the fine exacted by L. C. J. Jeffreys.
32. C.S.P.D. J.II, vol.2 § 153, 174.
33. C.S.P.D. J.II, vol.1, 2060, 2077.
34. C.S.P.D. J.II, vol.2, 265.
35. C.S.P.D. J.II, vol.2, 768.
36. Letters of the Duke of Somerset in Taunton Castle Museum, quoted in Fea, King Monmouth, P. 393, C.S.P.D. J.II, vol.2, 141, 254, 255, 750, 785.
37. Cold Caleb, ch.12.
38. Secret History, p. 123.
39. C.S.P.D. J.II, Vol.2 § 512, 625, 626, 627. P. Earle, 'Monmouth's Rebels', pp. 156-160.

Chapter 13
1. A long inscription in memory of William Oliver, M.D. F.R.S. mentions his Cornish descent. "He came into England an officer in King William's Army

in 1688 . . . till 1702 . . . And in the year 1714 he had the pleasure to have his Old Fellow Sailors committed to his Care".
2. C.S.P.D. W. III, 1690, Jan to April. The officer hanged at Taunton was not Col. Edward Matthews but Captain Arthur Matthews.
3. D.N.B.
4. C.S.P.D. J.II, vol.I 1212, 1423, 1430, 1512.
5. D.N.B. and 'Ferguson the Plotter.'
6 & 7. Wade, D.N.B. and C.S.P.D. J.II, vol.3, 559 and 1291.
8. Boswell's Johnson, vol.I, p. 582 in Everyman edition.
9. D.N.B.
10. 'Book of Nailsea Court'. S. Hope Evans.
11. See above pp. 77 and 9 n 27.
12. Harleian Ms 6845, 266-282, and Appendix.
13. Macaulay 1,347.
14. Somerset R.O. Roll of Meeting Houses registered at Quarter Sessions, Number 125.
15. Volume 37, Somerset Record Society.
16. Introduction to Coad's Memorandum, and Tablet in the church.
17. S&D N&Q Vol.21 p. 104.
18. Ecclesiastica, n.2 of ch.3.
19. Jeffreys' warrant, n.43 of ch.10, and Locke.
20. N.4 of ch.4.
21. N.2 of ch.12
22. Lansdowne 1152 A 242.
23. C.S.P.D. J.II, vol.I. 1277.
24-5. C.S.P.D. J.II, vol.2. 728, 792, and 1827.
26. Quoted in "Cold Caleb" p. 195.
27. C.S.P.D. J.II, vol.I, 1233.
28. C.S.P.D. J.II, vol.2, 646, Cold Caleb, p. 198.
29. Letter to John Caryll, quoted in "Cold Caleb" p. 213, facsimile opposite p. 156.
30. Cold Caleb, chapter 13.
31. D.N.B. and memorial tablet in South Harting Church, Sussex.

Postscript
1. I Will. and Mar. Cap.18, 1689: An Act for exempting their Majesties Protestant Subjects, dissenting from the Church of England, from the Penalties of certain Laws. Printed in Statutes of the Realm; in English Historical Documents, vol.viii; and in Grant Robertson: "Select Cases, Statutes and Documents".

Bibliography

ABBREVIATIONS
B.L. = British Library.
MSS = manuscripts.
Add. = Additional.
C.S.P.D. = Calendar of State Papers, Domestic.
C.S.P.Col. = Calendar of State Papers, Colonial.
C.O. = Colonial Office (papers).
P.R.O. = Public Record Office.
S.R.O. = Somerset Record Office.
H.M.C. = Historical Manuscripts Commission.
D.N.B. = Dictionary of National Biography.
S&D N&Q = Somerset and Dorset Notes and Queries.
J II = King James II.
W III = King William III.
fo = folio.
p = page.
ch = chapter.
n = note.
§ = paragraph.

MANUSCRIPT SOURCES
The most valuable is Nathaniel Wade's narrative, which is among the Harleian MSS 6845 in the British Library, and here printed as an Appendix. Also in Harleian 6845 are the papers of the Rev. Thomas Axe, which include some letters and his narrative, based on contemporary hearsay; two accounts of the capture of Wade; King James's account of the rebellion, based on his interrogation of captives and royal officers; and Dassell's account of Monmouth's landing (which has been printed in S & D N & Q Vol. XXVII).

Harleian MSS 7006 contain several of Monmouth's proclamations, and letters between the Duke of Albemarle, the Earl of Sunderland, and King James. Number 4689 is a beautiful fair copy of the Proceedings against the Rebels.

Lansdowne MSS 1152 A contain reports of a number of interrogations of captive rebels.

Among the Additional MSS number 4162 is the account written by the Rev. Andrew Paschall, Rector of Chedzoy, based on the information he received from his parishioners and, perhaps, others. Number 30077 is the Presentment of the Rebels; and Jeffreys' report to King James is Number 90 337. There are photostat copies of these two documents and of The Gaol Delivery Book in Somerset Record Office. The Gaol Book is printed (but with a few inaccuracies) in F. A. Inderwick's *Sidelights on the Stuarts*. Add MSS 31957 is a later version of Jeffreys' report, which is printed in the Treasury Books, 1685-88, vol. 8. Number 31956 is a transcript of Edward Dummer's Journal, the original of which is in the Pepysian Library at Magdalene College, Cambridge. Number 28050 contains two letters from Lord Dumblane to his father, then Earl of Danby, and subsequently Duke of Leeds.

Also in the British Library is Monmouth's Pocket Book, Egerton MS 1527.

The Gaol Delivery Book for the Western Circuit, 1685, is at the P.R.O. ASS1/23/3.

At the P.R.O. are Colonial Office papers, and among them lists of rebels transported on various ships to various destinations, records of deaths on the voyage, and of sales of the survivors. Some, but not all, of these lists were printed in J.C. Hotten's 'Original Lists of Emigrants, Exiles, Rebels, etc. who went from Great Britain to the American Plantations'. It was among these C.O. papers that I found the story of Daniel Manning.

Quaker documents now in Somerset Record Office include the Minute Books of 'the Western Division of Somerset Monthly Meeting' and the Quarterly Meeting of Bristol and Somerset Friends; and several letters between Friends in Ilchester and Friends in London. Another important letter is among the Clarke MSS in Somerset R.O.; where also is the Presentment of the Grand Jury at the Court Leet for the Manor of Taunton Deane, September 1685. The Phelips MSS include Sir Edward's letter about the disorderly retreat of the Somerset Militia from Axminster, and Dr Joseph Winter's bill for treating wounded rebels in Ilchester Gaol.

Nathaniel Pinney's account book is among the Pinney Papers in Bristol University Library, and George Wansey's ledger, with his observations on hearsay of the rebellion, is in Wiltshire R.O. at Trowbridge.

Documents in private hands include Depositions sworn in the case of

John Gardner, Clerk, v. Loder; and the defence of Joseph Holmes. I am grateful to Dr Dunning and Mr Stevens Cox for lending me photostat copies.

CONTEMPORARY SOURCES IN PRINT

Calendar of State Papers, Domestic: 3 vols, James II: warrants for arrests and pardons, etc. Vol.I of William III, 1689-90 for later history of some of Monmouth's officers.

Calendar of State Papers, Colonial: Transportation and sale of rebels.

Hotten, J.C.: Original Lists of Emigrants, etc.

Treasury Books, 1685-88, vol.8: Confiscations and sale of rebels' lands; Claims for rewards and compensation.

Stopford-Sackville MSS, H.M.C. vol.I contains Feversham's despatches to King James, written in French; also a very valuable anonymous narrative of the movements of Feversham's army; and other documents.

English Historical Documents, vol.8, 1660-1714, edited by Andrew Browning, M.A., D.Litt.

'A List of the Names of the Rebels that were executed', a broadsheet of 1686, recently reprinted. Not entirely accurate.

'The Bloody Assizes', also printed as 'The Western Martyrology', 1689 and several later editions. Reprinted in 1939, edited by W. Muddiman. Almost entirely accurate lists of sentences and executions. This edition also contains 'The Dying Speeches' and a valuable anonymous account of the rebellion by an officer who came with Monmouth but was probably not at Sedgemoor, perhaps Colonel Venner. Muddiman's list of those excepted from the General Pardon has omitted six names.

Ecclesiastica, the Book of Remembrance of Axminster Congregational Church, compiled in 1687, printed in 1874, and reprinted in 1976.

Records of a Church of Christ in Bristol, 1640-87, Bristol Record Society, vol.27. Broadmead Baptist Church. In a list of members some are marked as having had arms confiscated; some as 'strong supporters of the Duke of Monmouth'.

Dassell's account of Monmouth's landing is in S&D N&Q, vol.XXVII.

Coad, John, *A Memorandum of the Wonderful Providences of God to a poor unworthy creature,* printed in 1849.

Pitman, Henry, *A Relation of the Great Sufferings and Strange Adventures of Henry Pitman, Chyrurgion to the late Duke of Monmouth,* first printed in 1689, reprinted in 'Stuart Tracts', edited by Professor (subsequently Sir Charles) Firth, Constable.

Defoe, Daniel, *A Tour through the Whole Island of Great Britain,* 1724-26, reprinted in Everyman Library, 2 vols; also in Penguin, one vol. slightly abridged.

Ferguson, Robert, wrote an account of the rebellion for Archdeacon Eachard's History of England, but it is not in the first edition. Much of it is reprinted in *Robert Ferguson the Plotter* by James Ferguson, Edinburgh, 1887. Unreliable.

Grey, Lord, *The Secret History of the Rye House Plot and of Monmouth's Rebellion,* written in 1685, printed in 1754. Not very informative.

Oldmixon, John, *The History of England during the Reigns of the Royal House of Stuart,* 1730, includes personal recollections of the Sedgemoor days, when he was 12; also the escape of Dr Oliver.

Paschall, Rev. Andrew. His longer narrative is printed in S. Heywood's *Vindication of Mr Fox's History,* 1811. His shorter account was printed in S&D N&Q, vol.28.

Pinney, Rev. John, Letters of, 1679-99, edited by Geoffrey Nuttall, D. D. Oxford, 1939. Moving letters about the fate of his son after Sedgemoor.

Whiting, John, *Persecution Exposed.* Some of the book was written in 1685; 1st edition 1715; 2nd edition 1791. A Quaker in prison with several Monmouth men, and related by marriage to several more.

Ailesbury, Thomas, Earl of, Memoirs, Roxburgh Club, 1895. Though intensely loyal to King James, a personal friend of both Monmouth and Lady Henrietta Wentworth.

Pepys, Samuel, Diary, gives several pictures of the young Monmouth. Evelyn's Diary gives little of value about Monmouth or the rebellion.

Reresby, Sir John, *Memoirs and Travels,* several editions, e.g. Kegan Paul, 1904. The latest, edited by Dr Andrew Browning, Glasgow, 1936.

LATER BOOKS

Articles in the Dictionary of National Biography and Encyclopaedia Britannica.

Locke, Richard, *The Western Rebellion,* printed 1782, reprinted 1927. Largely an epitome of The Bloody Assizes; mainly accurate but not infallible.

Roberts, George, *The Life and Progresses of James, Duke of Monmouth,* 2 vols, 1844. The great pioneer work, based on tremendous research.

Macaulay, Lord, *History of England.* Also based on monumental research.

Fea, Allan, *King Monmouth,* 1902. A good biography, well researched.

D'Oyley, Elizabeth, *James, Duke of Monmouth,* 1938. Perhaps even better.

Bevan, Bryan, *James, Duke of Monmouth,* 1973, and

Wyndham, Violet, *The Protestant Duke*, 1976; much slighter biographies.

Little, Bryan, *The Monmouth Episode*, 1956, and

Trench, C. Chenevix, *The Western Rising*, 1969, are both very good accounts of the rebellion, though Mr Trench twice confuses Ilminster and Ilchester, while Mr Little hangs two rebels who were pardoned.

Parry, Sir Edward, *The Bloody Assizes*, 1929.

Curtis, C. D. *Sedgemoor and the Bloody Assize*, 1930.

Inderwick, F. A. *Sidelights on the Stuarts*, 2nd edition 1891. Misled by the absence of stars, meaning 'to be hanged', after the first day of the Assize at Taunton, Inderwick seriously underestimates the number of those hanged.

Keeton, Professor, *Lord Chancellor Jeffreys and the Stuart Cause*, 1972. Defending Jeffreys, Professor Keeton also underestimates the number hanged. His chapter on the Bloody Assizes contains a number of quite shocking errors of fact. See my article in S&D N&Q, vol.29, 1972.

Page, Maurice, *The Battle of Sedgemoor*, 1932.

Burne, Lt-Col. A. H. *The Battlefields of England*, 1950, and

Young, Brigadier Peter, and John Adair, *Hastings to Culloden*, 1964, both give excellent accounts of the Battle of Sedgemoor.

Childs, John, The Army of Charles II, 1976; for Monmouth's campaigns and his service as Captain General.

Price, Cecil, *Cold Caleb*, 1956, a very readable and well informed life of Lord Grey.

Evans, S. Hope, The Book of Nailsea Court, 1923, for Wade and his family.

Pares, Richard, *A West India Fortune*, 1950, for Azariah Pinney and his family.

Ashley, Maurice, *John Wildman, Plotter and Postmaster*, 1947, and

Morley, Iris, *A Thousand Lives*, 1954; both deal with the republican underground. Iris Morley credits Monmouth with more liberal political sense and strength than the evidence justifies.

Earle, Peter, *Monmouth's Rebels*, 1977. An important book, revealing for the first time the scheme of some escaped rebels to establish the manufacture of 'English cloth' on the continent.

APPENDIX

Wade's Narrative

PREFATORY NOTE

The narrative of Nathaniel Wade is among the Harleian Manuscripts 6845 in the British Library, and is here transcribed from the MS. Though it is the best contemporary account of the Monmouth Rebellion, it has not previously been printed in its entirety. A part was printed in 1778 in Volume 2 of the Hardwicke State Papers, which is not easily accessible. Its editor saw fit to omit the names of the officers Monmouth commissioned on the voyage from Holland, and to modernise both spelling and punctuation (which indeed was mostly conspicuous by its absence.) The MS mentions John, Hugh and Charles Speak, whose surname the editor printed as Speke, the spelling the family prefers. He misread German Ireton (Lord Grey's cousin and lawyer) as German Treton.

The narrative was compiled while Wade was a prisoner at Windsor Castle, moved there from the Tower by King James's order. It was signed by Wade, who was recovering from a very severe and nearly fatal wound, but is not in his handwriting. Whether he prepared a draft ot dictated the account we do not know, but it runs so smoothly and is so full, that a draft seems probable, of which the MS would be a fair copy. The first part bears the initials W^m B and the date October 4th; the second part, the printed half, was dated October 11th. W^m B may be the initials of William Blathwayt, who had served at The Hague as secretary to Sir William Temple, was Clerk to the Privy Council, and had recently become Secretary at War. Subsequently as Secretary to the Lords of Trade (or the Committee for Foreign Plantations) Blathwayt received much of the correspondence about the rebels who had been transported.

Wade was expected to reveal the names of many conspirators and rebels. In his narrative he says 'All the Persons I can positively charge to have been concerned in it are either outlawed, dead or executed', and more than once he uses the phrase 'whose name I do not know'. He had little compunction in mentioning Monmouth's friends in Holland; they were out of King James's reach. He mentions rebel officers, some of whom, like Capt. Francis Goodenough, had been killed at Sedgemoor; others, like Lt. Col. Holmes and Capt. Christopher Bettiscombe, had already been captured, tried and hanged (on September 12th); while Capt. Richard Goodenough, already captured, and the Rev. Robert Ferguson, who never was captured, were so well known to the Government that nothing Wade

149

could tell of them would add to their fate. Fletcher of Saltoun and Major Manley were already overseas and out of reach, though Fletcher, against whom the Government in Scotland had a grudge, was tried *in absentia*. Col. Danvers and Major Wildman were already accustomed to disappearing into hiding. Wade may well have had no sympathy for them or Lord Delamere, since their failure to aid the rebellion they had abetted, contributed substantially to its failure and the loss of a thousand lives at Sedgemoor.

The spelling of surnames in the MS calls for a brief comment. Some are easily phonetic. Dalby becoming Dolly; Hewlings, Hulins; and Askew, Ascough. One name has been a puzzle. The MS mentions Lt. Col. Basset as commanding the Blue Regiment, raised in Taunton. George Roberts infers that he came from London. The D.N.B. knows nothing of him. He is not to be found in the lists of New Model or Cromwellian officers. Various contemporary documents mention Col. Bovet, Richard Bovet, 'a gentleman of Taunton', who was hanged at Lord Stawell's gateway at Cothelstone. Where does he fit in? As locally Bovey Tracey is Buvvy, so Col. Bovet became Buffet[*], and was probably so written in the original of Wade's narrative. The amanuensis who made the fair copy misread the 'ff' as "long ss" and the 'u' as an 'a'. The colonel is mentioned as "old Buffet" in some contemporary writings.

In this transcript all contractions, such as y^e, y^t, y^m, have been expanded. 'The D.' has been allowed to stand, and military ranks have been left in their still usual forms. Punctuation has usually been left as it was, except where the addition of a comma has been helpful to the sense. It has not seemed necessary to add footnotes to the names mentioned; most of those active in the rebellion are mentioned in my book.

NATHANIEL WADE'S NARRATIVE

To the Right Hon. the Earl of Sunderland
    Principal Secretary of State.

                                Barnstable, the 31st July 1685.

My Lord,
        I here enclosed send your Lordship an account of the apprehending of Nathaniel Wade, one of the late rebells. I came to this towne to-day, and can, therefore, only give your Lordship what relation I have from the apothecary and chirurgeon which they had drawn up in a letter designed for Sir Bouchier Wrey; their examination of him is enclosed in the letter, to which I refer your Lordship. He continues very ill of a wound given him at his apprehending sixteen miles hence, at Braundon parish in Devon. I designe to examine him as soon as his condition will permitt, he promising to make large and considerable confessions: and herein, or if he dye, I humbly desire your Lordship's directions to me at

---

[*]This identification was first suggested by Mr Peter Earle in his valuable book *'Monmouth's Rebels'*, but he did not mention Lt. Col. Basset.

Barnstable, and shall herein proceed as becomes my duty to his Majesty and your Lordship.
My Lord,
 your Lordship's most humble Servant,
Richard Armsley.

To the Honorable Sir Bouchier Wrey, Kt. and Bart., in London.
Brendon, 30th July, '85

Honoured Sir,
 This comes to give you an account of one, not the least of the rebells, who was taken up last Monday night at a place called Fairleigh in the parish of Brendon. (Then follows an account of the wounding of Wade as he ran from John Burch's house, as told on page 77) The bullett past right under the pleura (They cut the bullet out.) He was very faint, having lost a great quantity of blood ... His spirits are much revived, only this day about ten of the clock he was taken with an aguish fitt, which I suppose was caused by his hard diet and cold lodging ever since the rout, he leaving his horse at Ilfordcombe. Ever since Tuesday last in the afternoon, Mr. Ravening and myself have bin with him, and cannot with safety move from him. We desire to know his Majesties pleasure what we shall due with his corps, if he dyes ... We will due what possible we can, for he hath assured us, that as soon as he is a little better, he will make a full discovery of all he knows, of which this enclosed is part, by which he hopes to have, but not by merits, his pardon. Here is noe one that comes to him that he will talk soe freely with as with us, if you will have any materiall questions of business or persons to be askt of him, pray give it in yours to us. We will be private, faithfull, to or King, whome God long preserve. Which is al at present from them who will ever make it their business to be
 Sir your most humble Servants
 Nicolas Cooke and Henry Ravening.

Mr. Nath. Wades Confession made before us undernamed the 29th Day of July. 1685.
 He came from Holland in M: owne ship with him and was made Major in his own Regiment. He was in every ingagement that the foot were ingaged in. He guarded the post at Shoote Hill. He commanded the right hand battalion at Weston moore. At Froome M: was about to goe away from his army privately.
 The cause of Wades leaving the Nation was Rumseys swearing him to be in the plott to kill the king, which, he protests, he never was, but was in that insurrection for the redressing of grievances. The bottom of it was for the Bill of Exclusion, and to declare M: Prince of Wales. That paper of James Holloway of Bristol gives a true account of him.
 He left Thompson, Captain of the blew Regiment, at Ilfordcombe, and Ferguson, who was chaplin to the Army. One Hook was M. domestick Chaplin. Batscomb was Captain Lieutenant of M. owne company.
 He sayeth that M., as to the best of his knowledge, did not bring with him from Holland not above £100 in gold and silver. He pawned all his

Jewels in Holland, and his great George to one Le Plon, a merchant in Amsterdam. About £500 in small bills were delivered to M: by several Englishmen that lived in Holland. Old Dare of Taunton was paymaster in Holland, who was killed at Lyme by one Fletcher, a Scotchman. Fletcher gott upon Dares horse. Dare bid him dismount. He told him he would not. Other words followed, and Fletcher shott him in the head with his pistole two days after they came into Lime. Since Dares death Goodenough was paymaster. One of their Chirurgions was called Oliver.

He was informed that Major Wildman of Barkshire was a man much concerned as an Abetter and assistant as to advise, but gave him noe money, for which he hath heard M. curse him; and one Mr. Hamden, that is or was in prison, was an Abetter. M expected Sir Walter Young, Sir Francis Rolle of Hampshire and other Gentlemen, but they all failing him made him grow very Malancolly. His intent was for Bristoll, being persuaded by Captain Tily that most of the Cityzens were for him, and then for Gloster, and so for London.

This is all he can do a present, but he will declare all he knows as soon as he is able, being despiratly wounded by a pistol shot almost through his body.

Nicholas Cooke
Henry Ravening.

The Horse	600
Bl(ue) Regt	600
Whit	400
Red	800
Green	600
Yellow	500

an Independent Company which came from Lime 80.

Mr. Wade's Further Information, October 4, 1685

I came acquainted with Col. John Romsey at an Election of Parliament men to serve in the last Parliament that sate at Westminster in the late Kings Reign, for the City of Bristol, to which City the Colonel came upon that occasion, and by this means I became known to my Lord Shaftesbury, the Duke of Monmouth etc. and consequently to Several Gentlemen of that Party, as Mr. West, Goodenough, Mr. John Trenchard and others. But my cheifest intimacy was with Col. Romsey, who always brought messages to me from my Lord Shaftesbury, and gave me an account as often as my Lord had a mind to Speak with me.

It was after the Dissolution of the Parliament at Oxford that I first heard of any discourse about having recourse to Arms. It was in Trinity Term next after that dissolution when Col. Romsey coming to my Chamber in the Middle Temple, told me that there was an Insurrection designed at Taunton presently after the end of that Term and that it was expected by my Lord Shaftesbury that I should take a part there, which I did not absolutely deny, but it being a thing new to me, made some hesitation thereat. He sayd I should Speedily have an account of Particulars. But in a few days after he came and informed me it was put off. From that time the matter slept, till about May the year following, when the late King being sick at Windsor, I was sent for by a footman of my Lord Shaftesbury's to come to his Lord, which I did with Mr. Ayloff. The footman brought us to Sir William Coopers house in Charterhouse-yard, where we found my Lord Shaftesbury, the Duke of Monmouth, my Lord Grey and Sir Thomas Armstrong. The first we spake with was my Lord Shaftesbury, who acquainted us with an insurrection designed that night being as I remember the night of the late King's birthday and required our assistance therein, demanding how many men we had in a readiness; We were much surprized at it, and Mr. Ayloff answerd my Lord, I know but of one, meaning himself, for indeed we had never heard of it before. Immediately the Duke of Monmouth, my Lord Grey and Sir Thomas Armstrong came into the room, of whom my Lord Shaftesbury demanded if they were in a readiness, but they answered that they had just now intelligence from Windsor, that the King was well recovered and so the business was over. My Lord Shaftesbury replyed that he understood that occasion was to have been made use of for the procuring the ends they had so often discoursed of, and not to have been longer delayed, and seemed to make complaint, that he was deserted and abused by them, although I believe he was in no manner provided for such an undertaking, but imagined to himself that he had many thousands at his Devotion in an hour's warning. For our parts we complained that we were abused by them all, in bringing us to discourse of things that should rather be done, than talked of, and so desiring to be no more concerned in that nature, we departed, resolving with some other to be gon into America, to a plantation in new Jersey purchased by Mr. West, and some others from whence sprang my more particular acquaintance with Mr. West, but finding the Grant to Mr. West and his Partners not so large as we were informed, we broke off from that Design.

    The later end of Trinity Term following or rather a little after the Term, Mr. Ferguson acquainted me that matters were wholely settled for a rising in two or three places in the Nation and that we should have a particular account of the Design sent us into the Country. I being then departing from London to Bristol, which followed me speedily by Mr. Tily of Bristol, who brought me this account, that the Duke of Monmouth intended a journy into Cheshire, to show himself to the People there, & settle matters with the Gentry of those Parts and that when he had effected that, he would come across the Country incognito into Wiltshire, and raising a body of Horse amongst his friends there, would fall into Bristol and master it by the assistance we were able to give him there and after that fall into Conjunction with the People of Taunton and of Devonshire, who were as he said to be headed by Mr. Trenchard, Sir William Courtney, Sir Walter Young & others that I do not remember, that at the same time an Insurrection was to be in Cheshire and the places adjacent under the conduct of my Lord Mackelsfeild, & in London by my Lord Shaftesbury, but that we were to expect a Messenger express, who should give us an exact account of time and place. Yet that it was necessary we should put things in a readiness for the occasion. But I having experience of the Unconstancy of those great Men, and their little resolution to execute what they had resolved, said, that the matter was not to be communicated to many, lest they starting from what they had resolved on, we might run the hazard of our lives by a discovery. Yet we agreed to consult with some few, whom we thought we might trust, of the meanes how we might surprize Bristol, which was our part in that affair.

The Persons consulted with were Benjamin Adlam, James Halloway, William Wade my Brother, and Thomas Tyler. We only discoursed of the Methods of doing of it, the number of men necessary, and made some remarks on several Persons we thought might be usefull to us in this design. But to acquaint any more with it, before we were fully satisfyed with the Resolutions of our Great Men we thought by no wayes advisable, and contented ourselves only by making some Provisions of Powder and Bullet & four small pieces of Canon which we put up in Mr. James Halloway's house, who was a Merchant that used to trade in such things, by which means the thing passed without suspition. At length all our expectations were frustrated by the Duke of Monmouth's rendering himself to a Messenger sent from the Council board to seize him, in that Cheshire progress. We looked upon ourselves as betrayed and abused, and for myself I then took up a resolucion to concern myself no more in those affairs. At Michaelmas this year I fell sick of a dangerous feaver which kept me in my chamber, and for the most part in my Bed in Bristol, until within a week of Christmas, when I was advised by my Physician to change the air as the only means to recover my health, which I did by going into Glocestershire, where I continued a month. From thence I returned to Bristol and so into Somersetshire, where I spent the greatest part of January about some affairs of my Lord Stamford to whom I was steward, and returning through Bristol and Glocester I came to London the beginning of february 1683. During this time of sickness it is that Col. Romsey charges me on Capt. Walcot's tryal to have been at a Consult in London, where the murther of his late and present Majestie was resolved on, yet in his depositions before the Council swears that I was alwaies against it.

When I came to London I met with Col. Romsey who acquainted me, that during my sickness in Bristol in November as I take it before there was a day prefixed for an Insurrection but that it was put off by Mr. John Trenchard's backwardness, he saying that his Taunton men were not in a readiness, which I very much admired at he having in Trinity Term before greatly complained to me at the trifling of the Lords and made large Professions of the great readiness of affairs at Taunton.

Col. Romsey then invited me to dine with him at the Ship Tavern, as I take it, in Grace-church street where I met him with Francis Shute son to the late Sheriff Shute. They then informed me of a design, that had been, but was disappointed, to have murthered the late King and his present Majestie either in his going to or coming from Newmarket I know not which, and asked of me what I thought of that undertaking, for they said the great Men had talkt them into treason and brought them in perill of their lives, but did not intend to do anything to save them, and therefore they were under a necessity of using this short and easy Method (as they called it) to save themselves. I spake my mind freely against it, and told them it was an Action so ungenerous and barbarous, that I could by no means be concerned in it, and that since they had been once disappointed in it, I hoped they would not make a second Attempt, for I said, in case the thing should be effected I could not see but that the effects of it would be the ruin of them and their Party. For even the Duke of Monmouth himself could not if he should be King, refuse the execution of Justice upon them for the murther of his Father and Uncle. They answered me that he must be served in the same manner, which I looked upon as idle distracted Talk and so this discourse ended, and as I thought the further design of that Project was wholely layd aside, but I perceived it shortly after to be otherwise by a letter wrote to me by Mr. West, and my enquiry of him what he meant by it, which story is at large set forth by Mr. Halloway, which part of his paper in relation to Me I own to be truth, and think that it need not be here reiterated. I left the town about the middle of March and returned in the beginning of May, as I take it, when I was attackt by my old friend Col. Romsey, who brought me to the Duke of Monmouth at his house in King's Square. The Duke had some discourse with me about the affairs of Bristol. I gave him this account that I thought it might be secured for him by the Presence of some great Man, taking the advantage of a surprize. He proposed Col. Romsey to me for the Great Man, who took it upon him, but I refused alledging his name and Interest was not considerable enough for such an undertaking. His answer was that he would consider of a fitt Person and so I departed without any further discourse. I then likewise learnt that there was a Council of several great Men who constantly mett to consult of and manage affairs in order to a Rising, and that they had sent Aaron Smith into Scotland, to invite several Gentlemen there up to London, who were then come to Town, but I had no acquaintance with any of them, only had this relation from Col. Romsey and Mr. Ferguson, whom I went sometimes to see at Mr. Brown's and Mr. Owen's, where he lodged. Thus things went on only in debate, and nothing as I perceived tended to Action. At length Col. Romsey and Mr. West desired me to meet them at the Young Devil Tavern within Temple-bar, and to bring Mr. Halloway of Bristol with me, who was then in Town, which I did. And there met us at that time (I think it was the beginning of June) Col. Romsey, Mr. West, Capt. Walcot, Mr. Richard Goodenough and his brother Francis, and Mr. Edward Norton. Col. Romsey began to speak and informed us that the Great Men after several consultations had taken no resolutions but that it was thought that all attempts would be to no purpose, unless the City of London could be secured, and the Guards beaten out from thence, which he said, was not to be don by talking and suppositions of a Party in readiness, but that there must be a certainty of 4000 men at the first onset, and that it was desired we would consult how such a Party might be gotogether at least that we would do our endeavours to see if such a number of Men were to be found to engage in this business within London the Hamlets and Westminister. We immediately fell into the method, that the whole should be divided into 20 parts, that a man should be chosen in every part, that should pitch on 10 men in his part, who should each bring 20, making up the number of 200 in each part, in all amounting to 4000 men, the number required. A map was bought in order to it, the Divisions were marked out & written each in a paper. Mr. R. Goodenough was the man pitcht upon to find out the men, being well acquainted in the whole. Only I was desired to speak to Mr. Bourn and Mr. Hix a Tobacconist in Friday street to be concerned in the Parts belonging to the Places where they dwelt, which I did; the former accepted of the charge, the latter would not hear any discourse of it. Mr. Goodenough brought us a good account of some parts, but as to the men concerned, he never told us, nor we never askt him. Many discourses we had together about the manner of managing the surprize of the Town, the Guards and the Tower, but they were only for to pass the time, all that being to have been submitted to the judgment of the Great Men, when we had been sure of the readiness of the 4000 men. But when we were but young in the business, we had notice by Keeling's brother that the whole was discovered, which we gave an account of to my Lord Russell by Mr. Norton and Mr. Nelthrop, desiring that they would immediately take their swords in their hands, but his answer was that it was better some private men should suffer, than the Public be precipitated. We could put no other construction upon it, than that they intended to abandon us, and therefore we resolved to depart the Kingdom, which we attempted by the way of London, and in order thereto mett at Capt. Tracy's in Goodmans feilds near Wapping, but suspecting the River might be stopt, we altered our resolutions, and shifted every man to find a way to transport himself, which I did afterwards with Mr. Nelthrop at Scarborough in Yorkshire, and landed at Roterdam the latter end of June 1683.

I have been the shorter in the Relation of what I was concerned in, before my departure out of England, because the same is more at large set forth by others, and all the Persons I can positively charge to have been concerned in it, are either outlawed, dead, or executed. But I shall be more particular in the account of what I know relating to the Invasions of England and Scotland by my Lord Argyle and the Duke of Monmouth, and in order thereunto it is necessary that I begin where I left off at my Landing at Roterdam, from whence I went the next day save one after my landing to Amsterdam, and meeting there with Mr. Thomas Dare, he informed us that there was no safety for us there, by reason of an order from the States General to seize us. I therefore resolved with my comrade Mr. Nelthrop to go into Swisserland as a place of safety, which we did, and began our journy the next day after our arrivall at Amsterdam, and came to Vivey in the canton of Bern in Swisse, the latter end of July, where we were kindly received by Col. Ludlow's Lady, and lived with them all the time of our abode there. About October after John Rowe came to us, who I suppose is still there. In April 1684 I received a letter from Mr. Ayloff then at Utrecht, desiring me to try whether Col. Ludlow might be prevailed with to come into Holland, and from thence to go into the West of England, to head a Party as General, and informing me, that there was a design on foot to make an Insurrection both in England and Scotland. He prayed me to come speedily to Holland, to give my assistance to the design. I did speak with Col. Ludlow as I was desired, but found him no wayes disposed to the thing, saying he had done his work he thought in the world and was resolved to leave it to others. I parted from Swisse in April and came into Holland in May 1684, where I found the business then on foot to be this. That one Mr. Rawlins a tradesman of london, then living at Utrecht, had fallen into acquaintance with my Lord Argyle and Madam Smith the wife of one Mr. Smith with whom my Lord Argyle then lived at Utrecht, and complaining of the backwardness of the Lords in the late Design, in not raising the £10,000 required by my Lord Argyle, for the Scotch Expedition, said that he believed he could yet raise £20,000 amongst his acquaintance in London, if a fitt Messenger could be found to be sent to them, and that he would give £1000 towards it himself. Mr. Ayloff offerd himself to go, and was, when I came into Holland, gon on that errand into England, but after some stay he returned without success. The Persons he spoke with I know not, but he said to me that he mett with such a character of himself as an Atheist and a man of no Conscience that the Nonconformist Ministers, who I understood were the Persons he was principally sent to, refused to Speak with him. There only followed him a letter, written in a mock hand, which I suppose was Mr. James Hooper's, and in a canting style, which Mr. Ayloff well understood, by which he was informed that Sir William Ellis had promised £2000. But now Mr. Rawlins was fallen from his promise, and would not give the £1000 he had offered, and Mr. Christopher Vane then living at Utrecht, who I understood had likewise promised £1000, was fallen from his, by the overruling power of his wife whom he had acquainted with the business. The business meeting these disappointments, the Expedition intended at Michaelmas 1684 was put off, and resolutions taken to endeavour what might be, to be ready against last Spring. It happened that Mr. Smith dyed and left his Wife the greatest part of his Estate, which being very considerable, and she willing to part with the most of it on this occasion, put new life into the business, and Mr. Rawlins began again to come on. It was therefore resolved that Preparations should be made against the Spring, yet with great privacy, because it had been observed that the last intended Expedition had been talked of in London and that, about the time it was intended, the King had appointed a Rendezvous of his English forces near London, and had caused several People in Scotland to be taken up and examined upon Oath if they knew of any Rebels or of any correspondence with my Lord Argyle; all which was esteemed to have risen from the too large spreading of the secret amongst our own friends. This was therefore kept very private, and the greatest difficulty was to hide it from our own Party. There happened about this time a thing very convenient for the affair. Sir William Waller had procured from the Duke of Lunenburg a promise of Protection for such as would retire thither. Some of our talking People were encouraged to go, & others on purpose went to other places that the thing might be carryed on with less observation. The whole winter was spent in Preparation, in which for the most part my Lord Argyle was an acter himself and had a little of mine & one Mr. Phelps assistance. The Scotch I had little or no acquaintance with, only with James Steward, on whom my Lord Argyle much relyed for his advice, not in War but Law and Policy. All this while the Duke of Monmouth and his Party knew nothing of this affair, but the King dying that matter created some difference amongst us. Some were for his not meddling at all in the matter, but that the Scotch should go on in their own business distinct from him, alledging that he must of necessity fall in in England if he had any regard to his own Interest. But this Party was very small even amongst the Scotch themselves. At length the Duke of Monmouth and my Lord Argyle had an Interview at Mr. Dare's in Amsterdam, where they immediately agreed and resolved to act in Conjunction.

But before I go further I shall give a particular account of the Duke of Monmouth. Immediately after his father's death he departed from the Hague to Bruxells, expecting some message from the great men his friends in England, and came to no manner of Correspondence with us, till the Marquis de Grana banisht him out of the Spanish Territoryes, when he came to Roterdam, and sent Capt. Matthews to try whether we were inclined to Correspond with him, for we had made complaints of him, that he had not made use of his interest with his father (which we supposed was great) in favour of us who had suffered for him. But we were immediately reconciled upon his coming to Amsterdam, & sending for us. He complained to us that all that while he had had no message from his friends in England, but at length there came one Mr. Cragg, who I then spoke not with, being gone into Fresland to my Lord Argyle. He as I understood by Mr. Ferguson who had spoken with him, came from Major Wildman in the name of all the other Gentlemen of the D's Party in England, to invite us to an agreement with the D. of M., assuring us that there was never a greater Spirit amongst the Common People in England for our purpose, and that if we would procure a good correspondence between my Lord Ar and the D. of M., that they might act with united councels, we should not want any reasonable Sum of mony for the carrying on our design. He was sent back by Mr. Ferguson with assurance, that Such a Correspondence should be settled according to their desire, and desired an Assistance of some thousands of pounds, which Mr. Cragg did not doubt, as he sayd, to procure. This message of Mr. C's and his confidence of having the mony (which indeed no man almost could have doubted of, considering the many protestations of Major Wildman & the Party of assisting the D. of M. in case of the death of the late King) put the D. upon entring into a promise to Ar. of invading England in near as short a time as he could land in Scotland in the Place he designed. A. was necessitated to put to Sea, because he had communicated the design to his Scotch friends, and drawn them all about him from Lunenburgh, out of the Prince of Orange's army, & other places. They were most of them poor and therefore to be maintained by him, which he was not able to bear long, and so given to tattle that the matter began to be talked as freely of in Amsterdam & Roterdam amongst the Dutchmen as any other news, & we expected every day to hear of it in their Public Gazettes. Thus my Lord A. was in a manner forced to sea before he was willing, and before matters could be well adjusted in relation to England. His equipage was 3 small ships, about 8000 arms, & 500 Barrels of Gunpowder, which cost about £9000. £1000 was given by Mr. Lock, and the rest I suppose by Madame Smith. Mr. Rawlins being before this time dead. I do not believe the Scotch advanced one peny towards this Equipage, although my Lord Melvin was very busy with his advice, yet as to his purse or Person he intended not to be concerned.

The D. of M. departs from Amsterdam incognito to Roterdam, from whence he sends Capt. Matthews into England to prepare his friends there for the business, and shortly after returns to Amsterdam, where understanding that Mr. Cragg lay at Roterdam waiting for a wind and made not the haste that the necessity of the affair required, he sent Mr. Bettescomb into England, who might pass by the speedy way of the Packet unsuspected. His errand was to speak to Major Wildman, to acquaint my Lord Mackelsfeild, Lord Delamere, Lord Brandon, etc. of his design of coming into England, and that he would have them manage the design in Cheshire, for that he intended to be himself in the West; and after he had so don he was to go into the West to speak with Sir Walter Young, Sir Francis Drake & Mr. Trenchard to desire them from the D. to meet him at his landing. But if he found Capt. Matthews in England before him, he was to leave the Cheshire business to him. The Place of Landing was not yet designed, but left to the West country Gentlemen to direct. Shortly after Mr. Bettescomb's departure, the D. receives a letter from Capt. Matthews, giving an account that he had spoken with Major Wildman, that he had spoke to him only in Hieriglyphics and was something shie of the matter, but that he beleived he should find the Cheshire Gentlemen in another humour. Mr. Cragg returns and acquaints the D. that Major Wildman and his friends in England were exceedingly rejoyced to hear that we were all agreed, and approved mightily of the Scotch Design, and that it was the Major's opinion that the D. should attend the success of that, and should come over incognito & lye hid in London, and brought no money, to save which we all beleived was the cause of his giving that advice, for we all knew the Major to be a great Husband. No further news was had of Capt. Matthews, none at all of Mr. Bettescomb, at which the D. very much wondered. But being engaged by his Promise to my Lord A. to make an attempt upon England, he resolved to put the matter into what forwardness* he could on his own Stock, for which end he goes again to Roterdam, pawns all his goods and Plate for about £3000 and returns to Amsterdam, having in the mean time left orders for myself to provide two small ships, and about 1500 foot arms, 1500 Curasses, 4 Pieces of Artillery mounted on feild carriages, 200 as I take it barrels of gunpowder, with some small quantity of Granado shells, match, and other things necessary for the undertaking, which I did by the assistance of Mr. Phelps and Mr. Arther merchants in Amsterdam, and gave him the account of it in a few days after, when he returned to Amsterdam, all which cost near £3000.

But before the Dukes return to Amsterdam Mr. Henry Ireton† came over, I suppose about some affairs of my Lord Grey's, yet likewise brought some messages from Major Wildman. One was to tell the D. that Henry 7th invaded England but with 140 men, and such like Dark sayings, but nothing positive, nor any mony. He was sent back by my Lord Grey, who

---

* 'readiness' was written first and struck through.

† Added in margin: Mr. Ireton as I understood knew of the designed Invasion and our Rebellion, and we had discourse to that purpose.

159

had orders from the D. of M. to that purpose, with messages like to the former as I take it in relation to mony. I forgot to give an account of the D's sending back Mr. Cragg again after his second coming, to tell Major Wildman that he must not dispute any longer, but must send him £4000, that he knew he could do it himself, yet he gave private instructions to Mr. Cragg that he should get what he could, and descended even to £1000. But Mr. Cragg returned shortly after with this answer from Major Wildman, that there was no need of Arms, the People were well armed, and so consequently no need of mony. Whereupon the D. resolved to proceed with what strength he had. A place was therefore thought of to land in the West, the furthest that might be from any standing force, and as near as could be to Taunton, and Resolutions were taken to trust to the People, who by all accounts were well disposed for the design. Lime was the place pitch upon as well affected, & of so small strength in itself, that we might be able to master it with our own strength, and the Duke doubted not when he was Landed, but that all these Gentlemen would fall in with him and make Insurrections in their Severall Stations. He likewise told us that he was assured that great Numbers of the King's standing forces, both officers and soldiers, would desert and come to him. But while we were thus consulting, Intelligence came that several of the King's men of war were on the Coast, which made us afraid to venture to sea with the two small ships, and was the occasion of our stay for almost 3 weekes, whilst a Ship of 32 guns was bought and fitted out. To pay for this Ship the D. was forct to pawn all he had in the World, even his biggest George, and sent it all to Amsterdam, where Mr. Daniel le Blon procured him the mony. But we had yet another difficulty to contest with, which was to ship the arms without observation. For his Majesties Consul took constantly an account of all arms entred in the Admiralty-books. This expedient was found by Mr. le Blon. They entred them as goods to be only transported from one of the United Provinces to another, and had a Passport for them as such; which Inland-Pasports are not entred in the Admiralty-books, & served to procure a Passage for the lighters out of the Booms, and afterwards a little mony prevailed with the Searchers at the Texel to let the Ships pass. This equipage of the D. of M. cost near £5500 as I remember. £400 was given by Mr. Lock, £100 by Will Rumball, £500 by Sir Patience Ward, and the rest was the D's own, for Sir William Ellis had fallen from his promise and would give nothing. So that all the mony for both Expeditions came meerly out of the purses of the People beyond the Seas. Mr. Cragg was dispatcht a third time to acquaint Major Wildman of the D's being ready to sail, and to desire the Major to inform the Lords and Gentlemen of the D. of M's Party of it, and to require them to leave off further consultations, and repair immediately Everyone to his Interest and to be in a readiness to joyn with him when they heard of his landing, but he was not intrusted with the place of his landing. A very little time before the departure of Mr. Cragg, came Mr. Jones. He was sent, as I understood, by Col. Danvers to see what we were doing, and to inform us the People were in earnest expectation of Us. He was dispatched back again with the Same Message as Mr. Cragg. Only thus much more was communicated to him (as I think) the Place of our Landing, where he promised to meet us with a considerable Party of Horse out of London, which he performed as to himself with about three others viz. Brand, Chaddock and Thompson. Shortly after his departure the D. set sail from Amsterdam, and was detained by contrary Winds and Calms three weekes at sea, before we landed at Lime, which was Thursday in the Whitson-week, with about 83 Persons, besides Dutch seamen.

Nath. Wade.

Windsor, October 4, 1685
  W^m B.

Mr. Wade's Further Information, Octob. 11. 1685
Whilst wee were on shipboard wee received severall commissions from the D. in paper (viz) in his own regiment Captaine Venner to be Lieutenant Coll, myselfe to be Major, Richard Goodenough to be eldest Captain, Joseph Tily Second Captain, Lieutenant Thompson 3rd Captain, James Hayes 4th Captain. Taylor to be Lieut. to Venner & adjutant, Dolly to be my youngest Lieut: and John Cragg to be my ensign. Mitchell & Lillington to be Lieutenants to R. Goodenough & Tho. Dare junor to be his Ensigne. William Hulin to be Lieut. to Capt. Tily, Mr. Sanford to be Ensigne to Capt. Thompson. Babbington to be ensigne to Capt. Hayes, & Vincent to be ensigne to the Duke.
  In the white Fouke Lieut. Coll
             Goodenough 1st Capt.
  In the yellow Fox Major.
  In the Green Holms Lieut.Coll. Parsons Major. Patchall 1st Capt.
             Blake Holmes' ensigne.
  Many others there were which I cannot remember but shall endeavour to sett them downe together in a place by themselves.

Wednesday night. When wee approached Lyme on the night before wee landed, wee came to an Anchor and in the night the D, sent Mr. Thomas Dare ashoare by the boat, who landed about 2 miles from Lyme with instructions to learne the present posture of the Country and inform Coll. Venner who was with him in the boat and to speed away for Taunton to raise that place and to bring what strength he could to Lyme.

Thursday. Att breake of the day the Tyde then serving wee wayed anchor and sett sayl for Lyme, and in our course mett the boate, which returning gave this accompt that they had put Mr. Dare ashoare, that that part of the country was cleare, no force thereabout, but that the Duke of Albemarle was gone to Exeter to raise the militia of Devonshire, and that the Somersetshire Forces were on foot and at Taunton; upon which the D. consulted whether wee ought to land; And it was resolved that wee ought. Wee came about noon to an Anchor in the bay before the Town, within a league of it, and immediately surprized a little fisherboat with 3 persons in it, by whom wee understood more perfectly the posture of the Town, and that wee should meett with no resistance in it as they beleived. Our 2 smaller ships sayld about halfe a mile nearer the town than the frigatt, which brought forth the Custome-house-boat & officers who were surprized by Mr. Hayes who commanded the ship of burden, on board of which they came, and brought prisoners on board the frigatt. The D. treated them very civilly & learned from them that no resistance could be made by the towne. After dinner when the Tyde served wee wayed Anchor and came as neare the town as wee could, and being then masters of 7 boats we gott all our land force on board of them and landed neare Lyme on the Strand being about Sunnsett, from whence wee marched very well armed and cloathed to Lyme in a military manner, the D. at the head of us, where wee were received by the shouts & acclamations of the people, the Major (mayor) being fled.

Our Company was by the D. divided into 3 parts, 2 thirds whereof were appointed to guard the Avenues of the Towne. The remaining third was to gett the arms & amunition from on board the ships. My part of it was to gett the 4 peices of Canon on shoare and see them mounted which I performed by break of day having good assistance of mariners and Townsmen. I forgott to mention that at our landing neare 60 younge fellows offered theyr Service to the D. and were immediately listed and had arms delivered them by break of day. Before the morning (the news of the D's landing being spread abroad into the country) many came in and offered theyr service, I suppose some hundreds. Some sayd that they were in bed when they heard the news but that they immediately arose and came away.

Friday. The next day great numbers presented themselves to the D. The method was that when they came the D. caused theyr names to be taken, and sent them by a messenger with the list of theyr names to the townhall where the arms were & persons to give them out, who immediately armed them and sent them by other messengers to the officers who guarded the Avenues, where they were put into order and exercised.

That day being Friday the morrow after our landing, all diligence imaginable was used to gett horses. Messengers were sent to seize all they could lay theyr hands on neare the Town. By noone considerable numbers were brought in. I suppose neare 40 or 50; and upon Intelligence that there were severall persons in Bridport 6 miles from Lyme ready to joyne us if the way were cleare of the constables guard then kept up in the Town, Major Manley was sent with 15 horse mounted for the most part by officers and gentlemen that came over with the D., to bring off the persons that were willing to joyn them, but they found not only the constables watch but a troope of militia horse to oppose them, which the major charged and routed killing 2 of the troopers and finding them supported with greater force retreated to Lyme without pursuit or a man wounded.

This being Friday, at night wee had a rendezvous of our forces and marched out of town with about 800 foot & 150 horse & 3 peices of canon to a crossway where wee posted ourselves advantageously in the hedges and streights to receive the D. of Albemarle who (as the D. was informed, yett falsely) intended to fall upon us that night. This night the foot lay on the ground with theyr arms in rank and file and the horsemen on the ground holding theyr bridles in theyr hands as theyr horses stood in squadron. This night I had no command of foot but of a party of horse, about 25 in number. There were left in towne about 200 foot & 1 peice of Canon.

Saturday. Early in the morning being Saturday a little after break of day Mr. Dare returned to us with a party of about 40 horse pretty well mounted but few of them armed and all but ordinary fellows; but himself very well mounted, for which horse in the evening Mr. Fletcher and he falling out, Mr. Dare received a shott in the head of which he instantly dyed, and Mr. Fletcher was committed prisoner to the Ship, which was a great loss to the D. in Mr. D who was the D's secretary and paymaster of his army, and in Mr. Fletcher who was his best horse officer and had received a commission to the Lieut. Coll. to my Lord Grey. By Mr. Dare we understood the Somersett militia was in the Town which kept it from rising. The same morning came to me Mr. Tyler of Peristole whom I presently made my Lieut.; he came from Exeter and gave the D. an accompt that the D. of Albemarle was in no condition to fall upon him in some days.

This day I formed the D's regiment and delivered every Capt. his command. The regiment as it then stood amounted to about 500 men. Coll. Holmes formed his this day amounting I beleive to neare the same number. Coll. Fouke his being I beleive about 350, and the yellow which was afterwards Matthews's began to be formed under the command of Major Fox. Neare the evening the D. told me I must prepare a party of 300 foot of his own regiment, to which he would add 100 of Foukes's under the command of Capt. Francis Goodenough, and a party of 40 horse commanded by my Lord Grey to fall upon the militia of Dorsetshire then at Bridport 6 miles of us; that we were to march all night and beat up theyr quarters by break of day; which I did. The order of our march was that Lieut.Mitchell should lead the vanguard being 40 Musqueteers and be followed with a hundred Musquetrs under the command of Capt. Thompson. The rest of the foot to follow commanded by Lieut.Coll. Venner, as the horse in the Reare commanded by my Lord Grey, who commanded the whole party in cheife but was ordered by the D. to take the advice of Coll. Venner.

Wee marched all night in great secrecy and by the way mett with information that the forces in the town were 1200 foot & 100 horse strong at the least which was an unequall match for us, but being positively commanded to attempt it wee were resolved to doe our best endeavours. Wee carryed the person prisoner with us that gave us the accompt and somewhat after broad day wee came to Briport being favored with a thick mist.

Sunday. They had no outguards at all but what wee mett with just at the Town's end; but before I speak of the action I shall sett down what I observed of the situation of the Towne. It is a long town of one broad street and a cross street, a bridge of stone at each end of the long street. The horse & some small party of the foot were in the towne; the rest of the foot were a meadow beyond the farthermost bridge. Wee entring the town mett with small resistance. The outguards retired with expedition to the maine guard, who were as speedy in theyr retreat, enduring only one volly of our vanguard of Musquettrs so that wee became masters of the town immediately and found many of the militia horses running up and down the streets without riders.

Wee having secured the entrance into the town by a stand of Pikes and 2 or 3 files of Musquetrs under the command of ensigne Askough, and the great cross street by 2 little partyes of foot commanded by the Lieuts Lillingstone and Brinscombe, least wee should be surrounded, the number of the enemy being so great. Wee advanced with a small body of foote to attacque the farthermost bridge under the command of Coll. Venner, and having drawn up another small body of foot behind them for theyr Succour I was commanded by Coll. Venner to desire my Lord Grey to advance with the horse to countenance the foott which he did but he was no sooner passed me then I found myself with my reserve of foot which I commanded engaged by some who fired att us out of the windows. This occasioned our breaking open the doors of the houses in which unhappy encounter those 2 gentlemen Mr. Strangways and Mr. Coker lost theyr lives. The latter was killed by Coll. Venner after he had shott the Coll. into the belly; the other was slaine by a musquet as he was endeavouring to pistoll Capt. Francis Goodenough after as wee thought he had taken quarter. After this was over wee advanced to the atacque of the bridge, to the defence of which the officers had with much adoe prevailed with theyr souldiers to stand. Our foot fired one volly upon them which they answered with another and killed us 2 men of the foot, at which my Lord Grey with the horse ran and never turned face till they came to Lyme, where they reported me to be slain and all the foot to be cutt off. This flight of my Lord Grey so discouraged the Vanguard of the foot that they threw down theyr arms and began to runne, but I bringing up another body to theyr succour they were perswaded to take theyr arms again all but such as ran into houses for shelter which was neare 16 or 17. Lieut. Coll. Venner being dismayed by his wound received from Mr. Coker commanded us to retreat and would not suffer us to make a second attaque upon the bridge and when he had so done he mounted and followed my Lord Grey to Lyme leaving us to retreat as we could. I drew off my guards on the cross streets and caused my men to retreat to the first bridge wee had possessed at the entrance of the town and there staying for about half an hour exspected that the enemy would have attaqued us as wee did them not doubting by an ambuscade of musqueteers that wee had near the bridge to give them good entertainment, but they contented themselves to repossess the middle of the town and shout at us out of musquet shott. Wee answered them alike, and by this bravo having a little established the staggering courage of our souldiers wee retreated in pretty good order with 12 or 14 prisoners and about 30 horses, sending 2 or 3 Captains before with a party of musquetts to dress some ambushes in case wee had been pursued but wee had no occasion of that matter.

When we were come within 2 miles of Lyme we were mett by the Duke at the head of a good body of horse to favour the retreat, as he thought, of his stragling forces but was surpized to see us marching in good order. He thanked me for bringing off his men and demaunded of me if it were true as it was reported that my Lord Grey ran away. I answered him yes, at which he seemed much surprized yett neverthelesse continued him in his command. Wee were much tired with our march, yett no sooner a little refreshed but the Duke told me I must be ready for the march early on the morrow morning & said that now Venner was wounded he exspected I should take the charge of the regiment on my selfe. He likewise acquainted me that he had intelligence of the Duke of Albemarle's march with the Devonshire and the march of the Somersetsheire forces to coup him up, and unless he marched early the next morning all was lost. I tooke little rest being sent by the Duke to fetch all the officers into the feild which I effected about 2 in the morning and layd me down in the ground till 3 when wee had orders to beat the drums. I perceived that in my absence the army was considerably encreased for on Monday.

Monday about 10 aclock wee marched out of Lyme neare 3000 strong. I had the vanguard that day of the foot. After wee had marched about 2 houres towards Axmister wee discovered on one side the march of the Devonshire forces, on the other of the Somersetsheire, to a conjunction as wee supposed in Axmister which caused us to double our march that we might prevent it. The scouts of the Somersetsheire forces had first entred the town but on the approach of ours they retired. The Duke possessed himself of the town and seized on the passes regarding each army, which he guarded with canon & musqueteers, the places by reason of the thick hedges and straight wayes being very advantageous for that purpose. I was posted with the Duke's Regiment regarding the Devonshire forces and had the German gentleman, now a prisoner, joyned to me by the Duke for my assistant. On our side the horse of the Devonshire forces advanced within half a quarter of a mile of our advanced post, But discovering that wee had lined the hedges they retreated. Wee advanced upon them but the Duke came and commanded us back telling us that the Somersetsheire forces were likewise retired on the other side, and said it was not his business at present to fight but to march on, so wee drew off our parties from theyr posts and encamped in a strong peice of ground on the other side of Axmister towards Chard, putting out very strong guards, where wee lodged that night.

Tuesday Wee marched early the next morning from thence to Chard where wee again encamped in a feild neare the town and lay there all the night. There happened nothing very remarkeable in this day's march save that Mr. John Speake came in to us with a company of ragged horse whose names I know not nor did not enquire being a company of ordinary fellows. And here began the first proposal of Mr. Fergason to proclaime the Duke of Mon. King; it was seconded by my Lord Grey but easily ran down by those that were against it. Here we likewise learnt that the retreat of the Somersetheire forces was little better than a flight, many of the souldiers coats & arms being recovered & brought in to us.

Wednesday This day wee marched to Ilmister and likewise encamped in a feild about halfe a mile beyond the town. Nothing at all hapned remarkeable in this dayes march.

Thursday. Wee marched to Taunton and encamped likewise in a feild neare the town and lay there all night, and the next day *Friday* when wee were presented with Colours by the maids of Taunton whose names I know not but I suppose they cannot be wanting. This day the Duke had intelligence of the Duke of Albemarle's having possessed himself of Wellington, a town within 5 miles of Taunton, which caused the Duke to make some small entrenchments on the roads leading that way and to putt out strong guards. I was commanded on the guard with the whole Duke's regiment where I continued that night and all the next day, *Saturday* till evening being Saturday when I was discharged and had quarters assigned me for the regiment. This was the first night wee lay in beds after our coming over. This evening wee received orders for a march early the next morning.

During our abode in Taunton I was called by the Duke to a councell of war, being the first I beleive that he held, doing all things before by his own judgement. It was proposed whither wee should march back and fight the Duke of Albemarle or march on, and it was resolved wee should march on. He then tooke me and some others aside and perswaded us that wee should consent to his being proclaimed King, alleadging that according to the intelligence he had received it was a great obstruction to his affaires and the only reason why the Gentlemen of the country came not in to him, being all averse to a commonwealth, which as he sayd they were all jealous wee intended to sett up, and promised us that he would the next day sett forth a proclamation whereby he would make fresh promises to the people of the libertyes were promised him by his Declaration. Wee submitted to it and it was done at the market cross at Taunton, being read by Mr. Tily.

The Duke's quarters in this town was at Mr. Hookers. During our stay here wee had slaine Cornett Legg in a horse skirmish neare the Towne.

Sunday Sunday morning wee marched to Bridgwater having an addition to our army of Lieut. Coll. Bassets regiment of foot which the officers sayd consisted of 800, to compleat which he had stoln from every regiment all the Taunton people that came to them at Lyme being I suppose at least 200 of Capt. Slapes company of Sithes & Musqueteers being 100 which were added to the Duke's regiment and of 2 Troops of horse, Capt. Hookers & Capt. Tuckers, making neare 160. I know of nothing remarkeable in this march save that wee had very good quarters at Bridgwater and for the most part free.

Monday Wee marched to Glasconbury being an exceeding rainy day wee quartered our foot in the Abby & Churches making very great fyers to drye and refresh our men and had provisions from the comissaries. In our march this day we were alarmd by a party of my Lord of Oxford's Horse and on the other side had news that the militia had left Wells and were retreated to Bath and Bristoll.

Tuesday Wee marched to Shepton Mallett and were quartered in houses. Here the Duke told me of his intent to attacque Bristoll and that on the Somersetsheire side and asked my opinion therein. I informed him that if it was on any part tenable it was there, and therefore that in my opinion he ought to pass the river Avon at Keynsham bridg (which is the midway between Bath and Bristol) and attacque it on the Glaucestersheire side where there were many advantages not to be found on the Somersetsheire side. He was satisfyed with what I sayd and resolved to doe accordingly. So in order to it *Wednesday* wee marched next day to Pensford. Wee were all this day alarmd in the reare by a party of Horse and Dragoons. Neverthelesse wee lodged quietly that night in Pensford within 5 miles of Bristoll where we mett with nothing remarkeable but that wee perceived a great fire in or neare Bristoll that night by the rednesse of the skye. Wee supposed that they had sett the suburbs on fire least wee should have possessed ourselves of it but it seems it was a ship accidently sett on fire.

Thursday Early in the morning wee marched towards Keynsham the Duke having the night before sent a troop of Horse under the command of Capt. Tily to possess themselves of the town and repair the bridge which wee had intelligence was broken downe to prevent our passage. At Capt. Tily's coming to the towne there was in it a troop of militia horse of Glaucestersheire who at his approach immediately retired and left behind them 2 horses and one of theyr party prisoner. By break of day the bridge was repaired and wee possessed ourselves thereof about 10 aclock in the morning marching over with our whole army but it proving very rainy weather and to (*gap of an inch*) the City of Bristoll which wee intended to fall upon that night having those in our camp that perfectly understood the city. Wee were ordered to march back againe and take up quarters in the town as if wee intended to lodge there all night but wee had hardly taken up our quarters but wee were alarmd by 2 parties of horse falling into the town at 2 severall places with whom our horse unadvisedly engaged and after the loss of about fourteen of our own party amongst whom was Brand Capt. of horse, they retired leaving us 3 prisoners from whom the Duke was informed that the kings army, being as they sayd about 4000 was at hand, upon which the Duke altered his resolution of attacquing Bristoll and debated it with his officers whether it was best to march forward to Glaucester and so breaking down the bridge there over Seavern and keeping the river on our flanck to march into Shropshire and Cheshire where he supposed he had freinds to joyn him, or to march into Wilshire where he was informed by Mr. Adlam who had come to him the day before, was a considerable body of horse would joyn him. The arguments against the march to Gloucester were that it was 4 days march, that our souldiers wanted shoes, that there was a considerable body of horse and dragoons in our Reer who would be continually retarding our march till the foot came up, and would necessitate us to fight before wee could reach Gloucester, that Wiltshire was neare at hand and that it would be better to march hither and having joyned those horse to fight before the Kings army grew stronger. The latter advice prevaild so we marcht away that night, and the next morning being *Friday* wee drew up before Bath and summonded it only in Bravado for wee had no expectation of its surrendry and from thence wee marched to Philipsnorton where wee lodged that night, the foot all in the feild. Here the Duke was very disconsolate and began to complain that all people had deserted him, for there was no appearance of the Wiltshire horse Mr. Adlam talked off although wee were neare enough to have joyned them if they had had any stomach to it. Indeed, the Duke was so dejected that wee could hardly gett orders from him. Wee lay all in the feild this night at the head of our men and were severall times alarmed but not in earnest till the morning being *Saturday* when we were faln upon by the Avaunt guard of the kings army just as wee were marching out of towne. There is a long lane that leads out of a plowed feild into the towne being neare a quarter of a mile long. On each side the inclosures are surrounded with good thick hedges. At the end of this lane the Duke had caused a Baracade to be made across the way for the security of his quarters which was guarded by 50 Musqueteers commanded by Capt. Vincent. Just by this barracade was a little byway which led into the back part of the town through a Gentleman's court, near to which court the foot were encamped in two feilds. The Grenadeers which were the forlorne hope of the Kings army advanced through the lane up to the Barracade, which the Duke having notice caused his own regiment of foot to march through the Gentleman's court up to the side of the lane and attaque them on the flank, which was done, and the regiment being much superior in number wee fell with a good part of them into theyr reare so that they were surrounded on all hands save the left flank by which way through the hedge many of them escaped. While wee were thus engaged with the Grenadeers in the lane, Lieut. Coll. Holmes was commanded to attaque a party of foot who lined the hedge that flanked us, which he did and after about an houres dispute having made them retire from hedge to hedge he gained the furthermost hedge near the feild, the Kings foot together with a party of horse that had likewise entred the lane retiring to the Kings army who were drawn up in the plowed feild about 500 paces from the hedge. Wee having gained the hedges next the feild drew up all our foot ranging in one line all along the hedges, our horse behind them, and drew up 2 peices of canon into the mouth of the lane and guarded them with a company of Sithmen. Our remaining 2 were planted on a little eminence on the right side of the lane. The Kings canon were likewise drawn in opposition to ours and so they beganne to canonade one another which lasted neare 6 houres without any great loss of either side. On ours wee lost only one man by the canon. Towards the evening Coll. Venner had perswaded the Duke (against all reason) to retreat, but it coming to a debate it was resolved to the contrary and resolutions taken to cutt passages through the hedges and come to a battle, and while wee were doing it, the kings army retreated and wee had no mind to pursue them because wee had no manner of confidence in our horse. In this action wee computed the loss on the Kings side to be about 80 men, on ours about 18, amongst which was 2 Captaines of Foot, Patchall and young Holms, both of Coll. Holms Regiment; Blake, Coll. Holms Lieut., and Chaddock a Capt. of horse, killed unfortunately by our owne men. Wee stayed in the feild till about 11 a clock at night, and then leaving great fires, wee marched (I suppose by the advice of Coll. Venner) to Froome in a miserable rainy night up to the knees in dirt, almost to the destruction of our foot. Wee came to Froome about 8 in the morning being *Sunday* where wee putt our men into quarters and stayed there all that day and the next to refresh our men.

Monday Here the Duke was very disconsolate complaining that all people had deserted him, that noboby stirred any where to make a division (diversion), that not one of the horse talked of by Mr. Adlam appeared, that he was likewise disappointed in the disertion he expected from the Kings forces, and that this must of necessity come to ruine, and therefore he thought it adviseable to leave his army and repair with his officers to some seaport town and make his escape with them beyond sea, which was mightily applauded by Coll. Venner, but my Lord Grey and others opposed it as a thing so base that it could never be forgiven by the people to be so deserted and that the Duke must never expect more to be trusted. At length it was layd aside and resolutions were taken by him to stick by his army. Nevertheless Coll. Venner & Major Parsons, Holmes's Major, went away privately. Monday night the Duke gave orders for a march on Tuesday morning and it was intended for Warmister but on the *Tuesday morning* wee had intelligence of a double nature, on the one hand that the Kings army were marched early that morning from Bradford to Westbury and so crossed our march to Warmister; on the other hand a quaker whose name I know not that had formerly been with the Duke at Glascenbury to inform him of a great Club army that were up in the marshes in Somersetshire about Axbridge, came now againe to the Duke and acquainted him that they were a 10000 strong and that if the Duke would retire towards them they would joyne him. This prevailed with the Duke to order his march to Shepton Mallett where wee came that night and were quarterd in houses. Here I suppose wee were at free quarters, mony being short.

Wednesday The next morning wee marched to Wells on information that there were some carriages left there of the Kings guarded by a small party of Dragoons, which wee took and quartered there all night.

Thursday Thursday morning wee marched towards Bridgwater thinking to meet with the great Club army which proved to be about a 160 instead of 10000. Wee lay in the moore all night and marched next day being *Friday* to Bridgwater to refresh our men and fix our arms which were very much out of order, sending warrants before to summon in the country people with spades and pickaxes to worke, as if wee intended to fortifye. Something of that nature was done but only to secure our quarters and amuse the world, intending nothing less than to stay there.

Saturday Saturday was spent in exercising our men and fixing our arms. This day great numbers went from us to Taunton to see theyr freinds, and returned for the most part againe on Sunday.

Sunday Sunday morning the Duke received an accompt of the march of the Kings army from Somerton, and therefore prepared himselfe to march from them, which he did intend to doe the evening following and to march all night to Axbridge, and from thence passing Keynsham bridge to march to Gloucester, and so passing the Seavern to take the formerly intended course into Shropsheire & Chesshire. Our carriages were loaded in order to it, But in the afternoone about 3 a clock having an accompt of the posture of the King's Army in Sedgmore that the foot were encamped in the feild, the horse going into the villages to quarter, that all the Canon were drawn up against the way to Bridgwater, and that wee might march upon them another way and avoyd theyr canon, he called the feild officers together and demaunded of them if they thought it adviseable to fight if wee could surprize them in the night; they all agreed it was; provided it was provided the foot did not entrench, upon which he sent back the spye that brought him the accompt to see if they entrenched or not, who brought answer that they did not, but tooke no notice of the ditch that lay in the way of our march. About a 11 aclock that night wee marched out of the Towne. I had the vanguard of the foot with the Duke's Regiment and wee marched in great silence along the road that leads from Bridgwater to Bristoll untill wee came to the lane that passed into the moore where the King's army was. Then wee made an halt for the horse to pass by and received our orders which was that the horse should advance first and push into the King's camp and mixing with the King's foote endeavour to keep them from coming together; that the Canon should follow the horse, and the foote the Canon, and draw all up in one line and so finish what the horse had began before the King's horse or canon could gett in order. The Horse advanced to the ditch and never farther, but on the firing of some of the King's foott rann out of the feild. By that time our foott came up wee found our Horse all gonn and the King's foote in order. I advanced within 30 or 40 paces of the ditch being opposite to the Scotch batalion of the Kings, as I learnt since, and there was forced to make a full stop to put the Batalion in some order, the Duke having caused them to march so exceeding swift after he saw his Horse runn, that they were all in confusion. By that time I had putt them in some order and was preparing to pass the ditch (not intending to fire till I had advanced these (? close) to our enemyes) Coll. Matthews was come up and began to fire at distance, upon which the Batalion I commanded fired likewise and after that I could not gett them to advance. Wee continued in that station firing for about an houre and an halfe, when, it being pretty light, I perceived all the Batalions on the left running (who as I since understood were broken by the King's horse of the left wing) and finding my own men not inclinable to stand, I caused them to face about and make a kind of disorderly retreat to a ditch a great way behind us where wee were charged by a party of horse & dragoons & routed; about 150 getting over the ditch, I marched with them on foott to Bridgwater, where I mett with 2 or 3 full Troops of horse that had rann away out of the feild without striking stroke. I gott my horses and with about 20 officers & others, amongst which was Ferguson, I went westward to meett 2 troops of horse who were gone to Minehead to fetch up 6 peices of Canon, being Capt. Hulins and Capt. Caryes Troops. With part of them amounting in all to neare 50, wee went to Ilfordcombe and seized on a vessell which wee victualed and putt to sea but were forced ashoare by 2 fregatts cruising on the coast, after which wee dispersed & fled into the woods. I for my part was alone from that time to the time I was taken coming out of the house of one John Birch in the parish of Brendin in the county of Devon.

Thus I have given an accompt of what I can remember which indeed amounts to little more than a journall of the marches and action of the army. It is the full of what I know. As to the persons that advanced mony I know of none nor have nor heard of the name of any. For my part I was never with the Duke but generally in the feild, unless when I came for orders or was at a councell of warr which was very seldome. Neither can I imagine the summe received to be very great, for it may be demonstrated that the whole expence of the Dukes army might be defrayed for £3000, not did I ever heare that there was any summe advanced towards it but what was was by ordinary and middlesort of people.

As to the annuity of my Lord Stamford granted to Coll. Romsey I cannot say anything positively to it; such a rumor I have heard, but whether it were so in truth, or only money lent I know not; it was transacted (if at all) while I was sick at Bristoll.

I know nothing more of Sir William Ellis then I have related, having never been in the gentlemans company in my life, nor doe I know him if I see him.

I know nothing more of the Cheshire affaire than what I have sett down, only that asking Capt. Matthews if the Cheshire gentlemen would not stirre. He answered Yes, surely, for he understood my Lord Delamere was gone into the country for that purpose.

The persons to have gone into America were John Ayloffe, Roger, a Quaker, myself, Thomas Merry. These were to have been concerned in the plantation as proprietors: Edmund Waller, Edward Norton, Richard Nelthrop, John Freke, Thomas Merry, Robert West. William Penn & severall other Quakers.

The persons of the Kings head club I can at present remember are John Trenchard, Henry Trenchard, John Ayloffe, Edward Norton, Richard Nelthrop, Richard Goodenough, Francis Goodenough, Robert West, John Romsey, Robert Blaney, Thomas Dore, James Hooper, Thomas Hooper, Daniel Blake, Peter Warburton, John Freke, Edmund Waller, Carleton Whitlock, Thomas Day, Joseph Tily, John Row, —Legg, Joseph Ashurst, Christopher Bettiscombe, Zechariah Bourn, William Clerk, —Clerk, Hugh Speak, Charles Speak, Francis Trenchard, John Allen, Thomas Shadwell, Henry Baker, Charles Umprevill, Aron Smith, Henry Starky, Hugh Westlake, —Ogle, German Ireton, Benjamin Rudyare, John Fanshaw, Thomas Merry, —Pratt, —Munckton.

I forgot to mention that Mr. Hooke, the Duke's Chaplain was sent to London to endeavour an insurrection there, but from whence or when I know not, for it was kept very secret and it was some time before I missed him; and that Major Manley's son came to Bridgwater from London the Saturday before the Battle at Weston and he and his father went towards London that Saturday night to endeavour a rising. I thinke that it was Sir Robert Payton that the Duke talked of for cheife in London.

Nath. Wade.

Index

Absalom and Achitophel 16
Adlam, Captain 51, 72, 154, 167-8
Ailesbury, Earl of 79-81, 84
Albemarle, 2nd Duke 35, 38, 40, 42, 44, 110, 161, 163, 165-6
Aldersey, Hugh 76, 138
Alford, Gregory, Mayor 34, 162
Alford, Richard 72
Argyll, Earl of 22-3, 28, 43, 157-8
Armsley, R. 150-1
Armstrong, Sir T. 153
Ascough, Ascue, Askew, Ensign 27, 39, 87, 164
Ashill, skirmish at 42, 63
Ashwood, J. 58, 123-4
Atkins, Jeremiah 107, 110
Austin, T. 107, 112
Axbridge 93, 169
Axe, Rev. T. 32-3, 59, 63
Axminster 40-1, 89, 90, 165
Axminster Book of Remembrance 33, 40-1, 117
Axminster Congregationalists 11, 41-2, 58, 123
Ayloff, John 153, 156-7, 171

Babbington, Ensign 27, 74, 161
Bach, Col. 100-1
Bagwell, P. 107
Barillon, 55
Bassett, see Bovet, R. and 150, 166
Bath 52, 93, 167
Battiscombe, C. 36, 87, 159, 171
Beaufort, Duke of 50
Berkeley, Lady Harriet 24-5
Birch, J. 77-8, 151, 170
Bishop, G. 116
Bisse, G. 116-7
Blake, Ensign 27; Lieut. 55, 161, 168, 171
Booth, Sir W. 87, 91
Bovet, Clement 74
Bovet, Richard, Col. 44, 46, 62, 92-3, 150
Bradford-on-Avon 55
Brand, Mr. 46, 50, 161, 167
Brandon, Mr. 46, 50, 161, 167
Brandon, Lord 159
Brendon 77-8, 170

Bridge, Mary 131
Bridgeman, W. 94
Bridgwater 48, 59, 60, 64-6, 69, 76, 90-1, 166, 169, 170
Bridport, skirmishes at 38-40, 63, 88, 162-4
Brinscombe, Lieut. 39, 164
Bristol 49-51, 71, 91, 93-4, 103, 122, 152-3, 166-7
Bristol, Broadmead Baptist Church 49
Brome, Jane and John 114. Also Thomas
Bruce, Capt. 28-9, 121
Bruce, Lord, see Ailesbury
Buccleuch, Anna, Duchess, 16, 80-1
Buccleuch, 6th Duke 15
Buffett, Col. see Bovet, Col. and 150
Burd, J. 93, 96
Burton, James 31, 94
Butcher, James 118
Buyse, Anton 28, 40, 67-8, 71, 78-9, 121, 165

Carrier, James 32, 118-9, 141
Cary, Capt. 77, 170
Castle Cary 90, 99
Chadwick, T. (Chaddock) 36, 55, 161, 168
Chamberlain, Hugh 28, 33, 118-9
Chamberlain (young) 74
Chard 41, 90, 165
Charles I, 9, 10, 71
Charles II, 11, 13, 15-6, 49, 71, 80, 154
Charmouth 115
Chedzoy 64-5, 68, 74
Chevalier Louis de Misiers 56, 131
Churchill, Charles, Lt. Col. 64
Churchill, John, Lord (Marlborough) 17, 35, 48-50, 52, 54, 64, 68, 92, 122
Churchill, Sir Winston 35
Clapp, J. 111
Clarke, W. 60
Clubmen 57-9, 169
Coad, John (or Thomas) 41, 50, 52-3, 55, 59, 75-6, 84, 97-102, 123
Cogan, R. 76
Coker, Lieut. 39, 164
Coleman, Edward 12
Collins, Mary 114

172

Colyton 89-90
Commonwealth 10
Compton, Sir F. 62, 64, 66, 70
Conventicle Acts 11
Cooke, Christopher 33, 120
Cooke, John 107
Cooke, Nicholas 151-2
Cooper, Sir W. 153
Cothelstone 90, 93
Courtney, Sir W. 153
Cox, Philip and Thomas 114
Cox, Richard 97
Cox, William 115, 120
Craddock, see Chadwick
Cragg, J. Ensign 27, 74, 161
Cragg, Mr. 158-60
Crewkerne 75, 90

Dalby (Dolly) Lieut. 27, 161
Danvers, Col. 23, 43, 160
Dare, Gideon 101, 111. Samuel 91
Dare, Thomas (the younger) 27, 29, 161
Dare, Thomas Heywood 28-9, 33-4, 39, 118, 152, 156, 158, 161, 163
Dassell, S. 34-5, 133
Defoe, Daniel 15, 36, 66, 122, 141
Delamere, Lord 51, 122, 124-5, 159, 171
de Misiers 56, 131
Dodds, J. 97
Dorchester Assize 86-8; Gaol 96
Douglas, Col. 64, 68
Drake, Sir F. 159
Dryden, J. 16
Dumbarton's Regiment 57, 62, 64, 68, 170
Dumblane, Lord 55-6, 60, 69
Dummer, Capt. 55, 70, 74, 135
Dunton, J. 93
Duras, Lord, see Feversham

Earle, Peter 120
Ellis, Sir W. 157, 160, 171
Ettrick, Anthony, J.P. 79
Evelyn, John 83
Exclusion Bills 12, 151
Exeter Assize 89; city 91, 161

Farrant, Amy 78-9
Ferguson, Rev. R. 28, 30, 33, 35, 41, 43, 47, 65-7, 77, 79, 121-2, 151, 153, 155, 158, 165, 170
Fernley, J. 94-5
Feversham, Louis Duras, 2nd Viscount, 29, 48-50, 52, 54-8, 60-1, 64, 68-9, 72, 82, 133

Fifth Monarchy Men 11, 132
Fletcher, Andrew, of Saltoun 26, 28, 39, 121, 152, 163
Foulkes, J. Col. 27, 62, 121, 161, 163
Fouracres, J. 89
Fox, James, Major 27, 38, 51, 121, 161, 163
Frome 56-7, 60, 93, 168-9

Gardner, Rev. J. 116, 123
Gaunt, Elizabeth 94-5
Gifford, Rev. A. 51
Gifford, John and Simon 115
Glastonbury 49, 74, 93, 166
Glisson, Samuel 87
Godfrey (guide) 65-6
Goodenough, Francis 27-8, 39, 74, 155, 161, 163-4, 171
Goodenough, Richard 27-8, 58, 60, 63, 124, 152, 155-6, 161, 171
Grafton, Duke of, 50, 52-5, 64
Green, Hugh 115
Grey, Ford, Lord Grey of Wark, 18, 24-5, 34, 39, 43, 58-9, 65-8, 71, 78-9, 119, 125, 153, 159, 163-5, 168-9
Grey, Lady 24-5, 125

Hallet, Mary and Joseph 114
Hampden, John (the younger) 13, 152
Harcourt, Simon 117
Hardy, W. 36, 59
Hawker, Joseph 99
Hayes, James, Capt. 27, 87, 161
Hellier, J. 83, 139
Henrietta Maria, Queen, 16
Hewling, Benjamin 27-8, 77, 92, 170
Hewling, Hannah 92
Hewling, William 27-8, 87, 161
Heywood, T. (sea-captain) 91, 94
Hickes, Rev. J. 15, 49, 86, 93-4, 134
Hobbes, E. (sheriff) 90
Hobson, H. (wounded at Sedgemoor) 114
Holloway, James 151, 154-5
Holmes, Abraham, Col. 27, 54-5, 62-3, 87, 161, 163, 168
Holmes, John Capt. 36, 55, 168
Holmes, Joseph 118-9
Holiday, Richard 78, 86, 88
Honiton 89, 90
Hook, Rev. N. 30, 58, 122, 171
Hooper, Mr. 46, 157, 171
Howard, Sir P. 87, 94
Howe, Grace 77
Hucker, Capt. 45, 66-7, 166

173

Ilchester 18, 36, 75, 84, 90, 96, 115
Ilfracombe 77, 170
Ilminster 41, 90, 93, 97, 118, 165
Inchiquin, Earl of 101-2
Ireton, German 171
Ireton, Henry (the younger) 25, 159

James I 9
James II (Duke of York) 12, 15, 16, 19, 23, 27, 49, 58-9, 62, 77, 79-80, 83-4, 86-7, 95, 99, 122, 125, 154
Jeanes, Dorothy 116
Jeffreys, Lord Chief Justice, 24, 67, 85-7, 90-1, 93-4, 111, 118-9
Jenkyn, W. 36
Johnson, Dr. S. 122
Jones, Capt. J. 36, 66-7, 160

Kay, Key, Samuel 33, 118-20
Ken, Bishop 80, 82
Keynsham 49-50, 63, 90, 166-7, 169
Kidd, J. Capt. 28, 30-1, 87
Kidder, Bishop 123
Kirke, Col. 48, 52, 74, 131
Kirke's Lambs 48, 61-2, 64, 68, 74-5, 97

Lane, T. 58
Langport 90, 95
Larke, Rev. Sampson 87
le Blon, D. 152, 160
Legg, Cornet 42, 166, 171
Lillington, Lieut. 27, 39, 74, 161, 164
Lisle, Dame Alice 86
Lock, Mr. 158, 160
Loder, Andrew 84, 112, 115-7
Long Sutton 75-6
Ludlow, Col. 26, 156
Lumley, Lord 79
Lunenburg, Duke of 157
Lyme Regis 34-40, 63, 87, 152, 161-5
Lyttleton, Sir C. 95

Macclesfield, Lord 153, 159
Macintosh, Capt. 64
Macaulay, Lord 82, 139
Maids of Taunton 44, 119, 134, 165
Mallack, Malachi 118
Manley, J. Major 28-9, 38, 65, 162, 171
Manning, Daniel 42, 48, 75, 124
Marders, Capt. 87
Martock 116
Mary, Princess 19; Queen 125
Mary of Modena, James II's Queen 90
Masters, R 97

Matthews, Arthur, Capt. 143
Matthews, Edward, Col. 46, 62, 65, 93, 121, 158-9, 170-1
Mead, Mary 44
Melcombe Regis 88
Melvin, Lord 158
Mews, Bishop 64, 68, 74, 79, 82
Middlezoy 56, 64, 70, 72-3, 76, 131
Militia: Devon 40, 161, 165
 Dorset 38-9, 54, 163
 Gloucester 50, 167
 Hampshire 57
 Oxfordshire 54
 Somerset 40-1, 54, 79, 128, 161, 163, 165
 Sussex 78-9
 Wilts 57, 64, 72, 74
Minehead 64, 77, 90, 170
Misiers, L de 56, 131
Mitchell, Lieut. 27, 39, 74, 161, 163
Monk, General, (1st Duke of Albemarle) 27
Monmouth, James Scott, Duke of 13, 15-6
 Military experience 17
 Progress in West 17-8
 In Holland 19, 22-3
 Pocket Book 19-22
 grants commissions 27
 his servants 28, 63
 lands at Lyme 34
 proclamation 35-6
 at Lyme 38-40
 at Taunton 43-7
 proclaimed king 44-5
 at Keynsham 51
 at Philip's Norton 52-6
 at Frome 57-8
 at Bridgwater 60, 65
 at Sedgemoor 66-7
 flight 71, 78
 captured 79-80
 Lord Ailesbury's description 80-1
 execution 81
 his children 81
 in Wade's narrative 152-5, 157-170
Monoux, Lieut. 42
Morgan, Edward 115
Musgrave, Sir C. 87, 90-1

Nelthorpe, R. 26, 28-9, 86, 94, 156, 171
Newton, B. (guide) 65-6
Nipho, Sir J. 87, 89, 94
Norton, Edward 155-6, 171
Nuthall, J. 106-7, 109-10

Oates, Titus 11-2
Occupations of rebels 36-7, 41, 46-7, 91, 112
Oglethorpe, Col. 50, 56-7, 62, 64-8
Oldmixon, John 65, 71, 82
Oliver, Dr. 30, 68, 71, 94, 121, 142-3, 152
Osborne, W. 114
Oxford, Lord Oxford's Horse 49, 166

Pacey, John 91
Parcet, Elizabeth 18
Parker, Capt. 50, 55
Parkin, Militiaman 79
Parry, John 91
Parsons, Major 27, 58, 161, 169
Paschall, Rev. A. 67
Patchall, Capt. 27, 55, 161, 168
Payton, Sir R. 171
Pembroke, Earl of 50, 56-7
Penn, William 122, 139, 171
Penne, George 103-4, 106
Pensford 49, 93, 166
Pepys, Samuel 11, 15-7, 122
Perrott, Robert 46, 51
Phelips, Col. Sir Edward 35, 40-1, 75-6, 116
Phelps, Mr. 157, 159
Phooce, Phooks T. 59
Pinney, Azariah 102-5, 141; family 102-5
Pinney, Robert 103
Pitman, Dr. Henry 46, 75, 84, 93, 106-10, 123, 141
Pitman, William 46, 106, 141
Plaice, Thomas 59, 112, 141, 169
Pollexfen, Henry 84-5
Popish Plot 11
Portman, Sir W. 33, 54, 79
Powell, Rev. R. 77-8
Presentment of the Rebels quoted 36, 41, 46-8, 83, 85, 133, 137, 139
Prideaux, Edmund 17, 34, 94, 117-9

Quakers 11, 18, 58-9, 64, 72, 75, 83, 86, 96, 136, 145, 169, 171

Rampson, S. 42
Ravening, H. 151-2
Rawlins, Mr. 157-8
Regiments: Royal 48, 52
　　Blue 46, 63, 152
　　Green 36, 38, 54-5, 63, 68, 152, 163, 168
　　Red 36, 38, 40, 42, 52, 54, 63, 65, 67, 74, 152, 163, 165, 168-9

White 38-9, 63, 68, 152, 163
　　Yellow 38, 51, 63, 67, 152, 163, 170
Reresby, Sir J. 51, 80
Ringwood 79
Roberts, George 58, 87, 147
Rochester, Earl of 79, 119
Rolle, Sir F. 152
Romsey, Col. 25-6, 151-2, 154-5, 170-1
Rose, Mr. 29, 74
Rumball, W. 160
Russell, Lord W. 156
Rye House Plot 13, 25-6, 28, 30-1, 119, 154

Sackville, Col. 64
St. John, Capt. 48, 75
Salisbury, Assize at 86
Saltatudos 108
Sands, Capt. 66
Sandford, Ensign 27, 74, 161
Savage, W. 67
Scott, Francis 45, 72-3
Sedgemoor 63-72, 169-70; those killed there 74, 131
Shaftesbury, Earl of 13, 15, 18, 152-3
Sheeres, Sir H. 50
Shepton Mallet 59, 60, 71, 93, 99, 166, 169
Sherborne 88, 94, 99
Shute, F. 154
Skinner, J. 115
Slade, J. and W. 97
Slape, Capt. 166
Smith, Aaron 155, 171
Smith, Mr. and Mrs. 157-8
Smith, Thomas 58, 123-4
Somerset, Duke of 50
Somerton 60, 90, 169
Sparke, W. 65
Spearing, Spiring, John 117
Speere, Rev. R. 100
Speke, Charles 41, 93, 118, 171
　　John 41, 58, 121, 165
　　George 17, 41, 115
　　William 32-3
Stamford, Lord 154, 170
Standerwick, J. 33, 118
Stapleton, Sir W. 87, 94
Stawel, Lord 75-6, 92-3
Storey, Samuel 31, 44, 60, 85
Strangways, Mr. 39, 164
Strode, Edward 71; William 17
Stuckey, G. 118-9
Sunderland, Earl of 44, 58, 77, 79-80, 118

175

Swain, J. 76
Sydenham, Sir J. 17

Taunton 43-7, 74, 90-2, 152, 154, 160, 165-6, 169
    Assize at 90-1
    Maids of 44, 119, 134, 165
Taylor, Lieut. 27, 74, 161
Tellier, J. 31, 58
Temple, Dr. 28, 30, 87
Tenison, Rev. Dr. 80-1
Thatcher, B. 93
Thompson, Capt. 27-8, 39, 151, 161, 163
Thompson, William 118-9
Tily, Joseph, Capt. 27, 50, 120-1, 152-3, 161, 166-7, 171
Tortuga 108
Towgood, Rev. S. 58
Trelawney's Regiment 62, 64, 68
Trenchard, J. 152-4, 159, 171
Tripp, Jacob 96
Tuchin, J. 96
Tucker, Capt. 166
Turner, Bishop 80
Turner, William 25, 31
Tyler, Lieut. 163; Thomas 154

Upham, blacksmith 42, 75

Vane, C. 157
Venner, Samuel 27, 39, 43, 56, 58, 121, 161, 163-5, 168-9
Venner, Thomas 27
Vickris, R. 86
Vincent, Ensign 27, Capt. 52, 161, 168

Wade, Nathaniel 26-7, 36, 38-42, 44, 49, 50, 54-6, 62-3, 67, 76-8, 119, 122-3, 149-71

Wade, Nathaniel quoted 49, 52, 54, 57, 65, 68
Wade, William 154
Walcott, Capt. 154-5
Waller, Sir W. 157
Walters, Lucy 15, 80
Ward, Sir P. 160
Warminster 169
Way, William 32, 141
Wayford 106
Wellington 90, 165
Wells 59, 93, 96, 169
    Assize at 83, 93-4, 99
Wentworth, Henrietta 19, 21, 23, 80-1
West, Mr. 152-3, 155, 171
Westbury 169
Weston Zoyland 61-2, 64, 70, 72-3
Weymouth 88-9, 91, 100, 106
Wheeler, Adam 72, 74
Whicker, John 107, 109-10
Whichehalse, John J.P. 77
Whiting, John 18, 45, 72, 75, 96
Whiting, John quoted 18, 37, 45-6, 73, 84, 86, 89, 90
White, Sir R. 91, 94
White, William 87
Wildman, Major 23, 43, 152, 158-60
William of Orange 27, 100, 111, 122, 125
Winchester 86
Winter, Dr. 76, 96-7, 141
Woodcock, W. 107
Wyatt, Zachery 44
Wyndham, Col. 57, 72, 74

Yeovil 90, 93, 132
Yonge, Young, Sir Walter 17, 111, 152-3, 159